Gen Z, Social Media, and News

Paula M. Poindexter

Gen Z, Social Media, and News

Implications for the Future of News Engagement, Journalism, the U.S., and Democracy

PETERLANG

New York · Berlin · Bruxelles · Chennai · Lausanne · Oxford

Library of Congress Cataloging-in-Publication Data

Names: Poindexter, Paula Maurie, author.
Title: Gen Z, social media, and news / Paula M. Poindexter.
Description: New York : Peter Lang, 2025. | Includes bibliographical references and index.
Identifiers: LCCN 2024059626 (print) | LCCN 2024059627 (ebook) | ISBN 9781636676340 (paperback) | ISBN 9781636676333 (hardback) | ISBN 9781636676357 (ebook) | ISBN 9781636676364 (epub)
Subjects: LCSH: News audiences–United States–History–21st century. | Generation Z. | Journalism–United States–History–21st century. | Social media–United States–History.
Classification: LCC PN4888.N47 P64 2025 (print) | LCC PN4888.N47 (ebook) | DDC 071/.3–dc23/eng/20250106
LC record available at https://lccn.loc.gov/2024059626
LC ebook record available at https://lccn.loc.gov/2024059627
DOI 10.3726/b22611

Bibliographic information published by the Deutsche Nationalbibliothek.
The German National Library lists this publication in the German
National Bibliography; detailed bibliographic data is available
on the Internet at http://dnb.d-nb.de.

Cover design by Peter Lang Group AG, with Paula M. Poindexter.

ISBN 9781636676340 (paperback)
ISBN 9781636676333 (hardback)
ISBN 9781636676357 (ebook)
ISBN 9781636676364 (epub)
DOI 10.3726/b22611

© 2025 Peter Lang Group AG, Lausanne

Published by Peter Lang Publishing Inc., New York, USA
info@peterlang.com—www.peterlang.com

All rights reserved.

All parts of this publication are protected by copyright.
Any utilization outside the strict limits of the copyright law, without the permission of the publisher, is forbidden and liable to prosecution.
This applies in particular to reproductions, translations, microfilming, and storage and processing in electronic retrieval systems.

This publication has been peer reviewed.

To News Engagement Day and My Gen Z Students

CONTENTS

List of Figures	ix
List of Tables	xi
Preface	xiii
Acknowledgments	xvii

Chapter 1	Who Is Gen Z and What Events and Issues Have Contributed to Defining this Generation?	1
Chapter 2	Social Media and News in the Lives of Gen Z	43
Chapter 3	How Social Media and Smartphones Disrupted the News Engagement Socialization Process and Redefined How Upcoming Generations Get News and Feel about Being Informed	63
Chapter 4	Gen Z Report Card on News, Journalism, Coverage of Their Generation	79
Chapter 5	The Gen Z Voter	91

| Chapter 6 | Barriers to a News Smart Gen Z | 109 |

| Chapter 7 | The Future of Journalism, the United States, and Democracy Depend on an Informed Gen Z and a Nationwide Belief That Being Informed is Essential and a Responsibility | 127 |

	Appendix A: List of End-of-Chapter Questions and Reflections	153
	Appendix B: How The National Gen Z, Social Media & News Engagement Survey was Conducted	157
	Appendix C: Questionnaire for The National Gen Z, Social Media & News Engagement Survey	161
	Appendix D: Celebrating 10 Years of News Engagement Day! Souvenir Program	177
	Appendix E: Voting & Engaging with News about the 2022 Midterm Elections	183

| | Index | 201 |

FIGURES

Figure 3.1	News Engagement Routines in Gen Z's Own Words	73
Figure 4.1	In Gen Z's Own Words: Reasons for Giving a High Grade to News Media Coverage	81
Figure 4.2	In Gen Z's Own Words: Reasons for Giving a Low Grade to News Media Coverage	81
Figure 4.3	In Gen Z's Own Words: What Gen Z Thinks of News Coverage of Their Generation	83
Figure 5.1	Why Gen Z Is Not Registered to Vote	100
Figure 5.2	Most Important Issues Facing Gen Z	101
Figure 5.3	Themes That Reflect Main Reasons Gen Z Will Vote in the 2024 Presidential Election	103
Figure 6.1	Barriers to a News Smart Gen Z	110
Figure 7.1	Select Constituent Groups that Have an Opportunity and Responsibility to Ensure Gen Z and Future Generations Are Informed, an Independent Press Thrives, and Democracy Is Protected	131
Figure 7.2	Gen Z's News Credibility Quick Check	136
Figure 7.3	News Media Action Plan for Covering and Engaging Gen Z	138

Figure A.1 Click a Topic and Get Answers to Your Questions About Registering and Voting 190
Figure A.2 Candidates and Issues on the Ballot for the 2022 Midterms 191

TABLES

Table 2.1	How the Demographic Portrait of Gen Z Compares with Millennials & Older Generations	45
Table 2.2	Social Media Use by Generation: Gen Z, Millennials, and Older Generations	47
Table 2.3	News Engagement by Generation: Gen Z, Millennials, and Older Generations	48
Table 2.4	Where Gen Z, Millennials, and Older Generations Get News	49
Table 2.5	Embracing Digital Platforms and Interpersonal Sources; Rejecting Legacy News Media: A Generational Comparison	51
Table 2.6	News Categories Gen Z, Millennials, and Older Generations Pay Attention To	56
Table 2.7	News Topics Gen Z, Millennials, and Older Generations Pay Attention To	57
Table 2.8	News Topics Paid Attention to from the Prism of Gender	58
Table 3.1	The Presence of News in the Homes of Gen Z, Millennials, and Older Generations While Growing Up	66
Table 3.2	Advice and School News Engagement Socialization	67
Table 3.3	Relationship Between News Engagement Routine and Engaging with News	71

Table 3.4	News Engagement Routine in the Lives of Gen Z, Millennials, and Older Generations	72
Table 4.1	Generations Grade News Media on Their News Coverage	80
Table 4.2	Grading Their Generation's News Coverage	82
Table 4.3	Agreement with Statements about News and the News Media	87
Table 5.1	Gen Z's Political Affiliations, Ideological Leanings, and Beliefs About the Importance of Voting	98
Table 5.2	Presidential Election Voting and Registration: How Gen Z Compares with Millennials and Older Generations	99
Table 6.1	Supplemental News Engagement Benefits	112
Table 6.2	Time Spent on Social Media	113
Table 6.3	How Gen Z Evaluates Trustworthiness of a News Story	117
Table 6.4	Familiarity with Term "Disinformation"	118
Table 6.5	Encountered Disinformation?	119
Table 6.6	Attitudes About the Cost of News on the Internet and the Purpose of News Subscriptions	120
Table 6.7	Types of Digital Subscriptions Paid for By Gen Z	120
Table 7.1	Grading News Media Coverage of Their Generation: Millennials in 2012 vs. Gen Z in 2023	137
Table 7.2	Select Rankings from Reporters Without Borders Index	142
Table 7.3	Civic Activities and Beliefs Perceived to Be Important to Being a Good Citizen	145
Table A.1	Registration and Voting in 2016 and 2020 U.S. Presidential Elections: Gen Z Citizens and All Citizens 18+	186

PREFACE

Gen Z, Social Media, and News: Implications for the Future of News Engagement, Journalism, the U.S., and Democracy is the third book in a trilogy that captures the intersection of generation change and news landscape transformation. This generation change, which began in the early 1980s with the birth of Millennials, continued with the arrival of Gen Z beginning in the late 1990s, then intersected with the transformation of the news landscape that accelerated in 2004 with the emergence of Facebook and Apple's 2007 unveiling of the iPhone.

The first two books in this trilogy, the 2012 *Millennials, News, and Social Media: Is News Engagement a Thing of the Past?* and *News for a Mobile-First Consumer*, published in 2016, set the stage for *Gen Z, Social Media, and News: Implications for the Future of News Engagement, Journalism, the U.S., and Democracy*. It was in the 2012 book, revised and updated in 2018, that because of my concern that the Millennial generation's engagement with news could become a thing of the past that I proposed a day to engage with news which would always be the first Tuesday of October, approximately one month before Election Day in November.

Two years later as president of the Association for Education in Journalism and Mass Communication (AEJMC), the largest association of journalism and communication educators, professionals, and graduate students and with the help of the News Engagement Day Committee that I chair and AEJMC's staff, I made News Engagement Day a reality.

The second book in the trilogy—*News for a Mobile-First Consumer*—was a recognition that something had changed dramatically, and it would affect news engagement, but not necessarily in a way that would increase news engagement. The bottom-line was that we needed to understand how smartphones might affect news engagement but at the time there was no research. So, one year after *Millennials, News, and Social Media* was published, I conducted a one-person "experiment" and canceled the two print newspapers that were delivered to my home every day and started reading the news on my iPhone, using news apps. Even when I traveled and there were print newspapers available for free on the plane and in my hotel, I ignored them and continued reading news only on my phone.

My one-person experiment enabled me to quickly learn how transformational getting news on your phone was. First, I never again had to wait for the newspaper to be delivered to my driveway or for NBC Nightly News to come on TV at 5:30 p.m. And I saved money because my digital subscriptions were significantly cheaper.

But as someone who has been researching the news audience since graduate school, developed and implemented news in K-12 classrooms in Los Angeles and Austin, encouraged my Millennial daughter to read newspapers while she was growing up, and devoted 10–15 minutes of my Thursday classes to discussing important and interesting news, I also realized that the important news engagement socialization process that had begun in homes that Baby Boomers had grown up in, was in jeopardy. Pre-smartphone, Baby Boomer, Generation X, and older Millennial children learned that it was important to get news by observing their parents read print newspapers, watch news on TV, or listen to news on the car radio while being driven to school or after-school activities. But if parents were engaging with news on their phones, how would their kids know?

This news engagement socialization process of learning the importance of keeping up with the news by observing one's parents disappeared when parents stopped reading print newspapers and started reading news on the sleek, elegant device they could hold in one hand.

Gen Z, born 1997 through 2012, is the first generation to grow up when the news engagement socialization process that we took for granted is virtually non-existent. Add to that, the fact that if Gen Z is engaging with news on social media and YouTube where disinformation is pushed, it's unknown how informed Gen Z is about news that can be trusted and what that may mean for the future of news engagement, journalism, the United States, and democracy. These are critical questions that must be answered and through a national survey conducted with adults 18 and over, which includes the oldest of Gen Z, Millennials, Generation X, Baby Boomers, and the Silent Generation, this book will answer these questions and much more.

ACKNOWLEDGMENTS

As the third book in a trilogy that first explored Millennials and is now examining Gen Z's coming of age in a news landscape transformed by social media, smart mobile devices, and disinformation, *Gen Z, Social Media, and News: Implications for the Future of News Engagement, Journalism, the U.S., and Democracy* ultimately answers the questions: Who is Gen Z? What is this generation's relationship to social media and news and what does that mean for the future of news engagement, journalism, the United States and democracy?

To understand Gen Z, born 1997 through 2012, and this generation's relationship with social media and news first requires understanding Millennials, born 1981 through 1996 which is why these acknowledgments begin with my Millennial daughter Alexandra Elizabeth Garrick and my Millennial students who provided insight that enabled me to ask the right questions in the national survey I conducted for the first book in the trilogy, *Millennials, News, and Social Media: Is News Engagement a Thing of the Past?*

While the second book in the trilogy, *News for a Mobile-First Consumer* focused on the rapid adoption of smart mobile devices and their transformational impact on news and news engagement, my third book in the trilogy is the reason I acknowledge my Gen Z students. My Gen Z students and I didn't just discuss some of the most consequential news events in our class, we experienced some together beginning with the deadly COVID-19 pandemic which meant Zoom replaced our in-person classroom on the campus of the University of Texas at Austin.

Post-pandemic when we were back in the physical classroom, class activities and discussions, including about the news, as well as informal chats before and after class, I obtained new insight that enabled me to write a questionnaire for the book's national survey that included questions that reflected Gen Z's news engagement socialization and relationship with news and what that might mean for the future of news engagement, journalism, the United States, and democracy.

I do want to single out one of my Gen Z students—Colton Winters—for a special acknowledgment. After Colton expressed an interest in helping me with my book, we met weekly during the last month of the spring semester and I shared the questionnaire I was developing for the national survey that would be the foundation for the book. During those meetings I was able to get a Gen Z perspective on phrasing LGBTQ+ demographic questions. While Gallup's report, "U.S. LGBT Identification Steady at 7.2%" provided me with some direction on question wording, the discussion with my Gen Z student gave me confidence in the final phrasing of two questions.

In the first question, survey participants could choose male, female, non-binary or other. In the follow-up question, survey participants were asked: "Which of the following do you consider yourself to be?" You can select as many as apply: (1) Straight or heterosexual; (2) lesbian; (3) gay; (4) bisexual; (5) transgender; (6) other (please specify). By asking the two questions, I was able to include insightful LGBTQ+ data about Gen Z that the book otherwise would not have had.

I also want to acknowledge Dynata, the international research firm I commissioned to collect the data for The National Gen Z, Social Media, and News Survey. We were partners from beginning to the delivery of the data for 1,504 respondents in an SPSS file, ready to analyze. A special acknowledgment is extended to Frank Markowitz, Senior Account Director, and John Ray Clarin, Project Manager who were patient, responsive, and simply wonderful to work with.

Elizabeth (Lizzie) Howard, Peter Lang Acquisitions Editor also deserves a special acknowledgment. Lizzie's support, patience, and straightforward feedback are greatly appreciated. Plus, Lizzie gave me several ideas that I included in the book and she helped me refine a new idea I wanted to add to the book—reflection questions. Based on Lizzie's feedback, I added end-of-chapter questions and reflections, a feature of the book I'm very excited about. And Lizzie encouraged me to share my ideas for the design of the book cover.

I also want to acknowledge everyone who has helped make News Engagement Day successful. I proposed "A Day to Engage with News" in the trilogy's first book *Millennials, News, and Social Media: Is News Engagement a Thing of the Past?*, published in 2012. As the 2013–2014 president of the Association for Education in Journalism and Mass Communication (AEJMC), I founded News Engagement Day as one of my most important presidential initiatives. An annual event, News Engagement Day is held the first Tuesday in October, approximately one month before Election Day. In 2024, we celebrated the 11th News Engagement Day Tues., Oct. 1, just over a month before what was expected to be the most consequential election of the twenty-first century.

News Engagement Day activities and events, which are organized by journalism and communication educators across the country and internationally, focus on engaging with news and learning about the principles and process of journalism. That's why in *Gen Z, Social Media, and News: Implications for News Engagement, Journalism, the U.S., and Democracy*, I recommend that news organizations embrace News Engagement Day to help increase news engagement and awareness about the importance of an informed public in our democracy.

Without Samantha Higgins, AEJMC's Communication Director, and Kyshia Brown, AEJMC's Website & Graphic Designer, News Engagement Day would not be the successful annual event that it is.

Finally, we are all indebted to someone or something that inspired us and deserves recognition for who we are, what we value, what we teach, research, and publish. I am indebted to my parents who taught me, by example, the importance of engaging with news. My parents Alfred and Rachael Poindexter subscribed to two newspapers that were delivered to our home seven days a week. Observing my parents read the daily newspaper and watch news on TV while growing up, taught me that engaging with news was important. I taught the same lesson to my daughter as she was growing up.

I learned a different but related lesson from Dr. Maxwell McCombs when I was a graduate student and research assistant in the Communications Research Center in the Newhouse School of Public Communications at Syracuse University that he directed. Not only did I learn the value of researching the news audience, I discovered published journal studies about those who engaged with news and those who didn't. In fact, one of those published studies sparked my interest in researching why some engage with news and others don't. What I learned in my research has made me an advocate for engaging with news and becoming informed and an advocate for more research in this transformed news landscape.

So, while scholars and graduate students across the globe know Maxwell McCombs as the co-founder with Donald Shaw of agenda-setting, one of the most significant theories in the field of journalism and communication, I want to acknowledge him as the person who introduced me to researching the news audience. Without Maxwell McCombs, my mentor, dissertation chair, former colleague, co-author, and friend, I likely would never have discovered researching the news audience or written *Gen Z, Social Media, and News: Implications for the Future of News Engagement, Journalism, the U.S., and Democracy* and the two other books that complete the trilogy. So, Max, thank you!

· 1 ·

WHO IS GEN Z AND WHAT EVENTS AND ISSUES HAVE CONTRIBUTED TO DEFINING THIS GENERATION?

At the beginning of the third decade of the twenty-first century, Gen Z was among the three largest living generations in the United States (Duffin, 2022). Millennials, who preceded Gen Z, were the biggest while Baby Boomers, who had spent every stage of their lives as the largest generation until Millennials arrived, had fallen to third place in percentage of the population, behind both Millennials and Gen Z (Duffin, 2022).

Defined by the birth years 1997 through 2012, Gen Z was born during two different centuries and three different decades (Dimock, 2019). In 2025, the youngest of Gen Z would be in high school; the oldest would be starting their late 20s. In contrast, Millennials, who immediately preceded Gen Z, were born during two decades, from 1981 through 1996. In 2025, the oldest Millennials would be in their 40s; the youngest would be in their early 30s.

These age differences within and between generations are a reminder that while the birth years of a generation are fixed, as the calendar changes, so do the ages, life stages such as college student, entry-level employee, married, parent, etc., and experiences. Some experiences are influenced by the times in which generations lived but generations can also have an impact on the times and even change the course of history.

And as generations grow up, they are not immune to the experiences of their parents' generation. For example, Baby Boomers, born 1946 through 1964, were no doubt influenced by the lessons their parents learned growing up during the Great Depression, which began in 1929 with the stock market crash and lasted 10 years (History.com editors, n.d.). Similarly, younger siblings can be influenced by the experiences of older siblings born in an earlier generation.

Because a generation's birth years represent a period of a decade and a half to two decades, the youngest and oldest members can be very different. Gen Z middle school students, of course, are very different from their older counterparts who may be college graduates, in the military, have started families, or are on a path to moving up in their second or third jobs. That's why in *Millennials, News, Social Media: Is News Engagement a Thing of the Past?*, I introduced the concept of Wave I for the older members of a generation and Wave II for a generation's youngest members to underscore that differences *within* a generation not only exist but they are significant (Poindexter, 2012). Wave I, the oldest members of a generation, may also have more in common with Wave II, the youngest members of the previous generation.

Differences are also related to the historic times in which generations were born as well as the economic, political, social, health, technology, climate, cultural, race, ethnicity, gender, LGBTQ+, and religious events and issues that were salient as they were coming of age. In some cases, these events and issues were so impactful that they inspired a generation to march and speak out for change. Across generations, journalists have reported on these marches for change as well as significant issues and historic events, producing the first draft of history. But journalists have also been slow to report and even failed to fairly and accurately report events of major historic significance such as the Civil Rights Movement, the Women's Movement, the Vietnam War, and the run-up to the war in Iraq.

Although Gen Z is now the second largest generation, it's too soon to know the impact this generation will have over its lifetime. But we do know enough about Gen Z to understand that because of its size and the historic events and trends it has experienced during its formative and coming-of-age years that this generation merits more attention and news coverage.

Whether reported widely in the news or not, so far, Gen Z has experienced or been exposed to at least 22 events and issues that will define and influence its members far into the future. These events and issues include: (1) pandemic reading and math loss; (2) active shooter drills; (3) video of murder of George Floyd by a white police officer; (4) social media and mental health harm; (5) once-in-a-century global pandemic; (6) unprecedented young voter political power; (7) historic diversity at highest levels of U.S. government; (8) Supreme Court's overturning of Roe v. Wade; (9) frenzy of new censorship laws and bans; (10) disinformation contamination; (11) attack on U.S. democracy from within; (12) emergence of TikTok which Gen Z embraced and governments banned; (13) climate change; (14) killing DEI; (15) LGBTQ+ State of Emergency declared; (16) youth vaping epidemic; (17) AI's new extraordinary, scary powers; (18) Barbie, Greta, Beyoncé, and Taylor; (19) women still earn less than men; (20) Hamas' attack on Israel and Israel's war on Hamas trigger Antisemitism and Islamophobia as well as protests and arrests on U.S. college campuses; (21) The 2024 Presidential Election: Biden vs. Trump rematch upended; (22) The reset of the 2024 Presidential Election: Vice President Kamala Harris vs. Former President Donald Trump.

1. Pandemic Reading and Math Loss

The COVID-19 pandemic didn't just shut down schools in 2020; it contributed to the learning loss of Gen Z's youngest. When classes were moved online, students were not just abruptly placed in an unfamiliar learning environment without their teacher explaining, guiding, and helping them learn, some students didn't even have computers, access to the internet, or a parent or caregiver available to log them on to the internet and lead them through the unfamiliar remote learning process.

As a result of the online learning that replaced in-class learning, some Gen Z kids fell behind in reading and math while others never acquired the reading and math skills in the first place. And three years after the pandemic began, school districts were still trying to get their students back on track in these two subjects that are essential for K-12 success as well as for navigating life's fundamentals. (NAEP, n.d.; Educators try to turn around, 2023).

2. Active Shooter Drills

Mass school shootings are terrorizing, traumatizing, heart-wrenching, and rare (Follman et al., 2023). But what is not rare are active shooter drills that are conducted in K-12 schools. According to Everytown, the gun violence prevention organization, during the 2005–2006 school year, 40% of public schools in the United States conducted active shooter drills; a decade later, 95% of schools conducted drills to teach students to hide and stay quiet in case an assailant with a gun breached their locked school. If during the years between 2005 and 2015, from 40% to 95% of K-12 public schools conducted active shooter drills, it would *not* be inaccurate to say that Gen Z is the only generation in which active shooter drills were a routine part of their school experience.

Routine, though, doesn't mean without consequences. According to Everytown, the same drills that were created to keep students safe from a shooter have been "associated" with harming students. Everytown's research suggests that the mere participation in active shooter drills is related to increasing depression, stress, and anxiety (The Impact of Active Shooter Drills, 2023).

3. Video of Murder of George Floyd by White Police Officer

If it hadn't been for a Gen Z high school student and her phone, we never would have known what really happened to George Floyd, a 46-year-old Black man who had moved from Houston to Minneapolis where he would get what the *New York Times* called a "fresh start" (Fernandez & Burch, 2021).

On May 25, 2020, Memorial Day, late in the afternoon outside Cup Foods in Minneapolis, a White police officer knelt on the neck of a 46-year-old Black man whose hands were cuffed behind his back. The Black man's 6-foot, 4-inch body was stretched out on the pavement on the street side of a parked patrol car. From time to time, the Black man would call out: "I can't breathe" as a dozen or so bystanders watching from the curb, pleaded with the police officer to get his knee off the man's neck. One of the bystanders, a 17-year-old high school student, with her phone and steady hands, video recorded the White police officer kneeling on the neck of the Black man until he breathed his last breath (Yan, 2021). And then she posted the video on Facebook (Levenson, 2021).

Local and national news outlets reported on the shocking video and social media users shared it with friends, family, and followers. The video which captured the last minutes of George Floyd's life sparked outrage and mass Black Lives Matter protests in cities and communities across the country and around the globe. These protests, which were the "largest racial justice protests in the United States since the Civil Rights Movement," (Silverstein, 2021) ignited a racial reckoning that touched federal, state, and local governments, corporations and non-profits, public and private universities, professional associations, science, medicine, and public health, professional sports teams, including the NFL, NBA, and WNBA, and even news organizations such as the *New York Times, Los Angeles Times*, and *Kansas City Star* (Alder, 2020; A call to action, n.d.; The Times Editorial Board, 2020; Wilson, 2020). These protests against a White cop's very public and seemingly nonchalant murder of an unarmed and hand-cuffed Black man were the first mass racial justice protests that Gen Z participated in, perhaps, securing their place in history as an activist generation.

4. Social Media and Mental Health Harm

In 2004, when Facebook was founded for college students, there was no evidence that the term "social media" had been used by more than a few people who had worked at AOL (Bercovici, 2010). As Facebook evolved from its beginnings in Mark Zuckerberg's Harvard dorm room to a virtual space open to everyone, regardless of whether or not they had a college ID, the term social media was adopted to describe a new type of platform in which an individual's opportunity to share a message, news, entertainment or other types of information was *equal* to the most influential news outlets, Fortune 500 companies, and even the president of the United States.

With its exponential growth in such a short period of time, social media became an essential, if not dominant, communication and social force, integrated into every aspect of twenty-first-century life in the United States and other democratic societies. According to Statista, "Facebook was the first social network to surpass one billion registered accounts and currently sits at more than three billion monthly active users." Meta, the parent company of Facebook, "owns four of the biggest social media platforms, all with one billion monthly active users each: Facebook (core platform), WhatsApp, Facebook Messenger, and Instagram" (Dixon, 2024). The top five social networks worldwide, based on monthly active users are: Facebook (3.049 billion); YouTube (2.491 billion); WhatsApp (2.0 billion); Instagram (2.0 billion); and TikTok (1.6 billion) (Dixon, 2024).

With domination, there can be effects, intended and unintended, beneficial and harmful. But it was the harmful effects exposed by a former Facebook manager turned whistleblower as well as research published in academic journals that caused alarm from local communities around the country to Capitol Hill and the Surgeon General.

In interviews with *The Wall Street Journal* and "60 Minutes" as well as testimony to the U.S. Senate Commerce Subcommittee, former Facebook product manager Frances Haugen disclosed that internal research showed that Instagram was detrimental to the mental health of teenage girls. The popular social media platform made girls feel negative about their bodies and contributed to anxiety, depression, and suicidal thoughts (Wells et al., 2021).

The negative effects of social media disclosed by the whistleblower were consistent with results from an earlier study published in the *Lancet Child & Adolescent Health* journal. That study found that frequent use of social media was bad for the mental health of girls between the ages of 13 and 16 because of more exposure to bullying and a decrease in activities such as sleeping and exercising that had a "positive impact" on mental health (Viner et al., 2019).

In a January 2023 CNN interview, U.S. Surgeon General Vivek Murthy cautioned the public about social media's detrimental effects. He said that although social media companies allowed 13-year-old children to join, 13 was too young because of social media's "skewed and often distorted environment" and children were "still developing their identity" (Gordon & Brown, 2023). Despite the Surgeon General's warning, eight percent of Gen Z, ages 13–17, were on Instagram worldwide (Dixon, 2023).

Warnings from the former Facebook manager and the U.S. Surgeon General as well as published scientific research no doubt prompted the American Psychological Association to publish a health advisory on social media use in adolescence that included 10 recommendations (Health advisory, n.d.).

By May 2023, social media's mental health toll on Gen Z youth had become an "urgent public health issue" that demanded the "nation's immediate awareness and action" (Social media, n.d.) That's why the U.S. Surgeon General Vivek Murthy issued the "Social Media and Youth Mental Health Advisory," alerting the public to "growing concerns about the effects of social media on youth mental health" (Social media, n.d.). The advisory described "current evidence on the positive and negative impacts of social media on children and adolescents." And it provided "actionable recommendations" for policymakers and technology companies as well as suggestions for parents, caregivers, young people, and researchers (Social media, n.d.).

5. Once-in-a-Century Global Pandemic

March 11, 2020, the *Washington Post* published the following headline: "WHO declares a pandemic of coronavirus disease covid-19" (Wan, 2020). Similar alarming headlines were published, posted, broadcast, tweeted, and talked about around the United States and across the globe. The *Washington Post* article quoted the World Health Organization director who said "more than 118,000 cases" of the coronavirus had been identified in "114 countries, and 4,291 people" had died (Wan, 2020). WHO's director expected that the number of coronavirus cases as well as deaths and countries affected would increase. Less than a month after the World Health Organization declared the pandemic, more than a half-million coronavirus (or what the WHO was now calling COVID-19) cases had been detected in the United States and 18,600 people had died (CDC COVID Timeline, n.d.).

And almost three years after the WHO's pandemic declaration, COVID-19 had infected 102,736,819 people in the United States and 1,110,364 people had died. Without the wearing of masks, social distancing, the development of tests to detect COVID-19 infections, and free vaccines to inoculate against the virus as well as the closing of schools, colleges, offices, and public events and venues, the number of COVID cases and deaths likely would have been significantly higher.

And without journalists' robust reporting of COVID updates from the White House and CDC as well as insightful interviews with independent infectious disease scientists and medical professionals who explained the scientifically based methods of protection, the deadly pandemic might have been more devastating and have lasted longer (COVID Data Tracker, n.d.).

The pandemic, though, didn't stop with the number of people infected and the men, women, and children who died. Small businesses were shut down. People lost their jobs and homes. Food insecurity increased. Children fell behind in school. And the "college-going rate" suffered its "steepest" decline (Binkley, 2023).

The pandemic also exposed racism and racial disparities in the United States which were vigorously reported on after a teenager posted her video of the murder of George Floyd, a Black man, by a White Minneapolis police officer. Black Lives Matter marches across the country and around the world protested both George Floyd's murder and the racism and racial disparities in policing, use of force, sentencing, and the criminal justice system overall.

But it was headlines like NPR's "CDC Director Declares Racism A 'Serious Public Health Threat'" (Wamsley, 2021) that connected the dots between racism built into the U.S. system prior to the Civil Rights Movement and passage of the 1964 Civil Rights Act and the racial disparities exposed by the pandemic that focused news coverage and grabbed the public's attention.

The CDC Director explained that the "disproportionate case counts and deaths" on communities of color "were not a result of COVID-19" but the pandemic had "illuminated inequities that have existed for generations and revealed for all of America a known, but often unaddressed, epidemic impacting public health: racism" (Media Statement from CDC Director, 2021). Explaining racism and its effects, the CDC Director said:

> Racism is not just the discrimination against one group based on the color of their skin or their race or ethnicity, but the structural barriers that impact racial and ethnic groups differently to influence where a person lives, where they work, where their children play, and where they worship and gather in community. These social determinants of health have life-long negative effects on the mental and physical health of individuals in communities of color. Over generations, these structural inequities have resulted in stark racial and ethnic health disparities that are severe, far-reaching and unacceptable. (Media Statement from CDC Director, 2021)

George Floyd's murder, the Black Lives Matter protests, and the CDC Director's declaration on racism as a serious public health threat shined a bright light on racial disparities, but it was the reporting with relevant context across platforms—network and local TV, cable and streaming as well as local and national newspapers, social media, radio, podcasts and smart speakers—that informed the public and contributed to a national racial reckoning.

And individuals, regardless of generation, public service volunteers, students, educators, journalists, TV and cable program hosts, social media influencers, athletes and entertainers, heads of corporations, non-profits, foundations, school districts, colleges, and universities as well as local, state, and national elected and appointed officials responded to the racial reckoning. And they appeared committed to addressing the racial inequities exposed by the pandemic. But that commitment for some was short-lived—the racial reckoning had also sparked a backlash, beginning with some state legislatures passing and governors signing laws that only allowed the teaching of a whitewashed racial history of the United States (Natanson et al., 2022).

6. Unprecedented Young Voter Political Power

Time magazine called the 2020 presidential election a "breakthrough moment" for young voters (Alter, 2021). CNBC described the "53% to 55%" young voter turnout rate as the "highest ever recorded in modern political history" (Hess, 2020). John Della Volpe, polling director of Harvard's Institute of Politics (IOP), predicted the 2022 Midterms would see a "Gen Z Wave," saying: "Youth today vote at levels that far exceed Millennials, Generation X and Baby Boomers when they were under 30" (Fall 2022 Harvard Youth Poll, 2022).

"Gen Z is a formidable voting bloc that demands to be heard," added Setti Warren, Director of the Institute of Politics. "Across geography, race, gender, and background, young Americans view the world from a starkly different lens than older generations. Elected officials should pay attention" (Fall 2022 Harvard Youth Poll, 2022).

Two factors—inspiration and fear—motivated Gen Z's unprecedented levels of voting, according to John Della Volpe, the Institute of Politics polling director (Fall 2022 Harvard Youth Poll, 2022). Gen Z's inspiration came from the Parkland, Florida high school students who survived what the History Channel described as the "deadliest shooting at a high school in United States history" (History.com, 2018). After a former student, carrying an "AR-15 semi-automatic rifle," breached the high school and shot and killed 17 students and staff and wounded 17 more, surviving Marjory Stoneman Douglas High School students didn't cower—they organized and mobilized. They created "Never Again MSD, an anti-gun violence organization and political action committee" (History.com, 2018). They marched, held rallies, lobbied elected officials for gun safety laws, and registered voters.

The fear that motivated Gen Z's unprecedented voting was three-fold, according to the polling director at Harvard's Institute of Politics: fear for their future; fear for the planet; and fear for their country (Fall 2022 Harvard Youth Poll, 2022). And fear of a future school shooting massacre like the one the Parkland students experienced may also have been on this young generation's mind once they were old enough to cast their first vote.

7. Historic Diversity at Highest Levels of U.S. Government

When the cabinet of Donald Trump, the 45th president, was complete, the *New York Times* described it as "more white and male than any cabinet since Ronald Reagan's" (*The New York Times*, 2017). Inaugurated as the 40th U.S. president 36 years before Donald Trump, Ronald Reagan served two terms during the 1980s, the decade in which the oldest Millennials were born.

In contrast to the Trump cabinet that included 20 White males, two White females, two Asian American females, and one Black male, Joe Biden, who was inaugurated January 20, 2021 as the 46th U.S. president, assembled a cabinet that not just reflected the diversity of the United States but also of Millennials and Gen Z, the most diverse generations ever. President Biden's cabinet included seven White males, four White females, two Black males and four Black females, three Hispanic males and one Hispanic female, two Asian American females, one Native American female, and one bi-racial (Black and Asian-American) female (The Cabinet, n.d.).

Diversity in the Biden administration wasn't limited to more women and people of color in the cabinet; there were also diversity-firsts in which women, people of color, and openly LGBTQ+ people were nominated for and appointed to positions they had never served in before. When Democratic presidential nominee Joe Biden picked Kamala Harris, a former U.S. senator and California attorney general, to be his vice-presidential running mate and they won, for the first time since the country's founding, the vice president of the United States was not a White male.

When Janet Yellen was confirmed as Secretary of Treasury, she became the first woman to hold that cabinet post. And with her confirmation as Secretary of the U.S. Department of Interior which "protects and manages the Nation's natural resources and cultural heritage; provides scientific and other information about those resources; and honors its trust responsibilities or special commitments to American Indians, Alaska Natives, and affiliated Island Communities," Deb Haaland, a member of the Pueblo of Laguna, became the first Native American to serve as a cabinet secretary (Secretary Deb Haaland, n.d.).

Separate from the cabinet post of Secretary of Treasury is the position of Treasurer of the United States which oversees the U.S. Mint, the Bureau of Engraving and Printing, and Fort Knox. When President Biden appointed Marilynn Malerba, the chief of the Mohegan Tribe, as Treasurer, she became the first Native American to hold the position. And because the Treasurer's signature is on U.S. currency, "for the first time in U.S. history, a Tribal leader and Native woman's signature" was printed on U.S. currency (Eddy, 2022; Rappeport, 2022).

And when the Senate voted 93-2 vote to confirm four-star Army General Lloyd Austin as President Biden's Secretary of Defense, for the first time in U.S. history, an African American would serve in that position (Booker, 2021).

Appointments in the Biden administration were also notable for LGBTQ+ firsts. When former mayor of South Bend, Indiana Pete Buttigieg was confirmed as Secretary of Transportation in the Biden administration, he became the first openly gay cabinet member in American history. The confirmation of pediatrician Rachel Levine, Pennsylvania's top health official, as the assistant secretary of health was also a historic first. Levine is an openly transgender female (Schmidt et al., 2021).

When in 1993, Bill Clinton, the 42nd U.S. president, appointed "Dee Dee" Myers White House Press Secretary, it was the first time a woman had held that position. In three of the four presidencies after Clinton, at least one woman served as White House Press Secretary. After Joe Biden's first press secretary Jen Psaki served two years in that position before joining MSNBC to host her own cable news program "Inside with Jen Psaki," President Biden appointed Karine Jean-Pierre (2022) as the new White House Press Secretary. Not only is Jean-Pierre the first Black woman to serve in that position, she is the first Black person to serve as White House Press Secretary. And she is the first openly gay White House Press Secretary.

Among the significant firsts of the Biden administration is Ketanji Brown Jackson. Since George Washington, the first president of the United States, nominated John Jay in 1789 to the Supreme Court, there have been 116 Supreme Court justices (FAQs—Supreme Court Justices, n.d.). It took 178 years for a non-White person to serve on the Supreme Court and 192 years before a woman became a Supreme Court justice.

When in 1967 President Lyndon B. Johnson nominated Thurgood Marshall to the Supreme Court, it was history-making. As head of the Legal Defense Fund (n.d.), which grew out of the NAACP, Thurgood Marshall brought segregated school cases to the Supreme Court, which led to the 1954 landmark Supreme Court ruling Brown v. Board of Education. With Thurgood Marshall's swearing in, for the first time since the founding of the United States, the Supreme Court had a Black justice. In President Ronald Reagan's 1981 nomination of Sandra Day O'Connor, for the first time, a woman would serve on the Supreme Court. With Barack Obama's nomination of Sonia Sotomayor in 2009, for the first time the Supreme Court included a person who was Hispanic. From 1991 to 2020, another Black male and three more White females would be appointed to the Supreme Court.

But not until the election of the 46th president of the United States would a Black woman be nominated to serve on the U.S. Supreme Court. And when on "June 30, 2022, Chief Justice John G. Roberts, Jr., administered the Constitutional Oath and Associate Justice Stephen G. Breyer (Retired) administered the Judicial Oath to the Honorable Ketanji Brown Jackson," for the first time since the nation's founding, an African American woman would serve on the U.S. Supreme Court (Oath Ceremony, n.d.).

8. Supreme Court's Overturning of Roe v. Wade

The June 24, 2022, *New York Times* headline said it all: "In 6-to-3 Ruling, Supreme Court Ends Nearly 50 Years of Abortion Rights" (Liptak, 2022). When the U.S. Supreme Court established a constitutional right to an abortion in its 1973 landmark 7-2 Roe v. Wade ruling, the oldest Baby Boomers were in their early to mid-twenties and Millennials and Gen Z weren't yet born. Roe v. Wade, a landmark Supreme Court ruling, issued on January 22, 1973, struck down a Texas statute banning abortion, effectively legalizing the procedure across the United States (History.com editors, 2022).

When almost a half-century later, the Supreme Court overturned the right to an abortion, the oldest of Gen Z were in their mid-twenties. A whopping 70% of 18-to-29-year-olds, which included Gen Z's oldest and the youngest Millennials, disapproved of the overturning of Roe v. Wade. In fact, the disapproval of young adults is eight points higher than the 62% of all Americans who say abortion "should be legal in all or most cases" (Majority of public disapproves, 2022). And within seven months of the Supreme Court ruling that made abortion illegal, 14 states outlawed or heavily restricted abortion (Knight et al., 2023). And by March 2023, Wyoming Gov. Mark Gordon had "signed into law the nation's first explicit ban on abortion pills" (Gruver, 2023).

9. Frenzy of New Censorship Laws and Bans

2020 will not just be remembered for the start of a once-in-a-century pandemic, the Black Lives Matter protests in the aftermath of the murder of

George Floyd, and a presidential election in which a sitting president lost, refused to concede, and pushed a lie that the election had been stolen from him. 2020 will also be known as the beginning of a frenzy of new censorship laws and bans of books, materials, and concepts to control what was taught and what was learned about diversity, primarily as it related to African Americans and LGBTQ+ communities.

One hundred and 55 years after the ratification of the 13th Amendment that freed Black people who were enslaved, 66 years after the 1954 landmark Brown v. Board of Education Supreme Court ruling that made segregated schools illegal, and 56 years after President Lyndon Johnson signed the 1964 Civil Rights Act that outlawed segregation in public facilities, and within months of the Black Lives Matter marches and the nation's collective racial reckoning, Republican-dominated state houses began passing laws that restricted teaching about race, racism, and slavery. And many of these same state houses, inspired by Florida's law, known as "Don't Say Gay," passed laws that limited, and in some cases, prohibited teachers from discussing LGBTQ+ issues in their classrooms (Erasing LGBTQ, 2023; Swidriski, 2022).

According to a *Washington Post* analysis, during a three-year period, 283 laws in 45 states were proposed to control how teachers taught about "race, racism, and American history" as well as what they said about "gender identity, sexuality and LGBTQ issues" (Natanson et al., 2022). These proposed laws would also give parents more control "over their children's education;" "limit students' access to school libraries and books;" restrict "the rights of transgender students; and/or promote what legislators defined as a 'patriotic' education" (Natanson et al., 2022). Of the proposed laws, 64 passed in 25 states with 28% of the laws limiting race-related instruction, and 23% restricting what teachers could discuss about LGBTQ-related issues.

By 2022, banning books in schools had reached a record high level. "From July 2021 to June 2022," PEN America's Index of School Book Bans "identified 2,532 instances of individual books being banned, affecting 1,648 unique book titles" (America's Censored Classrooms, 2022).

Specifically, PEN America found books had been banned in "138 school districts in 32 states, representing 5,049 schools with a combined enrollment of nearly 4 million students" (Banned in the USA, n.d.). Forty-one percent of the banned books had an LGBTQ+ theme or included prominent LGBTQ+ characters. Prominent characters of color were the focus of 40% of the banned books with 21% specifically addressing race and racism. But bans weren't limited to local school library books.

Within months of the 2020 murder of George Floyd by a White police officer, former President Donald Trump banned race-related training in federal agencies. The memorandum announcing the ban directed federal agencies to "cease and desist from using taxpayer dollars to fund" training on "critical race theory," "white privilege," or "any other training or propaganda effort that teaches or suggests either (1) that the United States is an inherently racist or evil country or (2) that any race or ethnicity is inherently racist or evil" (Memorandum, 2020).

Banning "critical race theory," which became a popular talking point for Republican politicians and pundits as well as hosts of conservative cable shows, radio broadcasts, and podcasts, was particularly notable because prior to the 2020 Black Lives Matter protests, few outside of law schools had heard the phrase or even knew what it meant. After the Black Lives Matter protests, many had heard of "critical race theory," especially if they watched Fox News on cable. In 2021, critical race theory was mentioned "1,860 times" on Fox News shows (Barr, 2021). Still, few could define the concept that late Harvard Law Professor Derrick Bell developed during the 1970s.

So, what is "critical race theory?" The *Washington Post*'s definition is one that non-legal scholars can understand. Critical race theory is an "academic framework centered on the idea that racism is systemic, and not just demonstrated by individual people with prejudices. The theory holds that racial inequality is woven into legal systems and negatively affects people of color in their schools, doctors' offices, the criminal justice system, and countless other parts of life" (Iati, 2021).

As a theory taught in law schools and written about in law journals, critical race theory is not being taught in K-12 classrooms. But scholars are using critical race theory as a framework for studying "how policies and practices in K-12 education contribute to persistent racial inequalities in education" (Sawchuck, 2021). According to *Education Week*, critical race theory has been the framework for studying "racially segregated schools, the underfunding of majority-Black and Latino school districts, disproportionate disciplining of Black students, barriers to gifted programs and selective-admission high schools, and curricula that reinforce racist ideas" (Sawchuck, 2021).

In addition to shutting down federal government diversity training programs and attacking "critical race theory," in Republican-dominated state houses across the country, laws were proposed and passed that banned the

"1619 Project," a series of essays published August 14, 2019, by *The New York Times Magazine* that commemorated the 400th anniversary of the date that enslaved Africans were brought to American colonies. Conceived by Nikole Hannah-Jones who won a Pulitzer Prize for the lead essay, "The 1619 Project" sought to "reframe the country's history by placing the consequences of slavery and the contributions of Black Americans at the very center of our national narrative" (The 1619 Project, 2019).

The Pulitzer Center (unrelated to journalism's most prestigious award, the Pulitzer Prize), created a multi-media curriculum, comprised of lesson plans, guides, and prompts, designed to facilitate teaching the *New York Times Magazine* project that reframed U.S. history about enslaved Africans and their impact (The 1619 Project Curriculum, n.d.).

Even the College Board's first-ever AP course for African American Studies that was created in consultation with "more than 300 professors" and "tried out" in "60 high schools around the country" was rejected by at least one state (Anderson & Rozsa, 2023). Although Florida did not pass a specific law to ban the advanced placement course that gave college credit to high school students who took the course and passed the AP exam, the education office rejected the course, saying it violated Florida law (Izaguirre, 2023).

10. Disinformation Contamination

Misinformation. Disinformation. Propaganda. Lies. The Big Lie. The name varies depending on the source—journalist, researcher, pundit, cable news show host, social media influencer, analyst, opinion columnist, politician, journalism educator—but the meaning is consistent with Merriam-Webster's definition. According to the online dictionary, disinformation is "false information deliberately and often covertly spread (as by the planting of rumors) in order to influence public opinion or obscure the truth" (Merriam-Webster, n.d.). Disinformation, which is purposeful and intended to deceive, can come in the form of half-truths, misleading statements and/or statistics, deceptive claims, conspiracy theories, and outright lies.

And disinformation doesn't stop with words; it can also arrive through video and audio called "deepfakes." A combination of the terms "deep learning" and "fake," deepfakes are "persuasive-looking but false video and audio files. Made using cutting-edge and relatively accessible AI (artificial intelligence) technology, they purport to show a real person doing or saying something they did not" (Metz, 2019). By 2023, with the development of new

AI tools, fake videos looked more realistic, making it easier to mislead when pushed across social media and video-sharing platforms (Duffy, 2023).

Gen Z likely first encountered disinformation on a national scale as those who were born in 1997 and 1998 prepared to vote in their first presidential election in 2016. Little did these 18- and 19-year-old first-time voters know that they were targets of a social media disinformation campaign created and executed by "Russian agents" to "drive down voter turnout" (Adler, 2018).

By 2018, two years after the 2016 presidential election in which Democratic nominee Hillary Clinton lost to Donald Trump, California established a new "Office of Elections Cybersecurity" with the goal of combatting Russia-backed social media disinformation campaigns that sought to "confuse voters or discourage them from casting ballots" (Adler, 2018).

Disinformation that targeted first-time Gen Z voters during the 2016 presidential election included: (1) "an image of actor Aziz Ansari holding a photoshopped sign urging Hillary Clinton supporters to save time by tweeting their votes from home;" (2) "an official-looking Clinton campaign graphic" urging Hillary Clinton supporters to "Vote from home" and to "Text 'Hillary' to 59925;" (3) social media posts directing voters to the "wrong polling place;" (4) claims that the "election was taking place on a different day;" (5) advising voters not to fill out provisional ballots because they wouldn't be counted even though "more than 90 percent of provisional ballots are ultimately counted" (Adler, 2018).

Additionally, according to reports commissioned by the U.S. Senate Intelligence Committee, "the Russian influence campaign on social media in the 2016 election made an extraordinary effort to target African-Americans" with the goal of suppressing their vote which was expected to favor Hillary Clinton over Donald Trump (Shane & Frenkel, 2018).

Disinformation campaigns, though, have not been limited to elections targeting first-time Gen Z voters or African Americans. And Russian agents have not been the only ones creating and pushing disinformation. Disinformation was widespread during the pandemic and the U.S. government's efforts to vaccinate Americans against the deadly virus. Disinformation about COVID-19 and the safe and effective vaccines developed to inoculate the public against being infected was so pervasive that the FDA (Food and Drug Administration) created a Web page to combat the lies. Called "Rumor Control," the web page was introduced with the following alert:

> The growing spread of rumors, misinformation and disinformation about science, medicine, and the FDA, is putting patients and consumers at risk. We're here to

provide the facts. Help stop rumors from spreading by doing three easy things: Don't believe the rumors. Don't pass them along. Get health information from trusted sources like the FDA and our government partners, such as usa.gov/health, coronavirus.gov and vaccines.gov. (Rumor Control, n.d.)

Because disinformation about the results of the 2020 presidential election began after the polls closed Election Day, November 3, on November 12, 2020, the Infrastructure Government Coordinating Council & the Election Infrastructure Sector Coordinating Executive Committee issued a joint statement that stressed the 2020 presidential election results could be trusted.

> The November 3rd election was the most secure in American history. Right now, across the country, election officials are reviewing and double checking the entire election process prior to finalizing the result.
>
> When states have close elections, many will recount ballots. All of the states with close results in the 2020 presidential race have paper records of each vote, allowing the ability to go back and count each ballot if necessary. This is an added benefit for security and resilience. This process allows for the identification and correction of any mistakes or errors. There is no evidence that any voting system deleted or lost votes, changed votes, or was in any way compromised. (Joint Statement, 2020)

This unprecedented joint statement about the security of the 2020 presidential election was necessary to counter what became known as "The Big Lie," which then-President Donald Trump began pushing within hours of the closing of the polls on November 3 (Final Report Select Committee, 2022). Despite the joint statement confirming the 2020 presidential election had been the most secure in history, Donald Trump lied and said that he had won the election but the election had been stolen from him. Donald Trump continued to repeat "The Big Lie" and so did his supporters. This disinformation was also repeated on Fox News by hosts and guests (Folkenflik, 2023). What became known as "The Big Lie" became the impetus for the Jan. 6, 2021 attack on the U.S. Capitol and American democracy.

In addition to disinformation about the global pandemic, Covid-19 vaccines, and the 2020 presidential election, disinformation has been found in official police reports in which a Black person died following an encounter with the police. A *Washington Post* examination of the 2015 "fatal injury" of Freddie Gray while he was in the custody of Baltimore police found the "initial police version of events was misleading, incomplete or wrong, with the first accounts consistently in conflict with the full set of facts once they finally emerged" (Parker & McDaniel, 2023).

The *Washington Post* also analyzed six other high-profile cases, including the initial police report on George Floyd who was murdered by a White Minneapolis police officer in 2020. The analysis found that "in cases where the police are later accused of excessive and unwarranted use of force, the first draft of history is almost always written in part by those same officers, who often portray the police in flattering ways and the alleged suspect in less flattering ones" (Parker & McDaniel, 2023).

11. Attack on U.S. Democracy from Within

In 2020, unbeknownst to first-time Gen Z voters as well as the millions of experienced voters who stood in line at polling places in their designated precincts to vote early or on election day, or mailed their ballot at the local post office or dropped it in a secure drop box, that what Americans had taken for granted for over two centuries about a post-presidential election period would not happen. Unlike losing candidates in past presidential elections, in 2020, the losing presidential candidate Donald Trump did not concede defeat and insisted that he had won the election and it had been stolen from him. And for the first time since this democracy was founded, the transfer of power was not peaceful.

On January 6, 2021, the day that the leaders and members of both houses of Congress as well as the Vice President of the United States, in his role as president of the Senate, were scheduled to gather in a Joint Session of Congress to certify the election of Joe Biden as the 46th President of the United States, the U.S. Capitol was violently attacked (Final Report Select Committee to Investigate the January 6th Attack, 2022). As supporters of then-President Donald Trump attacked the Capitol, the Vice President, senators, representatives, and staff fled and hid from the violent mob.

Since the closing of the polls on Election Day, Tuesday, November 3, 2020, and the counting of the in-person and mail-in ballots, former President Trump has lied to his supporters, telling them over and over that he won the 2020 presidential election and it had been stolen from him (Price, 2023). At the "Stop the Steal" rally held near the White House at Noon, January 6, 2021, prior to the Joint Session of Congress in which the Electoral College votes from each state would be counted and Joe Biden's winning of the presidency would be certified, Donald Trump told his supporters:

All of us here today do not want to see our election victory stolen by emboldened radical-left Democrats, which is what they're doing. And stolen by the fake news media. That's what they've done and what they're doing. We will never give up, we will never concede. It doesn't happen. You don't concede when there's theft involved.

Our country has had enough. We will not take it anymore and that's what this is all about. And to use a favorite term that all of you people really came up with: We will stop the steal. Today I will lay out just some of the evidence proving that we won this election and we won it by a landslide. (Transcript of Trump's speech at rally, 2021)

By the end of his rally speech, the former President told his supporters he would walk to the Capitol with them, but that did not happen. The Secret Service drove former President Trump back to the White House. Wrapping up his rally speech, the 45th President said: "You'll never take back our country with weakness. You have to show strength and you have to be strong. We have come to demand that Congress do the right thing and only count the electors who have been lawfully slated, lawfully slated" (Transcript of Trump's speech at rally, 2021). Former President Trump added: "I know that everyone here will soon be marching over to the Capitol building to peacefully and patriotically make your voices heard."

But by afternoon with the Vice President, serving in the role of President of the Senate, as well as members of the Senate and House having assembled to count the Electoral ballots and certify that Joe Biden would be the 46th President of the United States, Donald Trump's supporters pushed through the barricades, swarmed the Capitol steps, assaulted police, smashed the Capitol's windows, unlawfully entered the building, called for the hanging of the Vice President, and broke into the office of the Speaker of the House.

By 3:36 p.m., "more than two hours after protesters" first breached the Capitol grounds, White House press secretary Kayleigh McEnany tweeted that President Trump had "ordered the National Guard to the Capitol" (Lonsdorf et al., 2024). Shortly after 4 p.m., then-President-Elect Joe Biden addressed the nation: "I call on President Trump to go on national television now, to fulfill his oath and defend the Constitution and demand an end to this siege. This is not a protest—it is an insurrection" (Lonsdorf et al., 2024).

Despite frantic phone calls and tweets from Republican leaders and members of Congress who pleaded with President Trump to tell his supporters to go home, it wasn't until 4:17 p.m. that the President spoke to his supporters through a tweeted video. After telling his supporters that he knew their pain and hurt, he said: "We love you. You're very special. You've seen what happens. You've seen the way others are treated. ... I know how you feel, but go home, and go home in peace" (Lonsdorf et al., 2024).

The impact of the violent attack on the U.S. Capitol that lasted almost five hours can be measured by lives lost, the 140 police officers assaulted, the almost $3 million dollars of damage to the U.S. Capitol building, and the approximately 1,000 supporters of President Trump who were arrested and 351 who were sentenced within 24 months of January 6 (24 Months, n.d.).

January 6's impact can also be assessed by the terrifying moments suffered by members of Congress, their staff, and the shaken confidence in the belief that the democracy of the United States was strong, stable, and secure. But after the January 6 violent attack on the U.S. Capitol by supporters of the defeated 45th President of the United States, perhaps, for the first time, there were the seeds of a realization that the 2018 *New York Times* best-seller *How Democracies Die* (Levitsky & Ziblatt, 2018) may have been sending a message to the American people and telling them to "wake up."

12. Emergence of TikTok Which Gen Z Adored and Governments Banned

About a decade and a half after a Millennial and his Millennial friends created Facebook for Millennials, the Chinese tech company ByteDance merged three separate apps to create a single new app with a catchy name, and TikTok was born (Tidy & Galer, 2020). Just as Millennials enthusiastically adopted Facebook when it was founded during the first decade of the twenty-first century, Gen Z embraced TikTok with gusto during the beginning of the twenty-first century's third decade.

According to the Pew Research Center, TikTok "has become especially popular among teens—two-thirds of whom report using it in some way—as well as young adults" (Matsa, 2022). And "about a quarter of Americans in this age group (26%) say they regularly get news there" (Matsa, 2022). Plus, Gen Z is increasingly using TikTok as a tool for searching for information, which appears to have motivated Google to improve its search engine (Huang, 2022).

With TikTok describing its app as the "leading destination for short-form mobile video" with a mission "to inspire creativity and bring joy," it's not surprising that by February 2023, TikTok had 150 million monthly active users in the United States (Our mission, n.d.). What has been surprising is the unprecedented efforts by the federal government as well as state governments to ban the video-sharing app that Gen Z adores.

Initially, TikTok bans at the federal and state levels focused on government devices but that changed when the state of Montana, population about 1.1 million, passed a law that banned TikTok from personal devices (Fung, 2023). Public universities have also been affected by the bans—TikTok is no longer accessible on laptops and tablets distributed to faculty, staff, and students or even on instructional computers in classrooms. And some universities such as the University of Texas at Austin, Auburn University, and Boise State University have blocked TikTok from campus Wi-Fi, which automatically extended the TikTok ban to personal devices of students, faculty, and staff who relied on the university's Wi-Fi while on campus (Tolentino, 2023; Maheshwari, 2023).

The federal government and some state governments in the United States have not been alone in their TikTok bans. In addition to India, which banned TikTok in mid-2020, other government bodies implementing TikTok bans included Britain, Canada, France, Australia, New Zealand, and the European Union (Australia, 2023).

The reason for the ban? China. Because TikTok is owned by ByteDance, a Chinese company, governments became concerned that TikTok's parent company would give "sensitive user data" to the Chinese government (Maheshwari & Holpuch, 2025). Many in Gen Z and among the youngest Millennials are not happy with the banning of TikTok. Forty-six percent of adults under 30 oppose the U.S. government's TikTok ban. In contrast, the majority of older generations support banning TikTok (Silver & Clancy, 2023).

13. Climate Change

Seven-in-ten Americans say "they've felt sad about what is happening to the Earth, when they've seen news and information about climate change recently," according to a Pew Research Center report (Tyson & Kennedy, 2023). And 43% acknowledge that "climate change is causing harm to people in the U.S. today" (Tyson & Kennedy, 2023). Considering that the World Meteorological Association concluded that "2011–2020 was the warmest decade on record by a clear margin for both land and ocean" and "each successive decade since the 1990s has been warmer than all previous decades" (The global climate, n.d.), the emotions that are expressed in the Pew Research Center are not inconsistent with the impact that accelerated climate change is having. Even though climate change disinformation is still pushed, the science is well known. Perhaps, what is less well known is the impact that "severe floods, wildfires and hurricanes" can have on people who are in "financially and socially formative college years" (Hersher, 2024).

According to the study, "students whose families live in ZIP codes where there was a severe weather disaster" "get worse grades than their peers, are more likely to withdraw from difficult courses, and ultimately are more likely to default on their student loans after they graduate" (Hersher, 2024). The study also found that these climate change-induced disasters can even "keep students from entering college in the first place." It found that "students who are on the cusp of going to college when a disaster hits, are less likely to enroll, potentially leading to lower long-term earnings" (Hersher, 2024).

14. Killing DEI

Launched in the aftermath of the murder of George Floyd, DEI—Diversity, Equity, and Inclusion initiatives were created to address historic racial disparities exposed during the pandemic. But because of a Republican backlash, starting in the Trump White House and followed by states with Republican governors, many DEI initiatives were short-lived. According to the DEI Legislation Tracker (2024), 85 anti-DEI bills were introduced in 28 states and the U.S. Congress; 53 were "tabled, failed to pass or were vetoed"; "14 have final legislative approval"; and 14 have become law (DEI Legislation Tracker, 2024).

In 2023, Florida's Republican Gov. Ron DeSantis led the way in signing legislation "to defund diversity, equity and inclusion programs at all state universities" (Maher, 2023). As a result of Florida's new law, the University of Florida closed "the office of the Chief Diversity Officer," eliminated "13 full-time positions," ended 15 faculty administrative appointments, reallocated "$5M in funds," and discontinued "DEI-focused contracts with outside vendors" (Nottingham et al., 2024).

Texas followed Florida with similar anti-DEI legislation that Republican Gov. Greg Abbott signed into law. In addition to eliminating new DEI positions and closing new DEI offices at state universities and colleges, diversity statements in hiring and promotions were prohibited, and decades-old offices and programs that were established to support students and organizations of color were shut down under the new Texas law, SB 17 (SB 17, n.d.; McGee & Mohamed, 2024).

DEI proponents said the "recent backlash from lawmakers is an attempt to roll back decades of progress toward making college campuses and work environments diverse and inclusive to all" (Nottingham et al., 2024). University of Connecticut's vice president and chief diversity officer observed that there are "historic parallels between the growing outrage over DEI and the backlash to previous efforts to integrate education and expand civil rights" (Jones, 2024).

January 20, 2025, following his inauguration as the 47th President of the United States, Donald Trump signed the executive order "Ending Radical And Wasteful Government DEI Programs And Preferencing" (2025). His executive order affected all departments in the federal government as well as public universities, K-12 schools, public media, non-profits, and contractors that received federal dollars. Although not subject to President Trump's anti-DEI executive order, Target and other Fortune 500 companies minimized, and in some cases, eliminated their DEI initiatives, backtracking on a commitment to diversity in the aftermath of the murder of George Floyd and Black Lives Matter protests (Meyersohn, 2025).

15. LGBTQ+ State of Emergency Declared

"Following an unprecedented state legislative session in 2023, the Human Rights Campaign officially declared a state of emergency for LGBTQ+ people in the United States for the first time ever." In 2023, "over 75 anti-LGBTQ+ bills were signed into law" "with a laser focus on transgender and non-binary youth." Twenty-one "gender-affirming care ban bills" were passed, "effectively eliminating access for youth to age-appropriate, medically-necessary health care." "Anti-LGBTQ+ legislation also included bills undermining the inclusion of LGBTQ+ topics and support systems in schools as well as intentional misgendering, and forcible outing" (2023 State Equality Index, n.d.).

State officials continued anti-LGBTQ+ policies in 2024: "Florida officials revoked transgender residents' ability to update gender markers on driver's licenses and ID cards; Utah passed a bill banning transgender people from bathrooms corresponding to their gender identity; and Texas' attorney general pressed a clinic in Georgia for medical records of transgender young people who used telehealth to obtain gender-affirming care there" (Ramirez, 2024).

16. Youth Vaping Epidemic

Six years after the U.S. Surgeon General declared vaping an epidemic, U.S. senators said the "unchecked sales" of "e-cigarettes in vivid colors and candy flavors" that "attract young people who could become addicted to nicotine" "pose a tremendous public health threat" (Jewett, 2024).

The World Health Organization (WHO), calling for "urgent action," documented this public health threat by saying 13-to-15-year-olds were "using e-cigarettes at rates higher than adults in all WHO regions." In Canada, according to the WHO, "rates of e-cigarette use among 16–19-year-olds doubled between 2017–2022," and in England (the United Kingdom) the number of young people using e-cigarettes "tripled in the past three years."

The World Health Organization also underscored that "e-cigarettes have been allowed on the open market and aggressively marketed to young people" (Urgent action, 2023). Although "34 countries ban the sale of e-cigarettes, 88 countries have no minimum age at which e-cigarettes can be bought and 74 countries have no regulations in place for these harmful products" (Urgent action, 2023).

In the United States, the Gallup Poll found eight percent of adults "smoked e-cigarettes in the past week" with "those under age 30 more than twice as likely as any other age group to smoke e-cigarettes." In fact, according to the Gallup Poll, "vaping is now more common than cigarette smoking among young adults (18% vs. 10%, respectively)."

Although vaping is viewed as less harmful than cigarettes, a majority (54%) of Americans say vaping is "very harmful" (Jones, 2023). And while the Gallup Poll found 55% of Americans would like to see stricter vaping laws and regulations, other countries are taking action against vaping.

The British Prime Minister "unveiled a package of measures to ban single-use vapes, restrict flavors, and regulate packaging and displays" (Specia, 2024). "Australia introduced sweeping legislation late last year that bans all vaping without a prescription. French lawmakers have backed a proposal to ban single-use vapes. And New Zealand has introduced regulations on marketing vapes to children" (Specia, 2024).

17. AI's New Extraordinary, Scary Powers

Because we were accustomed to Siri and Alexa promptly responding to simple requests and virtual assistants helping us shop, bank, refill prescriptions, and do our taxes online, we learned to trust them, took them for granted, and didn't feel a need to pay close attention. But when ChatGPT burst on the scene spring 2023 (Metz, 2023), the world, from news outlets, social media, governments, and businesses to researchers, educators, Gen Z, and older generations, paid close attention—especially after "more than 1,000 technology leaders and researchers" issued a warning in an open letter (Metz & Schmidt, 2023).

The open letter called for a pause in the development of these powerful "AI systems" because they were capable of "profound risks to society and humanity" (Pause, 2023). The letter's FAQs (2023) identified at least seven ways these AI systems could cause harm: "discrimination and bias, misinformation, the concentration of economic power, adverse impact on labor, weaponization, and environmental degradation."

But just because the open letter called on technology leaders to pause AI development, it didn't mean Gen Z students wouldn't explore ChatGPT or educators wouldn't assume their Gen Z students might use it to cheat as a professor did at Texas A&M-Commerce. The professor not only falsely accused his whole class of using ChatGPT to write their final paper, he gave them incompletes and required them to prove they *didn't* cheat which jeopardized their graduation (Verma, 2023).

Educators are also advocating for the incorporation of AI into teaching. That's what Ken Fleishmann, a professor in the School of Information at the University of Texas at Austin, is doing. Fleishmann said that instead of trying to catch students cheat, faculty should "modify assignments to make them more AI-proof" (Baskar, 2023).

Students at the University of Texas at Austin are not "forbidden from using AI in the process of curating or enhancing one's work," according to the Vice Provost for Academic Affairs. However, according to the UT-Austin vice provost: "At no point should anyone turn in an assignment that uses (AI) without acknowledging how it was used" (Baskar, 2023).

18. A Dream Cultural Moment for Barbie, Greta, Beyoncé, and Taylor

If you can dream it—there's no limit—could be the theme song for Barbie, Greta, Beyoncé, and Taylor. But, of course, Barbie can't dream because she's a doll. Created in 1959, according to History.com (n.d.), Barbie was re-imagined and re-born with a brain and feelings in 2023 by Greta Gerwig who co-wrote and directed "Barbie" which "grossed more than $1.4 billion at the box office, making it the biggest movie of the year, and the highest-grossing film ever directed by a woman" (Lansky, 2024).

"Barbie," which a Statista report (Worldwide box office, 2024) called a "very pink fantasy-comedy" "has since become a pop-culture phenomenon" (Lansky, 2024). "Gerwig's story is as much about commerce as it is about art: her films are humane, emotional, and playful; she is the only director in history to have their first three solo feature films nominated for Best Picture at the Oscars. Yet her movies also clean up at the box office" (Lansky, 2024).

Just as every girl and woman of a certain generation played with Barbie growing up, the younger generations sang along with and danced to a Beyoncé song or attended a Beyoncé concert. Beyoncé's "Renaissance" World Tour concert which was scheduled to play 57 cities by the tour's end is projected by *Forbes* magazine to "clear nearly $2.1 billion." And this number doesn't include theater ticket and streaming sales from "Renaissance: A Film by Beyoncé" (Asmelash, 2023). And then non-country artist Beyoncé, perhaps realizing a dream, ventured into country with the release of "Texas Hold 'Em," which "debuted in the top spot of Billboard's Hot Country Songs chart" (Rosenbloom, 2024). Not long afterward, Beyoncé dropped her first country album—"Cowboy Carter."

"After launching a record-shattering global tour and becoming the world's most-streamed musical artist in 2023," Taylor Swift entered new territory when she bypassed "studios and streamers" and released the concert film "Taylor Swift: The Eras Tour" with AMC, giving the theater chain "its highest single-day ticket sales in history" (Gutterman, 2023). And then *Time* magazine named Taylor Swift the 2023 "Person of the Year," making her "the first person to be selected because of her achievement in the arts" (Shah, 2023).

19. Women Still Earn Less than Men

On Equal Pay Day in 2024, the president and CEO of the Institute for Women's Policy Research (IWPR) called the gender pay gap in the United States a "national disgrace" (Sahadi, 2024). An analysis of wage data found that in the United States, women have to work "14.5 months" to make "12 months' worth of a man's median wages" (Sahadi, 2024).

Or, according to the National Committee on Pay Equity and the Equal Pay Today campaign, for every dollar a man earns, a woman is paid 84 cents (Here are the other equal pay dates, n.d.). And even in professions that are "typically dominated by women, men earn more for doing the same job"

(Sahadi, 2024). Whether men and women work in the same occupation or different occupations, women still earn less than men (Institute for Women's Policy, 2024).

However, there is a point in a lifetime of work that the gender pay gap is almost but not completely closed: When "men and women are in their early-to mid-20s" (Sahadi, 2024). When the pay of White men is compared to Black, Hispanic, or Native American women, the difference in pay is "typically widest" (Sahadi, 2024).

20. Hamas' Attack on Israel and Israel's War on Hamas Trigger Antisemitism and Islamophobia as well as Protests and Arrests on U.S. College Campuses

Israel's war to destroy Hamas in Gaza after Hamas' surprise Oct. 7, 2023 attack in which 1,200 were killed and 250 men, women, and children were taken hostage has resulted in the deaths of "more than 40,000 Palestinians" during the war's first 10 months (Shurafa & Frankel, 2024). Additionally, the war has contributed to a devastating humanitarian crisis, including food insecurity, scarce clean water, bombed-out hospitals, damaged medical equipment, insufficient medicine and supplies, and disease-inducing unsanitary conditions.

As the first news reports about Hamas' attack on Israel and Israel's war to destroy Hamas spread across the globe, on some college campuses in the United States, there was an emergence of Islamophobia and antisemitism (Smith, 2023). Six months and a half months later, "pro-Palestinian demonstrations" had "sprung up at more than 150 colleges and universities across the country" (Rosenzweig-Ziff, et al., 2024). "On more than 80 campuses, state, local and campus police, sometimes in riot gear" "monitored or dispersed crowds" (Rosenzweig-Ziff, et al., 2024). And from mid-April through May 2, "more than 2,000 people" were arrested on college and university campuses, from Columbia University and the University of Wisconsin, Madison to the University of Texas at Austin and the University of Southern California (Rosenzweig-Ziff, et al., 2024).

According to the *New York Times*, "historians who study student movements say the United States hasn't seen such a large number of people arrested in campus protests in 50 years. While millions of students participated in protests against the Vietnam War, there were about 4,000 arrests at campus protests in the spring of 1969, during the most intense period of activity." New York University historian Robert Cohen asserts that "the pro-Palestinian activism is a relatively small movement," however, "the arrests are almost comparable to the height of the Vietnam protests" (Tate et al., 2024).

With students returning to campus Fall 2024, college administrators are preparing for the resumption of protests, including the establishment of encampments on campus grounds. While the future of protests ultimately may be tied to whether Israel and Hamas agree to the latest "cease-fire and hostage deal" proposal from the "United States and its allies," college administrators and students are expecting that the protests will pick up where they left off at the end of spring semester 2024 (Hudson et al., 2024; The Associated Press, 2024). And students' demands driving the protests will continue. In addition to "demanding an end to Israel's war in Gaza," students are demanding their colleges and universities "divest from, or cut financial ties with, Israel or companies profiting from its invasion of Gaza" (Edmonds et al., 2024). Additionally, Yale and Cornell students are demanding that their schools "stop investing in weapons manufacturers" and Columbia students "want their school to sell holdings in Google, which has a large contract with the Israeli government, and Airbnb, which allows listings in Israeli settlements on the occupied West Bank" (Edmonds et al., 2024).

21. The 2024 Presidential Election Biden vs. Trump Rematch Upended

It wasn't the 2024 presidential election that voters wanted but it was the election that voters thought they would have when on Tuesday, March 12, 2024, both President Joe Biden, age 81, and former President Donald Trump, age 78, secured their party's nomination (Knowles & Olorunnipa, 2024). With little movement in the polls or visible enthusiasm for the rematch, the Biden campaign sought to inject something fresh into the race by challenging the former president to two debates with the first one to be held in June and hosted by CNN. But President Biden's "disastrous" debate performance on June 27 (Lee et al. 2024) wasn't the "new beginning" Democrats had hoped for. It was a "moment of panic" (Korecki et al., 2024). June 28, 2024, the day after the debate, the *New York Times* Editorial Board called on President Biden to step aside, saying:

"At Thursday's debate, the president needed to convince the American public that he was equal to the formidable demands of the office he is seeking to hold for another term. Voters, however, cannot be expected to ignore what was instead plain to see: Mr. Biden is not the man he was four years ago" (To serve his country, 2024).

Despite calls from Democrats in the House and eventually, the Senate, for President Biden to drop out, President Biden insisted he would continue his presidential campaign. But on Sunday afternoon, July 21, 2024, President Biden announced he would no longer seek a second term as president of the United States (Joseph R. Biden, 2024). And then, he endorsed his Vice President to be the Democratic Party's 2024 nominee for president (Biden, 2024).

22. Reset of the 2024 Presidential Election: Vice President Kamala Harris vs. Former President Donald Trump

So, 91 days before Election Day, there was no longer a race between a 78-year-old former president and an 81-year-old current president. The 78-year-old former president would now be running against the Vice President—the first woman of color—Black and South Asian—to be the nominee of a major political party. And Kamala Harris was 19 years younger than Donald Trump.

Would Gen Z Turn Out to Vote in the Most Consequential Presidential Election in Their Young Lives?

In two of the past four presidential elections—2008 and 2020—over half of young voters turned out to vote. In 2020, 55% voted, making it the second-largest young voter turnout in almost a half century (Youth voter, n.d.). The largest young voter turnout—55.4%—was 1972 after the July 1, 1971 ratification of the Twenty-Sixth Amendment (n.d.) to the U.S. Constitution which extended the right to vote to 18-, 19-, and 20-year-olds who were able to vote for the first time. Between 1972, the first U.S. presidential election in which young voters, ages 18–20, were eligible to vote and 2020 when President Joe Biden defeated former President Donald Trump, the lowest young voter turnout during a presidential election was 1996 when only 39.6% of young voters voted.

With the resetting of the 2024 presidential race— Vice President Kamala Harris vs. former President Donald Trump— what would Gen Z voter turnout be? And how informed would Gen Z be? Would Gen Z's sources of information about the election and where the candidates stood on issues important to them and their generation be trustworthy? And what would Gen Z do when confronted with disinformation that pushed false information about the election? And how would Gen Z vote in 2024 when a woman of color—Black and South Asian—was the nominee for president for a major political party? Regardless of the outcome, the historic significance of the 2024 presidential election would no doubt contribute to defining this generation born during the years 1997 through 2012.

Gen Z, Social Media, and News: Implications for the Future of News Engagement, Journalism, the U.S., and Democracy: An Overview

Gen Z is one of seven generations born since 1901. From the oldest to the youngest, the generations are: Greatest Generation (1901–1924); Silent Generation (1925–1945); Baby Boomers (1946–1964); Generation X (1965–1980); Millennials (1981–1996); Gen Z (1997–2012); Post-Gen Z (2013–?).

The years born represent only one of many factors that make Gen Z and other generations unique. Events and issues that a generation experiences while coming of age can contribute to defining it and so can the technology that transforms how they communicate, work, travel, socialize, entertain themselves, and get and make news part of their lives.

And let's not forget other factors that can leave a defining imprint on a generation: A war; the election of the first Black president in the United States; the election of the first woman vice president who is also a person of color; a health, economic or education crisis; the passage of a transformational law; the Supreme Court's overturning of a half-century of abortion rights across the nation and the passage of laws that ban abortion at the state level; marching and advocating for civil rights, voting rights, social justice, gun safety, clean air, etc.; the failure to peacefully transfer presidential power from a defeated U.S. president to a newly elected U.S. president as insurrectionists attacked the Capitol and our democracy.

As we think about the generations that came before Gen Z and those that will come after, it is important to keep in mind what Michael Dimock (2023), president of the Pew Research Center, said: "generational categories are not scientifically defined." That lack of scientific rigor is why a generation's birth years may vary depending on the expert (Dimock, 2019; Howe & Strauss, 2000; Twenge, 2023). And the naming of generations also lacks scientific rigor. In fact, a generation's name is more likely to be the result of its frequent use in the media than a scientific measurement.

Even so, the lack of scientific rigor in designating years born and naming a generation do not change the fact that each of the 22 events and issues outlined in Chapter 1 that Gen Z personally experienced or learned about through social media and news outlets, will always be a distinctive part of their generation's history. Millennials, Generation X, and Baby Boomers will also have experienced and learned about the events through social media and news but will likely see them from the vantage point of an older, more established generation.

Although the 22 events and issues described in Chapter 1 helped answer the question: Who is Gen Z?, by the chapter's end, it was clear that we know a lot more about the events and issues that have contributed to defining Gen Z than we know about the generation born during the years 1997 through 2012.

The obvious reason that we don't know more about Gen Z is that it will be 2030 before everyone in this post-Millennial generation is 18 years or older. Gen Z's youngest aren't yet in high school; they're too young to drive and too young to vote. And although kids only have to be 13 to join social media, parental permission is required for anyone under 18 to participate in a research study or news poll.

A less obvious reason that we don't know more about Gen Z is the data have been mixed with data about Millennials. Polls will report on adults "under 30" but that age range of 18–29 includes the youngest Millennials. And as you'll learn later, another part of the reason our Gen Z knowledge is limited is that, whether consciously or unconsciously, the news media have not regularly included young adults in their news reports unless they've committed or been a victim of a crime, have excelled in the world of sports and entertainment or have done something so extraordinary that it would be journalism malpractice not to report about them (Poindexter, 2018).

While the data about this generation, born 1997 through 2012, is incomplete and somewhat muddied, the 22 events and issues that have helped define Gen Z are clear. Unfortunately, many of the events and issues discussed in Chapter 1 have been a source of harm and that harm has not been limited to the generation born after Millennials.

Whether the murder of George Floyd, a Black man, by a White police officer, a once-in-a-century pandemic and the reading and math loss that followed, active shooter drills for kindergarteners to high school seniors, the Supreme Court's overturning of a half-century constitutional right to an abortion, states restricting what teachers can teach about African American history and LGBTQ+ issues, exposure to detrimental social media content, disinformation pushed on social media, cable news channels, and even at the dinner table, and attacks, large and small, on our democracy, these events and issues have immediate and long-term harmful consequences that can impede Gen Z's growth and potential and even set the country back decades.

While these events and issues have been reported in the news, the subjects of tweets on Twitter which Elon Musk bought and renamed X, and cable news chatter, the impetus for marches, partisan talking points, statehouse banning bills and the focus of disinformation, it is not known how informed Gen Z has been about some of them. More detail is needed about the sources Gen Z has relied on to learn about events and issues reported in the news. And because Gen Z, unlike previous generations, has come of age in a social media-smartphone world infected with disinformation, it's not even known if what Gen Z has learned was from news reported by journalists guided by ethical principles, lies that prime-time cable news and podcast hosts pushed, or inaccurate information unwittingly shared by a family member or friend.

Although Gen Z is the second largest living generation, we know less about Gen Z than we knew about Millennials at the same stage of their coming of age. But that changes with *Gen Z, Social Media, and News: Implications for the Future of News Engagement, Journalism, the U.S., and Democracy*. The National Gen Z, Social Media & News Engagement Survey that this book is based on provides significant insight into this generation's relationship with social media and news and attitudes about journalism.

Results from the demographic questions tell us who Gen Z is and the questions on political party, ideology, and past and future voting behavior help us understand the Gen Z voter. Using crosstabulation analysis, percentages that tell us about Gen Z enable us to compare their answers to Millennials and older generations which are combined into one group. Plus, with answers to several open-ended questions, we learn more about Gen Z through their own words.

In addition to painting a demographic portrait, Chapter 2 examines social media and news in the lives of Gen Z, including preferred news topics and platforms. Plus, gender differences in news interests are analyzed. The focus of Chapter 3 is the news engagement socialization process, which has been disrupted by the smartphone, social media, and a decline in legacy media. This chapter also defines and explores news engagement routines and the important role they play in increasing engaging with news. In Chapter 4, Gen Z grades, from A to F, social media and other digital news platforms as well as the news in general, journalism, and coverage of their generation. As the "fastest-growing segment of the electorate," (Marquez, 2023), the Gen Z voter is the focus of Chapter 5. Barriers to a news smart Gen Z, from a broken news engagement socialization process to avoidances, disinformation, and a lack of knowledge about how journalism works are examined in Chapter 6.

Finally, Chapter 7 will speak to the book's subtitle and help answer the question of where we are: Inflection Point? Tipping Point? Point of No Return? By the end of *Gen Z, Social Media, and News*, readers will have the information, the data, and the insight needed to begin answering those critical questions about social media and news as well as the future of news engagement, journalism, the United States, and our democracy.

Questions and Reflections

Please Note: Questions to answer, research, and reflect on are at the end of each chapter. For your convenience, a complete list of all end-of-chapter questions is included in the Appendix.

1. Review the 22 events and issues described in Chapter 1. What event or issue do you think has most contributed to defining Gen Z? Why did you select that event or issue?
2. What event or issue would you add to defining Gen Z? Explain your rationale for adding that event or issue.

References

24 Months since the January 6 attack on the Capitol. (n.d.). https://www.justice.gov/usao-dc/24-months-january-6-attack-capitol

1619 Project, The. (2019). https://www.nytimes.com/interactive/2019/08/14/magazine/1619-america-slavery.html

1619 Project Curriculum, The. (n.d.). https://pulitzercenter.org/lesson-plan-grouping/1619-project-curriculum

2023 State Equality Index: A review of state legislation affecting the lesbian, gay, bisexual, transgender and queer community and a look ahead in 2024.

2023 *State Equality Index* (n.d.). https://reports.hrc.org/2023-state-equality-index?_ga=2. 872 07082.300447684.1706811924-465285443.1704472908

A call to action: Building a culture that works for all of us. (n.d.). https://www.nytco.com/company/diversity-and-inclusion/a-call-to-action/#our-plan

Adler, B. (2018). *California launches new effort to fight election disinformation.* https://www.npr.org/2018/09/23/649524683/california-launches-new-effort-to-fight-election-disinformation

Alder, E. (2020). *"Brutes" and murderers: Black people overlooked in KC coverage—except for crime.* https://www.kansascity.com/news/local/article247235584.html

Alter, C. (2021). *The 2020 election was a breakthrough moment for young voters.* https://time.com/6049270/2020-election-young-voters/

America's Censored Classrooms. (2022). https://pen.org/report/americas-censored-classrooms/

Anderson, N., & Rozsa., L. (2023). *Amid DeSantis attacks, AP African American studies course is updated.* https://www.washingtonpost.com/education/2023/02/01/ap-african-american-studies-curriculum-desantis/

Asmelash, L. (2023). *Everything you need to know about Beyoncé's "Renaissance" movie.* https://www.cnn.com/2023/11/26/entertainment/beyonce-renaissance-movie-preview-cec/index.html

Associated Press, The. (2024). *U.S. colleges revise rules on free speech in hopes of containing anti-war demonstrations.* https://www.nbcnews.com/news/us-news/us-colleges-revise-rules-free-speech-hopes-containing-anti-war-demonst-rcna166866

Australia bans TikTok from federal government devices. (2023). https://www.npr.org/2023/04/04/1167878286/australia-bans-tiktok-from-federal-government-devices

Banned in the USA: The growing movement to censor books in schools. (n.d.). https://pen.org/report/banned-usa-growing-movement-to-censor-books-in-schools/

Barr, J. (2021). *Critical race theory is the hottest topic on Fox News. And it's only getting hotter.* https://www.washingtonpost.com/media/2021/06/24/critical-race-theory-fox-news/

Baskar, K. (2023). *UT professors embracing, preparing for AI use in classrooms.* https://www.kxan.com/news/education/ut-professors-embracing-preparing-for-ai-use-in-classrooms/

Bercovici, J. (2010). *Who coined "social media"? Web pioneers compete for credit.* https://www.forbes.com/sites/jeffbercovici/2010/12/09/who-coined-social-media-web-pioneers-compete-for-credit/amp/

Biden, J. (2024). *My fellow Democrats.* https://x.com/JoeBiden/status/1815087772216303933

Binkley, C. (2023). *Jaded with education, more Americans are skipping college.* https://apnews.com/article/skipping-college-student-loans-trade-jobs-efc1f6d6067ab770f6e512b3f7719cc0

Booker, B. (2021). *Lloyd Austin confirmed as Defense Secretary, becomes 1st Black Pentagon Chief.* https://www.npr.org/sections/president-biden-takes-office/2021/01/22/959581977/lloyd-austin-confirmed-as-secretary-of-defense-becomes-first-black-pentagon-chie

Cabinet, The. (n.d.). https://www.whitehouse.gov/administration/cabinet/

CDC Covid Timeline. (n.d.). https://www.cdc.gov/museum/timeline/covid19.html

COVID Data Tracker. (n.d.). https://covid.cdc.gov/covid-data-tracker/#cases-deaths-testing-trends

DEI Legislation Tracker. (2024). https://www.chronicle.com/article/here-are-the-states-where-lawmakers-are-seeking-to-ban-colleges-dei-efforts

Dimock, M. (2023). *5 things to keep in mind when you hear about Gen Z, Millennials, Boomers and other generations*. https://www.pewresearch.org/short-reads/2023/05/22/5-things-to-keep-in-mind-when-you-hear-about-gen-z-millennials-boomers-and-other-generations/

Dimock, M. (2019). *Defining generations: Where Millennials end and Generation Z begins*. https://www.pewresearch.org/fact-tank/2019/01/17/where-millennials-end-and-generation-z-begins

Dixon, S. (2024). *Global social networks ranked by number of users 2024*. https://www.statista.com/statistics/272014/global-social-networks-ranked-by-number-of-users/

Dixon, S. (2023). *Distribution of Instagram users worldwide as of January 2023, by age group*. https://www.statista.com/statistics/325587/instagram-global-age-group/

Duffin, E. (2022). *U.S. population share by generation 2021*. https://www.statista.com/statistics/296974/us-population-share-by-generation/

Duffy, C. (2023). *Puffer coat Pope. Musk on a date with GM CEO. Fake AI "news" images are fooling social media users*. https://www.cnn.com/2023/04/02/tech/ai-generated-images-social-media

Eddy, K. (2022). *Treasury applauds appointment of Chief Lynn Malerba as Treasurer of the United States*. https://home.treasury.gov/news/featured-stories/treasury-applauds-appointment-of-chief-lynn-malerba-as-treasurer-of-the-united-states

Editorial Board. (2024). *To serve his country, President Biden should leave the race*. https://www.nytimes.com/2024/06/28/opinion/biden-election-debate-trump.html?smid=nytcore-ios-share&referringSource=articleShare&sgrp=c-cb

Edmonds, C., Betts, A., & Hartocollis, A. (2024). *What to know about the campus protests over the Israel-Hamas War*. https://www.nytimes.com/2024/04/17/us/college-protests-israel-hamas-war-antisemitism.html?smid=nytcore-ios-share&referringSource=articleShare&sgrp=c-cb

Educators try to turn around pandemic-era learning loss. (2023). PBS News Weekend. https://www.pbs.org/newshour/show/educators-try-to-turn-around-pandemic-era-learning-loss

Ellis, N. T. (2024). *NAACP, DEI supporters call on Black athletes to avoid colleges in states with anti-DEI laws*. https://www.cnn.com/2024/03/11/us/naacp-black-athletes-anti-dei-laws/index.html?iid=cnn_buildContentRecirc_end_recirc

Ending radical and wasteful government DEI programs and preferencing. (2025). https://www.whitehouse.gov/presidential-actions/2025/01/ending-radical-and-wasteful-government-dei-programs-and-preferencing/

Erasing LGBTQ People from Schools and Public Life. (2023). https://www.mapresearch.org/file/MAP-Under-Fire-Erasing-LGBTQ-People_2023.pdf

FAQs—Supreme Court Justices. (n.d.). https://www.supremecourt.gov/about/faq_justices.aspx

FAQs about FLI's open letter calling for a pause on giant AI experiments. (2023). https://futureoflife.org/ai/faqs-about-flis-open-letter-calling-for-a-pause-on-giant-ai-experiments/

Fernandez, M., & Burch, A. D. S. (2021). *George Floyd, from "I Want to Touch the World" to "I Can't Breathe."* https://www.nytimes.com/article/george-floyd-who-is.html

Final Report Select Committee to Investigate the January 6th Attack on the United States Capitol. (2022). https://www.govinfo.gov/content/pkg/GPO-J6-REPORT/pdf/GPO-J6-REPORT.pdf

Folkenflik, D. (2023). *Rupert Murdoch says Fox stars "endorsed" lies about 2020. He chose not to stop them.* https://www.npr.org/2023/02/28/1159819849/fox-news-dominion-voting-rupert-murdoch-2020-election-fraud

Follman, M., Aronsen, G. & Pan, D. (2023). *US mass shootings, 1982–2023: Data from Mother Jones' investigation.* https://www.motherjones.com/politics/2012/12/mass-shootings-mother-jones-full-data/

Fung, B. (2023). *Montana lawmakers vote to completely ban TikTok in the state.* https://www.cnn.com/2023/04/14/tech/montana-house-tiktok-ban

The global climate 2011–2020: A decade of accelerating climate change. (n.d.). https://library.wmo.int/viewer/68585/download?file=1338_Decadal_State_Climate-HG_en.pdf&type=pdf&navigator=1

Gordon, A., & Brown, P. (2023). *Surgeon General says 13 is "too early" to join social media.* https://www.cnn.com/2023/01/29/health/surgeon-general-social-media

Gruver, M. (2023). *Wyoming governor signs measure prohibiting abortion pills.* https://apnews.com/article/wyoming-medication-abortion-ban-gordon-8120493afa25f7a2d4233192dc612cb3

Gutterman, A. (2023). *"I bet on myself." How Taylor Swift's deal with AMC came together.* https://time.com/6342992/taylor-swift-amc-eras-tour-movie-deal/

Harvard Youth Poll. (2022). https://iop.harvard.edu/youth-poll/44th-edition-fall-2022

Health advisory on social media use in adolescence. (n.d.). https://www.apa.org/topics/social-media-internet/health-advisory-adolescent-social-media-use

Here are the other equal pay dates for 2024. (n.d.). https://www.pay-equity.org/

Hersher, R. (2024). *The unexpected links between climate change, student debt and lower lifetime earnings.* https://www.npr.org/2024/02/27/1230002959/debt-missed-classes-and-anxiety-how-climate-driven-disasters-hurt-college-studen

Hess, A. J. (2020). *The 2020 election shows Gen Z's voting power for years to come.* https://www.cnbc.com/2020/11/18/the-2020-election-shows-gen-zs-voting-power-for-years-to-come.html

History.com. (n.d.). *The Barbie doll makes its debut.* https://www.history.com/this-day-in-history/barbie-makes-her-debut

History.com. (2018). *Teen gunman kills 17, injures 17 at Parkland, Florida high school.* https://www.history.com/this-day-in-history/parkland-marjory-stoneman-douglas-school-shooting

History.com editors. (2022). *Roe v. Wade.* https://www.history.com/.amp/topics/womens-history/roe-v-wade

Howe, N., & Strauss, B. (2000). *Millennials rising: The next great generation.* Vintage Books.

Huang, K. (2022). *For Gen Z, TikTok is the new search engine.* https://www.nytimes.com/2022/09/16/technology/gen-z-tiktok-search-engine.html?smid=nytcore-ios-share&referringSource=articleShare

Hudson, J., Vinall, F., Bisset, V., & Balousha, H. (2024). *U.S. proposes final Gaza cease-fire plan, seeking agreement by next week.* https://www.washingtonpost.com/world/2024/08/16/israel-gaza-war-ceasefire-news-hamas/

Iati, M. (2021). *What is critical race theory, and why do Republicans want to ban it in schools?* https://www.washingtonpost.com/education/2021/05/29/critical-race-theory-bans-schools/

The impact of active shooter drills in schools: Time to rethink reactive school safety strategies. (2023). Everytown. https://everytownresearch.org/report/the-impact-of-active-shooter-drills-in-schools/#intro

Institute for women's policy research fact sheet. (2024). https://iwpr.org/wp-content/uploads/2024/03/Occupational-Wage-Gap-2024-Fact-Sheet-1.pdf

Izaguirre, A. (2023). *Florida blocks high school African American studies class.* https://apnews.com/article/ron-desantis-florida-race-and-ethnicity-education-353417231de0a790c8e290479a5e52b8

Jewett, C. (2024). *Top senators urge stores to stop selling illicit vapes.* https://www.nytimes.com/2024/03/07/health/vaping-senators-warning-fda.html?smid=nytcore-ios-share&referringSource=articleShare&sgrp=c-cb

Joint Statement from Elections Infrastructure Government Coordinating Council & the Election Infrastructure Sector Coordinating Executive Committees. (2020). https://www.cisa.gov/news-events/news/joint-statement-elections-infrastructure-government-coordinating-council-election

Jones, A. (2024). *DEI supporters see echoes of America's fraught racial history in attacks on diversity efforts.* https://www.cnn.com/2024/02/23/us/dei-defenders-see-historic-backlash-reaj/index.html

Jones, J. M. (2023a). *U.S. cigarette smoking rate steady near historical low.* https://news.gallup.com/poll/509720/cigarette-smoking-rate-steady-near-historical-low.aspx

Joseph R. Biden, Jr. (2024). https://static01.nyt.com/newsgraphics/documenttools/5c749e32c65e55c0/37384880-full.pdf

Karine Jean-Pierre to be next White House press secretary. (2022). https://www.pbs.org/newshour/politics/karine-jean-pierre-to-be-next-white-house-press-secretary

Knight, S., Davis, W., Gourlay, K., Wroth, C., Chu, H., & Daugert, K. (2023). *Here's where abortions are now banned or severely restricted.* https://www.npr.org/sections/health-shots/2022/06/24/1107126432/abortion-bans-supreme-court-roe-v-wade

Knowles, H., & Olorunnipa, T. (2024). *Biden and Trump secure their parties' presidential nominations.* https://www.washingtonpost.com/politics/2024/03/12/biden-trump-win-presidential-nomination/

Korecki, N., Dixon, M., & Allen, J. (2024). *Babbling' and "hoarse": Biden's debate performance sends Democrats into a panic.* https://www.nbcnews.com/politics/2024-election/biden-debate-performance-democrats-panic-rcna157279

Lansky, S. (2024). *Greta Gerwig's next big swing.* https://time.com/collection/women-of-the-year/6692799/greta-gerwig-interview/

Lee, C. E., Welker, K., Allen, J., Memoli, M., & Alba, M. (2024). *"It's a mess": Biden turns to family on his path forward after his disastrous debate.* https://www.nbcnews.com/news/amp/rcna159591

Legal Defense Fund. (n.d.). https://www.naacpldf.org/about-us/history/full

Levenson, E. (2021). *Former officer knelt on George Floyd for 9 minutes and 29 seconds—not the infamous 8:46.* https://www.cnn.com/2021/03/29/us/george-floyd-timing-929-846/index.html

Levitsky, S., & Ziblatt, D. (2018). *How democracies die.* Broadway Books.

Liptak, A. (2022). *In 6-to-3 ruling, Supreme court ends nearly 50 years of abortion rights.* https://www.nytimes.com/2022/06/24/us/roe-wade-overturned-supreme-court.html

Lonsdorf, K., Dorning, C., Isackson, A., Kelly, M. L., & Chang, A. (2024). *A timeline of the Jan. 6 Capitol attack—including when and how Trump responded* https://www.npr.org/2022/01/05/1069977469/a-timeline-of-how-the-jan-6-attack-unfolded-including-who-said-what-and-when

Maher, K. (2023). *DeSantis signs bill to defund DEI programs at Florida public colleges* https://www.cnn.com/2023/05/15/politics/desantis-signs-dei-defunding-bill/index.html

Maheshwari, S. (2023). *Auburn banned TikTok, and students can't stop talking about it.* https://www.nytimes.com/2023/01/15/business/auburn-tiktok-ban-students.html

Maheshwari, S., & Holpuch, A. (2025). *Why TikTok Is Facing a U.S. Ban, and What Could Happen Next.* https://www.nytimes.com/article/tiktok-ban.html?smid=nytcore-ios-share&referringSource=articleShare

Majority of Public Disapproves of Supreme Court's Decision To Overturn Roe v. Wade. (2022). https://www.pewresearch.org/politics/2022/07/06/majority-of-public-disapproves-of-supreme-courts-decision-to-overturn-roe-v-wade/

Marquez, A. (2023). *Generation Z is the most racially diverse and fastest-growing segment of the electorate.* https://www.nbcnews.com/meet-the-press/meetthepressblog/gen-z-diverse-fastest-growing-segment-electorate-rcna66517

Matsa, K. E. (2022). *More Americans are getting news on TikTok, bucking the trend on other social media sites.* https://www.pewresearch.org/fact-tank/2022/10/21/more-americans-are-getting-news-on-tiktok-bucking-the-trend-on-other-social-media-sites/

McGee, K., & Mohamed, I. (2024). *As doors close and funding fades, students worry UT-Austin is taking Texas' new DEI ban too far.* https://www.texastribune.org/2024/02/26/university-texas-austin-dei-ban-students/

Media Statement from CDC Director Rochelle P. Walensky, MD, MPH, on Racism and Health. (2021). https://www.cdc.gov/media/releases/2021/s0408-racism-health.html

Memorandum for the Heads of Executive Departments and Agencies. (2020). https://www.whitehouse.gov/wp-content/uploads/2020/09/M-20-34.pdf?fbclid=IwAR1r7Ej2V0gZ8pNhIEjLtHDDNlfeYvBkzEgUfbrU3cXfot7RP2XKPwnCDe4

Merriam-Webster. (n.d.). https://www.merriam-webster.com/dictionary/disinformation

Metz, R. (2019). *The fight to stay ahead of deepfake videos before the 2020 US election.* https://www.cnn.com/2019/06/12/tech/deepfake-2020-detection/index.html

Metz, C. (2023). *'The Godfather of A.I.' Leaves Google and Warns of Danger Ahead.* https://www.nytimes.com/2023/05/01/technology/ai-google-chatbot-engineer-quits-hinton.html?smid=nytcore-ios-share&referringSource=articleShare&sgrp=c-cb

Metz, C., & Schmidt, G. (2023). *Elon Musk and Others Call for Pause on A.I., Citing 'Profound Risks to Society'.* https://www.nytimes.com/2023/03/29/technology/ai-artificial-intelligence-musk-risks.html

Meyersohn, N. (2025). *Target retreated on DEI. Then came the backlash.* https://amp.cnn.com/cnn/2025/02/19/business/target-dei-boycott

NAEP. (n.d.). *2022 Mathematics and Reading Report Cards at Grades 4 and 8.* https://www.nationsreportcard.gov/media.aspx

Natanson, H., Morse, C. E., Narayanswamy, A., & Brause, C. (2022). *An explosion of culture war laws is changing schools. Here's how.* https://www.washingtonpost.com/education/2022/10/18/education-laws-culture-war/

Nottingham, S., Suarez, C., & Ellis, T. E. (2024). *University of Florida eliminates DEI office to comply with state regulations.* https://www.cnn.com/2024/03/01/us/university-florida-shutters-dei-office-reaj/index.html

Oath Ceremony: The Honorable Ketanji Brown Jackson. (n.d.). https://www.supremecourt.gov/publicinfo/press/oath/oath_Jackson.aspx

Our Mission. (n.d.). www.tiktok.com

Parker, A., & McDaniel, J. (2023). *From Freddie Gray to Tyre Nichols, early police claims often misleading* https://www.washingtonpost.com/nation/2023/02/17/police-shootings-false-misleading/

Pause giant AI experiments: An open letter. (2023). https://futureoflife.org/open-letter/pause-giant-ai-experiments/

Poindexter, P. M. (2018). *Millennials, news, and social media: Is news engagement a thing of the past?* (2nd ed.). Peter Lang.

Poindexter, P. M. (2012). *Millennials, news, and social media: Is news engagement a thing of the past?* Peter Lang.

Price, M. L. (2023). *What to know about Trump's CNN town hall: Lies about election and abortion, attacks on accuser.* https://apnews.com/article/trump-cnn-town-hall-things-to-know-7be863292956dd2663537880dfbd8c3f

Ramirez, M. (2024). *As anti-trans legislation proliferates in 2024, community fears erasure from public view.* https://www.usatoday.com/story/news/nation/2024/02/06/anti-trans-bills-grow-2024/72353716007/

Rappeport, A. (2022). *Yellen is first female treasury secretary with signature on U.S. dollar.* https://www.nytimes.com/2022/12/08/business/janet-yellen-signature-dollar.html

Rosenbloom, A. (2024). *Beyoncé debuts at No. 1 on Billboard's Hot Country Songs chart and makes history.* https://www.cnn.com/2024/02/20/entertainment/beyonce-no-1-country-chart?cid=ios_app

Rosenzweig-Ziff, D., Morse, C. E., Svrluga, S., Cornejo, D., Dormido, H., & Ledur, J. (2024). *Riot police and over 2,000 arrests: A look at 2 weeks of campus protests.* https://www.washingtonpost.com/nation/interactive/2024/university-antiwar-campus-protests-arrests-data/

Rumor Control. (n.d.). https://www.fda.gov/news-events/rumor-control

Sahadi, J. (2024). *March 12 marks equal pay day this year.* https://www.cnn.com/2024/03/12/success/equal-pay-day-2024?cid=ios_app

Sawchuck, S. (2021). *What is critical race theory, and why is it under attack?* https://www.edweek.org/leadership/what-is-critical-race-theory-and-why-is-it-under-attack/2021/05

SB 17. (n.d.). https://capitol.texas.gov/tlodocs/88R/billtext/pdf/SB00017F.pdf#navpanes=0

Schmidt, S., Wagner, J., & Armus, T. (2021). *Biden selects transgender doctor Rachel Levine as assistant health secretary.* https://www.washingtonpost.com/health/2021/01/19/rachel-levine-transgender-biden-hhs-pick/

Secretary Deb Haaland. (n.d.). https://www.doi.gov/secretary-deb-haaland

Shah, S. (2023). *Taylor Swift makes history as person of the year. Here's how.* https://time.com/6343069/taylor-swift-history-person-of-the-year/

Shane, S., & Frenkel, S. (2018). *Russian 2016 influence operation targeted African-Americans on social media.* https://www.nytimes.com/2018/12/17/us/politics/russia-2016-influence-campaign.html

Shurafa, W., & Frankel, J. (2024). *More than 40,000 Palestinians have been killed in Gaza, the territory's Health Ministry says.* https://apnews.com/article/gaza-death-toll-hamas-war-israel-40000-32a79e03c8eb62669412dab23d03219e

Silver, L., & Clancy, L. (2023). *By more than two-to-one, Americans support U.S. government banning TikTok.* https://www.pewresearch.org/fact-tank/2023/03/31/by-a-more-than-two-to-one-margin-americans-support-us-government-banning-tiktok/

Silverstein, J. (2021). *The global impact of George Floyd: How Black Lives Matter protests shaped movements around the world.* https://www.cbsnews.com/amp/news/george-floyd-black-lives-matter-impact/#app

Smith, T. (2023). *Colleges face pressure to curb antisemitism and Islamophobia.* https://www.npr.org/2023/11/11/1211234951/colleges-face-pressure-to-curb-antisemitism-and-islamophobia

Social media and youth mental health: The U.S. Surgeon General's Advisory. (n.d.). https://www.hhs.gov/sites/default/files/sg-youth-mental-health-social-media-advisory.pdf

Specia, M. (2024). *U.K. to ban disposable vapes in plan to combat use by children.* https://www.nytimes.com/2024/01/29/world/europe/uk-vaping-ban.html

Swidriski, E. (2022). *Florida's "Don't Say Gay" law raises serious legal questions.* https://www.americanbar.org/groups/labor_law/publications/labor_employment_law_news/fall-2022/florida-do-not-say-gay-law/

Tate, I., Lemonides, A., Gamio, L., & Betts, A. (2024). *Campus protests led to more than 3,100 Arrests, but many charges have been dropped.*

New York Times, The. (2017). *Donald Trump's cabinet is complete. Here's the full list.* https://www.nytimes.com/interactive/2016/us/politics/donald-trump-administration.html

Times Editorial Board, The. (2020). *Editorial: An examination of The Times' failures on race, our apology and a path forward.* https://www.latimes.com/opinion/story/2020-09-27/los-angeles-times-apology-racism

Tidy, J., & Galer, S. S. (2020). *TikTok: The story of a social media giant.* https://www.bbc.com/news/technology-53640724

To serve his country, President Biden should leave the race. (2024). https://www.nytimes.com/2024/06/28/opinion/biden-election-debate-trump.html?smid=nytcore-ios-share&referringSource=articleShare&sgrp=c-cb

Tolentino, D. (2023). *These are all the public universities that have instituted TikTok bans.* https://www.nbcnews.com/tech/tiktok-bans-public-universities-list-rcna66185

Transcript of Trump's speech at rally before US Capitol riot. (2021). https://apnews.com/article/election-2020-joe-biden-donald-trump-capitol-siege-media-e79eb5164613d6718e9f4502eb471f27

Twenge, J. M. (2023). *Generations: The real differences between Gen Z, Millennials, Gen X, Boomers, and Silents-and what they mean for America's future.* Atria Books.

Twenty-Sixth Amendment. (n.d.). https://constitution.congress.gov/constitution/amendment-26/

Tyson, A., & Kennedy, B. (2023). *How Americans view future harms from climate change in their community and around the U.S.* https://www.pewresearch.org/science/2023/10/25/how-americans-view-future-harms-from-climate-change-in-their-community-and-around-the-u-s/

Urgent action needed to protect children and prevent the uptake of e-cigarettes. (2023). https://www.who.int/news/item/14-12-2023-urgent-action-needed-to-protect-children-and-prevent-the-uptake-of-e-cigarettes

Verma, P. (2023). *A professor accused his class of using ChatGPT, putting diplomas in jeopardy.* https://www.washingtonpost.com/technology/2023/05/18/texas-professor-threatened-fail-class-chatgpt-cheating/

Viner, R., Gireesh, A., Stiglic, N., Hudson, L. D., Goddings, A.-L., Ward, J. L., & Nicholls, D. E. (2019). *Roles of cyberbullying, sleep, and physical activity in mediating the effects of social media use on mental health and wellbeing among young people in England: A secondary analysis of longitudinal data.* https://www.thelancet.com/journals/lanchi/article/PIIS2352-4642(19)30186-5/fulltext

Wamsley, L. (2021). *CDC director declares racism a "serious public health threat."* https://www.npr.org/2021/04/08/985524494/cdc-director-declares-racism-a-serious-public-health-threat

Wan, W. (2020). *WHO declares a pandemic of coronavirus disease COVID-19.* https://www.washingtonpost.com/health/2020/03/11/who-declares-pandemic-coronavirus-disease-covid-19/

Wells, G., Horowitz, J., & Seetharaman, D. (2021, September 15, 2021). *The Facebook Files: Facebook Knows Instagram Is Toxic for Teen Girls, Its Research Shows—Internal documents show a youth mental-health issue that Facebook plays down in public.* https://www.wsj.com/articles/facebook-knows-instagram-is-toxic-for-teen-girls-company-documents-show-11631620739?mod=hp_lead_pos7&mod=article_inline

Wilson, C. C. (2020). *Opinion: How racism at the L.A. Times shaped my journalism career.* https://www.latimes.com/opinion/story/2020-10-03/career-as-a-black-journalist-was-shaped-by-the-l-a-times-racism

Worldwide box office revenue of "Barbie" 2024, by region. https://www.statista.com/statistics/1401601/global-box-office-revenue-barbie-by-region-worldwide/#:~:text=As%20of%20January%2010%2C%202024,film%20directed%20by%20a%20woman.

Yan, H. (2021). *A teen with "a cell phone and sheer guts" is credited for Derek Chauvin's murder conviction.* https://www.cnn.com/2021/04/21/us/darnella-frazier-derek-chauvin-reaction/index.html

Youth voter turnout in presidential elections in the United States from 1972 to 2020. (n.d.). https://www.statista.com/statistics/984745/youth-voter-turnout-presidential-elections-us/

· 2 ·

SOCIAL MEDIA AND NEWS IN THE LIVES OF GEN Z

As Gen Z, born 1997 through 2012, fully comes into adulthood, this generation will likely be scrutinized for the role social media has played in their lives and they will be compared with Millennials on the demographic characteristics of race, ethnicity, and education. Will Gen Z surpass Millennials as the most racially and ethnically diverse generation? Will Gen Z be more educated than the most educated generation born in the twentieth century? And what other demographics, if any, will distinguish Gen Z from earlier generations?

Demographic characteristics just like the events and issues discussed in Chapter 1 as well as the transformational technologies that generations adopt provide insight that birth years alone cannot. The results from The National Gen Z, Social Media & News Engagement Survey provide a detailed demographic portrait of Gen Z that enables us to compare the generation born during the years 1997 through 2012 with older generations. As Table 2.1 is examined, it's important to keep in mind that we don't yet have a complete picture because only the oldest of Gen Z, those ages 18 through 26 in 2023, were included in the national survey of 1,504 U.S. adults.

Comparing Gen Z Demographics with Older Generations

Still, the data in Table 2.1 suggest Gen Z will be more racially and ethnically diverse than the three oldest generations (Generation X, Baby Boomers, and the Silent Generation) that were combined into one group and labeled "Older Generations." But it's too early to know for certain if that statistical conclusion will hold when comparing Gen Z and Millennials. According to Table 2.1, Gen Z is less racially and ethnically diverse than Millennials; 39% of Gen Z, 18 or older, identified as Black/African American, Hispanic/Latino, Asian American, Native American, Other or Two or More Races compared to 50% of Millennials.

Similarly, it's premature to draw conclusions as to whether or not, Gen Z will be more educated than Millennials, the generation with the most college degrees. Because the United States has yet to make up for the pandemic learning loss discussed in Chapter 1, it's unknown whether the educational setback in K-12 schools will be temporary or permanent (Goldstein, 2023a). But if the ACT test results for the high school class of 2023 are any indication, Gen Z "would not be able to earn Bs or Cs in entry-level college coursework" in "English, reading, math and science," which would make earning a college degree challenging for this generation (Goldstein, 2023b).

However, it is reasonable to conclude from Table 2.1 that Gen Z will stand out demographically from previous generations by their diverse gender identity. Four percent of Gen Z self-identified as "non-binary or other" while 52% identified as female and 44% male. Gen Z (73%) was significantly less likely to self-identify as "straight or heterosexual" compared to Millennials (89%) and the Older Generations group (94%). Additionally, and significantly, Gen Z (20%) was almost three times more likely than Millennials (7%) and 10 times more likely than the Older Generations group (2%) to self-identify as bisexual. And two percent of Gen Z identified as transgender while none of the Millennial or Older Generations group identified as transgender, according to the survey. The LGBTQ+ self-identification for Gen Z, Millennials, and the Older Generations group matches well with Gallup's 2023 LGBTQ+ survey and generational analysis (Jones, 2023).

Table 2.1 How the Demographic Portrait of Gen Z Compares with Millennials & Older Generations

	Gen Z	Millennials	Older Generations (Gen X, Baby Boomers & Silent)
Gender			
Male	44%	46%	52%
Female	52%	54%	48%
Non-Binary	3%	0.3%	0%
Other	1%	0.3%	0%
Self-Identified As			
Straight or Heterosexual	73%	89%	94%
Bisexual	20%	7%	2%
Gay	2%	3%	3%
Lesbian	1%	1%	1%
Transgender	2%	0%	0%
Race/Ethnicity			
White	60%	50%	67%
Black/African American	17%	21%	12%
Hispanic/Latino	14%	18%	10%
Asian American	5%	5%	8%
Native American	1%	3%	2%
Two or More Races/Other	2%	3%	3%
Education			
High School Degree or Less	41%	24%	19%
Some College or Technical School	29%	30%	27%
College Grad & Some Grad or Professional School	26%	34%	38%
Masters, M.D. or Doctorate	3%	12%	17%

(*continued*)

Table 2.1 Continued

	Gen Z	Millennials	Older Generations (Gen X, Baby Boomers & Silent)
Income			
Under $50,000	56%	45%	41%
$50,000 to $99,999	30%	33%	32%
$100,000-Plus	14%	22%	27%

Note: Generations are defined by years born: Gen Z, 1997–2012; Millennials, 1981–1996; Generation X, 1965–1980; Baby Boomers, 1946–1964; Silent Generation 1928–1945 (Dimock, 2019). However, when The National Gen Z, Social Media & News Engagement Survey was conducted in 2023, only the oldest Gen Z members, those between ages 18 and 26, were surveyed. Due to rounding error, total percentages for each demographic group may be slightly larger or smaller than 100%. For the questionnaire and details on the survey's methodology, please see Appendix.

Technology Distinguishes Generations as They Come of Age

Every generation born since the Golden Age of Radio which began in the late 1920s, has been known for its enthusiastic embrace of a consumer-oriented technology that changed how they communicated, engaged with entertainment, information, and news, and shopped for goods and services. Radio, during its Golden Age, was adopted by the Silent Generation; Baby Boomers were wild about TV which delivered entertainment, news, and advertising directly into their homes; and beginning in the 1980s when Gen X began navigating their teenage years, there was enthusiasm about VCR's which could record favorite TV programs that teens and their families could watch on their own time (Overly, 2016). Millennials were devoted to Gameboy as kids, iPods as teens, and by college, they swooned over Facebook, the new social media platform created by Millennials for Millennials that would become the dominant social media platform on the planet.

And when the oldest of Gen Z started to approach the preteen years, Steve Jobs introduced the iPhone that transformed our lives because it put us in charge of how, when, and where we communicated, searched for, accessed, and shared information, informed ourselves about the latest news, posted on social media, entertained ourselves, listened to our favorite music, and shopped. Plus, with the iPhone, we could take great photos, including of ourselves, and with a few finger taps, we could shoot and edit high-quality videos that we were excited to share. And we were able to accomplish all of that whenever we wanted, wherever we were with an elegant, sleek device that we could hold in one hand.

In 2018, *Wired* magazine said the iPhone was not only the "best-selling gadget ever created," but "probably the most influential one too" (Pierce & Goode, 2018). *Wired* added that the iPhone "put the world in our pockets" and "there's no denying that the iPhone has utterly transformed our lives." Although technically not iPhone natives since Gen Z's oldest were 10 and the youngest were five when Steve Jobs introduced the iPhone in 2007, iPhones and other smartphone brands were in the homes that Gen Z grew up in, making their growing up distinct from the generations that preceded them and potentially having an impact on news engagement socialization as we'll learn in Chapter 3.

Social Media Use Is Integral to Gen Z Lives

Table 2.2 reminds us that while Millennials may have been the first social media generation, Gen Z has matched them in their daily social media use with almost two-thirds of both generations using social media daily. And when it comes to number of hours, a larger percentage of Gen Z (25%) than Millennials (19%) is spending five or more hours per day on social media. Finally, Table 2.2 underscores that although the two youngest generations as well as the Older Generations group use social media, these platforms are essential in Gen Z and Millennial lives.

Almost two-thirds of Gen Z and Millennials use social media daily but only half of the Older Generations group are daily social media users. One quarter (25%) of Gen Z and one-fifth (19%) of Millennials spend five or more

Table 2.2 Social Media Use by Generation: Gen Z, Millennials, and Older Generations

	Gen Z	Millennials	Older Generations (Gen X, Baby Boomers & Silent)
Use Social Media Daily	64%	63%	50%
Spend 5+ Hours on Social Media Daily	25%	19%	7%
Use Social Media 0 Days Weekly	2%	4%	21%

hours on social media daily while only seven percent of the Older Generations group devotes as many hours to social media daily. And as Table 2.2 shows, one-fifth (21%) are not on social media at all.

The Intersection of Social Media Use and News Engagement

The Pew Research Center first documented the intersection of social media use and engaging with news in 2008, four years after Facebook was founded for college students. The oldest Millennials were college age or just graduating college and the oldest of Gen Z were starting elementary school. The 2008 Pew study found that 10% of those with a profile on the social networking sites Facebook and MySpace regularly engaged with news (Key News Audiences, 2008). Over the next decade and a half that percentage would not only grow exponentially, but every generation, whether young or old, would turn to social media for news. But getting news from social media does not guarantee regular engagement with news.

In fact, according to Table 2.3, Gen Z is the generation that is least likely to get or seek news daily. And although more than two-fifths (44%) of Gen Z get news at least three times per day, a larger percentage (56%) of Millennials and the Older Generations group (55%) get news three times or more during a 24-hour period. Perhaps, the most insightful statistic in Table 2.3 is about seeking news, especially because news is around to get even when you're not seeking it as older generations do. The Older Generations group is far more likely to seek news than the two youngest generations: 52% of older generations seek news daily compared to 22% of Millennials and 10% of Gen Z.

Table 2.3 News Engagement by Generation: Gen Z, Millennials, and Older Generations

	Gen Z	Millennials	Older Generations (Gen X, Baby Boomers & Silent)
Get News Daily	25%	38%	64%
Seek News Daily	10%	22%	52%
Get News 3+ Times in 24-Hour Period	44%	56%	55%

Where Gen Z Gets News

While 44% of Gen Z report they're getting news three or more times a day, it doesn't necessarily mean they're intentionally getting news. It could simply mean they're *seeing* news on social media. Regardless, whether actively seeking or passively seeing news, Gen Z's most popular place to get news, according to Table 2.4, is social media. In fact, over three-quarters (78%) of the youngest generation often gets news from social media. Not surprisingly, social media is number one with Millennials too; over three-fifths (62%) often get news from social media platforms. But for the Older Generations group that combines Generation X, Baby Boomers, and the Silent Generation, only 22% report often getting news from social media.

What is surprising in Table 2.4 is that the second most popular source of news for Gen Z is family; almost three-fifths (56%) of Gen Z get news from family often. This reliance on family for news far outpaces Millennials (34%) and the Older Generations group (18%). Plus, for Gen Z, friends, as a source of news, are as popular as YouTube. Almost half (49%) of Gen Z often get news from friends and YouTube. For Millennials, friends, which tie with family, rank seventh as a source for news. One-third (34%) of Millennials get news from family and friends.

Table 2.4 also reveals that the *same* platforms are in the top seven for both Gen Z and Millennials; however, the preference order differs and in the case of social media, which ranks first for both, there is a 16-percentage point difference between the two youngest generations in using social media *often* for news. A whopping 78% of Gen Z often gets news from social media but that percentage drops 16 points for Millennials. Although social media platforms are the number one place for getting news often for Millennials, only three-fifths (62%) of Millennials often get news from social networking sites.

Table 2.4 Where Gen Z, Millennials, and Older Generations Get News

	% Saying Often Get News From Platform		
	Gen Z	Millennials	Older Generations (Gen X, Baby Boomers & Silent)
Social Media	78% (1)*	62% (1)	22% (6)
Family	56% (2)	34% (7)	18% (9)
Friends	49% (3)	34% (7)	17% (10)

(*continued*)

Table 2.4 Continued

% Saying Often Get News From Platform			
	Gen Z	Millennials	Older Generations (Gen X, Baby Boomers & Silent)
YouTube	49% (3)	40% (4)	17% (10)
Google or Other Search Engine	48% (4)	51% (2)	26% (4)
Notifications	40% (5)	36% (6)	19% (8)
News Apps	30% (6)	38% (5)	24% (5)
Local TV	29% (7)	45% (3)	61% (1)
Radio	24% (8)	33% (8)	24% (5)
Network TV	23% (9)	33% (8)	48% (2)
Cable	22% (10)	34% (7)	40% (3)
Podcasts	18% (11)	24% (9)	7% (12)
Newsletters	16% (12)	19% (10)	6% (13)
Print Newspapers	13% (13)	18% (11)	21% (7)
Smart Speaker	12% (14)	14% (13)	5% (14)
Print Magazines	10% (15)	15% (12)	10% (11)
Other	9% (16)	11% (14)	5% (14)

*Rank Order

When the 17 different news platforms, including Other, in Table 2.4 are sorted into three platform categories—Digital, Interpersonal, and Legacy—another surprising picture emerges. Interpersonal news sources (family and friends) are embraced by Gen Z and the rejection of legacy print newspapers and magazines is not limited to the younger generations (see Table 2.5).

Setting 45% as a threshold, a point at which digital, interpersonal, and legacy platforms matter as sources of news for Gen Z, Millennials, and the Older Generations group, it's clear from Table 2.5 that three of the eight digital platforms (social media, YouTube, search engine) and both interpersonal sources family and friends are embraced by Gen Z. Furthermore, Gen Z rejects all legacy news media platforms, including broadcast (local TV, network TV, and radio), cable, and print newspapers and magazines. So, while 48% or more of Gen Z often get news from social media, YouTube, or family and friends, this generation barely gets news from legacy media, especially the print form.

Table 2.5 Embracing Digital Platforms and Interpersonal Sources; Rejecting Legacy News Media: A Generational Comparison

	% Saying Often Get News from Platform		
Source	Gen Z	Millennials	Older Generations
Digital			
Social Media	78%	62%	22%
YouTube	49%	40%	17%
Google or Other Search Engine	48%	51%	26%
Notifications	40%	36%	19%
News Apps	30%	38%	24%
Podcasts	18%	24%	7%
Newsletter	16%	19%	6%
Smart Speaker	12%	14%	5%
Interpersonal			
Family	56%	34%	18%
Friends	49%	34%	17%
Legacy			
Local TV	29%	45%	61%
Radio	24%	33%	24%
Network TV	23%	33%	48%
Cable	22%	34%	40%
Print Newspapers	13%	18%	21%
Print Magazines	10%	15%	10%

Explaining Legacy Media

Legacy media is described by the *Oxford Dictionary of Journalism* as a "term popular amongst advocates of new media, especially in the USA" (Harcup, 2014, p. 157). Print newspapers and magazines as well as TV, radio, and cable, which were created long before the arrival of Facebook and other twenty-first-century media platforms, are examples of legacy media. Print newspapers began publishing in the United States before the Declaration of Independence was written and print magazines date back to 1741, according to the authors of *The Press and America: An Interpretive History of the Mass Media* (Emery et al., 1996.) *Time*, a newsweekly magazine founded a century ago (Emery et al., 1996), may be best known to Gen Z for its "Person of the Year" cover because *Time* named Taylor Swift "Person of the Year" in 2023 (Shah, 2023).

Electronic media—radio and TV—are also examples of legacy media. Radio's "Golden Age" was in the 1930s and 1940s (De Fleur & Ball-Rokeach, 1975, p. 92) and TV started taking off in the 1950s with a heavy dose of entertainment programming and must-watch network evening news brought to you by trusted news anchors who informed the public about major events and issues, including the assassinations of President John F. Kennedy and Dr. Martin Luther King Jr. as well as the Civil Rights Movement, protests against the Vietnam War, and U.S. presidential elections. By 1970, TV was so popular in the homes that Baby Boomers were growing up in, that one television set was in every household (De Fleur & Ball-Rokeach, 1975).

"Cable TV started as Community Area TV (CATV) in 1948 in the remote areas of Pennsylvania, Oregon and Arkansas," according to *Forbes* magazine (Adgate, 2020). "CATV gave households the opportunity to get a TV signal," which meant access to TV's entertainment programs and news (Adgate, 2020). After the FCC began deregulating cable in the 1970s, over the next decade, new types of programs became available to subscribing cable households. New programming included sports (ESPN), music (MTV), movies (HBO), kids programs (Nickelodeon), and news. In 1980, Ted Turner founded Cable News Network (CNN), the first 24-hour news channel, and in 1996, Fox News and MSNBC were launched (Defining Moments, 2020; Ray, 2024; MSNBC, 2010).

By the time the calendar turned from the twentieth to the twenty-first century and new types of platforms sprang up in the media landscape, references to legacy media meant before the twenty-first century. After Facebook and other social media platforms as well as smartphones exploded on the scene during the first decade and a half of the twenty-first century, the business models of some legacy media companies were no longer winning formulas. As a result, some legacy media companies shut down; others created digital extensions of their print, broadcast, and cable platforms such as news apps, podcasts, and newsletters. And they established a presence on social media and YouTube, but it was never the same in terms of advertising revenue or profits and the relationship varied depending on generation.

How Legacy Media's Relationship Differs by Generation

Applying the 45% threshold, a point at which digital, interpersonal, and legacy platforms matter as sources of news for Gen Z, Millennials, and the Older Generations group, legacy media still have a place in the lives of older generations. Forty-five percent of Millennials often get news from local TV while three-fifths (61%) of older generations (Generation X, Baby Boomers, and Silent) often get news from local TV and almost half (48%) turn to network TV news often (see Table 2.5).

Millennials also embrace some of the same digital platforms—social media and search engines—that Gen Z embraces. However, Table 2.5 shows Millennials are more like older generations—Generation X, Baby Boomers, and Silent—in not relying on family and friends for news. Additionally, older generations (Generation X, Baby Boomers, and Silent) fall well below the 45% threshold for the eight digital platforms. About one-quarter get news from apps as well as Google or another search engine. But for the most part, older generations reject digital platforms for news, according to Table 2.5.

Gen Z's News Categories and Topics

Gen Z's preferred news platforms are only part of the story; the rest of the story is in the news categories and topics this generation pays attention to. Fully understanding the story, though, requires some context about content and how legacy news organizations organize the content for the public's consumption. The roots of legacy news in the United States can be found in the first of 10 Amendments to the U.S. Constitution. Ratified December 15, 1791, the first 10 Amendments form what is known as the "Bill of Rights" (The U.S. Bill of Rights, n.d.).

The First Amendment, which speaks to freedom of the press as well as four other freedoms says: "Congress shall make no law respecting an establishment of religion, or prohibiting the free exercise thereof; or abridging the freedom of speech, or of the press; or the right of the people peaceably to assemble, and to petition the Government for a redress of grievances" (The U.S. Bill of Rights, n.d.). In other words, the First Amendment empowered the press to independently determine, without government interference, the type of content it would publish.

"In the 1890s, 'objectivity' became codified as the great law of journalism" (Mindich, 1998, p. 114) and in 1922, newspaper editors organized to address "common problems" and promote their "common ideals" (Emery et al., 1996, p. 521). The next year, a "code of ethics, called the 'Canons of Journalism,' was presented to the first annual meeting" of the new American Society of Newspaper Editors (ASNE) (Emery et al., 1996, p. 521).

As journalism matured as a profession, newspapers established clear boundaries between news and non-news content, that is, opinion, advertising, and promotions. News, reported by journalists who were guided by a code of ethics, was published on the front page of the paper and the first page of news sections. Both news and advertising were published inside sections but the distinction between the two was made clear.

Traditionally, up to two news pages within the first or second section of a newspaper, were reserved exclusively for opinion. Generally, the first page of opinion, called the editorial page, was written by the publisher or editorial page editor and/or editorial board. Opposite the editorial page, known as the "op-ed" page, experts were invited to share their opinions about pressing issues of the day. Generally, invited "op-ed" columns were approximately 800 words. Letters to the editor, written by readers of the newspaper, were also published in the newspaper's opinion section. By the digital age, letters to the editor were transformed into comments that readers could post at the end of a story and there were no limits to how many comments could be posted, unlike the number of reader letters that could be published in a print newspaper.

A newspaper's front page was not for any news; the front page was reserved for the most important news of the day as decided by the top editors. Introduced with compelling headlines, these front-page stories could be about a devastating tornado, a once-in-a-generation earthquake, the results of a presidential election, a mass school shooting, a health scare or medical breakthrough, large employee layoffs, employee strikes at major companies, the closing of a major business, introduction of an innovative new technology, a consequential Supreme Court ruling, an important sports or entertainment story or the death of a major figure. Traditionally, the front page of a newspaper had the highest readership so stories that were published on the front page were not just newsworthy, they were news stories the public thought about and talked about.

The effect that front page news stories had on what the public thought about was called agenda-setting by Maxwell McCombs and Donald Shaw, journalism scholars who conducted the first agenda-setting study on undecided voters in Chapel Hill, North Carolina during the 1968 U.S. presidential election (McCombs, 2004). Over the next half-century, generations of scholars in the United States and around the world would conduct agenda-setting studies to increase understanding about the effects news stories, when published, broadcast, or posted, could have on the public and under what conditions, that is, if the public were paying attention to the important news of the day.

Beyond the front page, newspapers organized news stories into five to eight categories of news that ranged from geography such as international, national, state, and local to essential subjects such as weather, business, and education. And then there were news categories with passionate followers: politics, sports, and entertainment. There were also so-called "women's pages" that were filled with what the author of *A Place in the News: From the Women's Pages to the Front Page* described as soft news, a category of news, that was distinct from hard news:

> Hard news? Soft news? Where did these terms come from? Their sexual implications fairly leap from the page. Hard news is news about foreign policy, the federal deficit, bank robberies. Historically, men's stuff. The right stuff. Soft news is news about the Four F's—family, food, fashion, and furnishings. Women's stuff. Back of the book. Plays, movies, books. Lifestyle. (Mills, 1988, p. 110)

One category of news that was not available in an exclusively print newspaper and magazine world was, of course, "Breaking News." In today's digital news landscape, news can break any time of the day on any topic and the public knows about it, that is, if a smartphone's breaking news notification has been activated. And because digital platforms update and break news any time of the day, legacy print newspapers and magazines are not just at a disadvantage, according to Table 2.5, they barely register with Gen Z.

Table 2.6 shows breaking news is popular with Gen Z—over half (53%)—often pay attention to this news category. But unlike for Millennials and Older Generations, in which breaking news is the top news category, breaking news ranks fourth for Gen Z.

While platform and category are important to understanding Gen Z's engagement with news, specific news topics provide the most insight. Unlike news categories which don't vary, the news dictates the topics that are published, posted, and broadcast, leading to a changing variety of topics that are published and posted from day to day, hour to hour, and sometimes minute to minute. Table 2.7 shows the variety of news topics and which of the 16 topics are paid attention to most often.

Table 2.6 News Categories Gen Z, Millennials, and Older Generations Pay Attention To

	% Saying Often		
News Categories	Gen Z	Millennials	Older Generations (Gen X, Baby Boomers & Silent)
Local News	65% (1)*	59% (2)	45% (2)
National News	59% (2)	45% (4)	37% (5)
Weather	57% (3)	45% (4)	43% (3)
Breaking News	53% (4)	61% (1)	66% (1)
State News	52% (5)	49% (3)	35% (6)
Entertainment, Arts & Culture	26% (6)	30% (6)	14% (9)
International News	24% (7)	29% (7)	38% (4)
Sports	22% (8)	34% (5)	28% (7)
Business & Consumer News	13% (9)	19% (8)	19% (8)

*Rank Order

According to Table 2.7, crime news is the number one topic for Gen Z with just under two-fifths (38%) paying attention to this news topic often. News about abortion rights restrictions (36%) is the second topic paid attention to, followed by health news (28%), gun violence news (27%), and news about student loan debt (26%).

Crime is also the top news topic for Millennials; 42% pay attention to this topic often. But for the three oldest generations, presidential election news ranks number one with over two-fifths of Generation X, Baby Boomers, and Silent saying they pay attention to this topic often.

From one-fifth (20%) to one-fourth (25%) of Gen Z pay attention to eight topics often: climate change (25%); state laws restricting teaching about Black history (24%); presidential elections news (23%); Supreme Court cases & rulings (23%); news about the President of the United States (21%); technology news (21%); news about voting (20%) and politics (20%). News about democracy safeguards & threats as well as news about Congress and immigration were news topics that the smallest percentage of Gen Z paid attention to often, according to Table 2.7.

Table 2.7 News Topics Gen Z, Millennials, and Older Generations Pay Attention To

	% Saying Often		
News Topics	Gen Z	Millennials	Older Generations (Gen X, Baby Boomers & Silent)
Crime News	38% (1)*	42% (1)	37% (3)
Restrictions on Abortion Rights	36% (2)	31% (4)	31% (8)
Health News	28% (3)	34% (2)	31% (8)
News about Gun Violence	27% (4)	30% (5)	31% (8)
News about Student Loan Debt	26% (5)	24% (9)	18% (12)
Climate Change	25% (6)	30% (5)	27% (10)
State Laws Restricting Teaching About Black History	24% (7)	27% (7)	24% (11)
Presidential Election News	23% (8)	32% (3)	42% (1)
Supreme Court Cases & Rulings	23% (8)	25% (8)	36% (4)
News about the President	21% (9)	27% (7)	41% (2)
Technology News	21% (9)	27% (7)	17% (13)
News about Voting	20% (10)	23% (10)	33% (7)
Politics	20% (10)	28% (6)	36% (4)
News about Democracy Safeguards & Threats	18% (11)	27% (7)	35% (5)
News about Congress	18% (11)	24% (9)	34% (6)
Immigration News	17% (12)	25% (8)	29% (9)

*Rank Order

A Women's Pages Legacy?

If newspapers' separate women's pages no longer exist, does that mean gender is not a factor in news topics that are paid attention to? According to Table 2.8, gender matters even when the news is not specifically about an issue that resonates with women. Table 2.8, which compares news topics that males and females pay attention to, independent of generation belonged to, confirms gender matters. The third column of Table 2.8 shows the percentage point difference in news topics. Not only is there a difference in the top news topics that males and females pay attention, but a statistically significant gender gap exists for 10 of the 16 news topics.

The top three news topics that males often pay attention to are: (1) presidential election news; (2) news about the president; and (3) politics. For females, the top three news topics are (1) crime; (2) restrictions on abortion rights; and (3) health news. When Table 2.8 is examined by the size of the gender gap in terms of percentage points, the following news topics have the largest statistically significant gap: presidential election news (14 points); politics (13 points); news about Congress (12 points); technology news (10 points); Supreme Court cases & rulings (10 points); news about the president (9 points); crime news (9 points); and news about voting (9 points). Crime news, which has a 9- point gender gap, is the only news topic in which significantly more females than males (43% vs. 34%) pay attention to it.

For two news topics—climate change news and state laws restricting teaching about Black history—there is no gender gap and for news about restrictions on abortion rights, there is a small numerical difference, but it is not a statistically significant difference.

Table 2.8 News Topics Paid Attention to from the Prism of Gender

	% Saying Often		
News Topics	Male	Female	Gender Gap Percentage Point Difference
Presidential Election News	42% (1)*	28% (5)	14
News about the President	38% (2)	29% (4)	9
Politics	37% (3)	24% (8)	13
Supreme Court Cases & Rulings	35% (4)	25% (7)	10
News about Congress	34% (5)	22% (10)	12
Crime News	34% (5)	43% (1)	9

Table 2.8 Continued

	% Saying Often		
News about Democracy Safeguards & Threats	33% (6)	25% (7)	8
News about Voting	32% (7)	23% (9)	9
News about Gun Violence	31% (8)	29% (4)	2**
Restrictions on Abortion Rights	30% (9)	34% (2)	4**
Health News	30% (9)	32% (3)	2**
Immigration News	29% (10)	22% (10)	7
Climate Change News	27% (11)	27% (6)	0
State Laws Restricting Teaching about Black History	25% (12)	25% (7)	0
Technology News	25% (12)	15% (11)	10
News about Student Loan Debt	20% (13)	22% (10)	2**

*Rank Order

**Gender Difference is *not* statistically significant

Note: With only 12 respondents identifying as non-binary and 3 identifying as Other, the groups were too small to be of statistical significance and were not included in the Table 2.8 analysis.

Gen Z's Embrace of Interpersonal Sources for News is Important to Know

While there are similarities between Gen Z and Millennials when it comes to demographics, using social media daily, and preferences for some types of news, Gen Z couldn't be more different than the Older Generations group in engagement with social media and news. While it was unsurprising that Gen Z rejected all forms of legacy media, it was a surprise to learn that Gen Z embraces interpersonal (family and friends) sources for news. Knowing interpersonal sources are almost as important to Gen Z as social media means this dynamic should not be ignored when contemplating the future of news engagement, journalism, the United States, and democracy.

Questions and Reflections

1. The questionnaire for The National Gen Z, Social Media & News Engagement Survey is in the Appendix. Make a copy of the questionnaire, then fill it out.
2. Compare your answers to the Gen Z responses reported in Tables 2.4, 2.5, and 2.7. If any of your questionnaire answers differ from Gen Z responses in the three tables, reflect on the reasons for the differences.

References

Adgate, B. (2020). The rise and fall of cable television *Forbes*. *Defining moments from 40 years of CNN*. https://www.cnn.com/2020/05/30/world/gallery/cnn-history/index.html

De Fleur, M. L., & Ball-Rokeach, S. (1975). *Theories of Mass Communication* (Third ed.). David McKay Company, Inc.

Defining moments from 40 years of CNN. (2020). https://www.cnn.com/2020/05/30/world/gallery/cnn-history/index.html

Dimock, M. (2019). *Defining generations: Where Millennials end and Generation Z begins*. https://www.pewresearch.org/fact-tank/2019/01/17/where-millennials-end-and-generation-z-begins

Emery, M., Emery, E., & Roberts, N. L. (1996). *The press and America: An interpretive history of the mass media* (8th ed.). Allyn and Bacon.

Goldstein, D. (2023a). *What the new, low test scores for 13-year-olds say about U.S. education now*. https://www.nytimes.com/2023/06/21/us/naep-test-results-education.html

Goldstein, D. (2023b). *ACT reports record low scores as admissions landscape shifts*. https://www.nytimes.com/2023/10/11/us/act-scores-college-admissions.html

Harcup, T. (2014). *Oxford dictionary of journalism*. Oxford University Press.

Jones, J. M. (2023). *U.S. LGBT identification steady at 7.2%*. https://news.gallup.com/poll/470708/lgbt-identification-steady.aspx

Key news audiences now blend online and traditional sources. (2008). https://www.pewresearch.org/politics/2008/08/17/key-news-audiences-now-blend-online-and-traditional-sources/

McCombs, M. (2004). *Setting the agenda: The mass media and public opinion*. Polity Press.

Mills, K. (1988). *A place in the news: From the women's pages to the front page*. Columbia University Press.

Mindich, D. T. Z. (1998). *Just the facts. How "objectivity" came to define American journalism*. New York University Press.

MSNBC.com's history. (2010). https://www.nbcnews.com/slideshow/amp/msnbc-coms-history-35541370

Overly, S. (2016, July 22). The VCR is officially dead. Yes, it was still alive. *Washington Post.* https://www.washingtonpost.com/news/innovations/wp/2016/07/22/rip-to-the-vcr/

Pierce, D., & Goode, L. (2018). *The Wired guide to the iPhone.* https://www.wired.com/story/guide-iphone/

Ray, M. (2024). *Fox News Channel.* https://www.britannica.com/money/Fox-News-Channel

Shah, S. (2023). *Taylor Swift makes history as person of the year. Here's how.* https://time.com/6343069/taylor-swift-history-person-of-the-year/

U.S. Bill of Rights, The. (n.d.). https://www.archives.gov/founding-docs/bill-of-rights-transcript#toc-amendment-i

· 3 ·

HOW SOCIAL MEDIA AND SMARTPHONES DISRUPTED THE NEWS ENGAGEMENT SOCIALIZATION PROCESS AND REDEFINED HOW UPCOMING GENERATIONS GET NEWS AND FEEL ABOUT BEING INFORMED

After *Journalism Quarterly* published "A Profile of the Daily Newspaper Non-Reader" in 1964 (Westley & Severin, 1964), the next six decades would see dozens of studies that would try to understand why newspapers as well as TV news and eventually digital news platforms were paid attention to by some and ignored by others (Newman et al., 2022; Newman et al., 2023; Poindexter, 2008). And while it would take through the end of the second decade of the twenty-first century for the wide variety of digital platforms and formats to be adopted and accessed on the go or wherever one might be, questions about why some engaged with news and others didn't, remained the same.

That 1964 *Journalism Quarterly* newspaper non-reader study identified socio-economic factors, including less education and income as well as age, both young and old, as reasons that some didn't read newspapers (Westley & Severin, 1964). When follow-up studies analyzed why some ignored newspapers, a variety of answers ranging from lack of time and a newspaper's cost to disinterest, bias, and distrust were identified (Poindexter, 2008). Additionally, adults who didn't embrace the belief that being informed was important or a civic duty were less likely to read newspapers or watch news on TV (Poindexter & McCombs, 2001).

With studies querying adults about the reasons for engaging with or ignoring news, it's important to emphasize that long before reaching the age to vote, kids learned whether reading newspapers or watching news on TV was important. Kids observed their parents reading print newspapers and watching television news, key contributors to news engagement socialization.

Defining News Engagement Socialization

Sociologist Charles Wright who analyzed mass communication from a sociological perspective defined socialization as the "social process by which individuals come to belong to a society and acquire some of its values, beliefs, perspectives, knowledge, social norms, and preferences—in short its culture" (Wright, 1986, p. 185). This socialization process begins when we're born and continues "throughout life" (Wright, 1986, p. 185). News engagement socialization, therefore, is the process by which individuals learn about news platforms from print and broadcast to digital, develop beliefs, norms, likes and dislikes about them, and choose to incorporate engagement with news in their lives or not.

Unlike learning to read, write, and do math, news engagement socialization can begin before kids start walking because it is learning through observation, a psychological process that Stanford University social psychologist Albert Bandura called modeling. Modeling helps explain how traditionally without parents saying a word, kids learned that reading print newspapers and watching news on TV were important things that grownups did and when they became adults, they, too, would do these important grownup things (Bandura, 2001; Edgerly et al., 2018; Maccormick, 2021; Poindexter, 2018).

So, what does modeling as a factor in news engagement socialization look like? Table 3.1 suggests that it's the presence of news in the home while growing up as well as interpersonal communications. Correctly interpreting Table 3.1 requires remembering that generations grew up during different time periods with access to different news media and platforms. The Older Generations group, which includes Silent, born 1928 through 1945, Baby Boomers, born 1946 through 1964, and Generation X, born 1965 through 1980, grew up in a pre-digital news landscape. Millennials born 1981 through 1996 grew up during a news landscape transition, from primarily print newspapers and television news, to a variety of digital platforms, including websites, apps, social media, and search engines, where news could be accessed.

By the time Gen Z, born 1997–2012, started high school around 2011, the iPhone, unveiled in 2007, had redefined how, when, and where news could be accessed. And in this new mobile-digital news world, consumers with a few finger swipes and taps on their smartphones—*not* newspaper and broadcast news executives—controlled when, where, and how long they engaged with news.

Did consumer-controlled news access on their smartphones disrupt the news engagement socialization process as we knew it? What impact, if any, was there in the homes that Gen Z grew up in? Answers to these questions will likely play a role in the news engagement socialization process for generations that come after Gen Z.

News in Homes Kids Grew Up In

Table 3.1 does provide some insight into those news engagement socialization questions for the oldest members of Gen Z, born 1997 to 2005, which would make them ages 18–26 when the survey was conducted. As the first members of Gen Z grew up, the mobile-digital transformation of the news landscape would eventually affect the homes that Gen Z grew up in. In fact, in three of the four questions asked about news in the home, Gen Z was less likely than Millennials and older generations to say they grew up in homes in which news was present. Only one-third (32%) of Gen Z said they grew up in a home in which news was around "all or most of the time" while a larger percentage of Millennials (43%) and older generations (39%) said news was present.

But just because news was less present in Gen Z homes, it didn't mean they weren't raised to believe being informed about news wasn't important. In fact, according to Table 3.1, the majority of Gen Z (57%) as well as Millennials (68%), and the Older Generations group (69%) were raised to believe being informed about news was important.

In homes that older generations and Millennials grew up in, newspapers were also around and news was on TV during dinner. Almost two-thirds (64%) of older generations and almost half (46%) of Millennials said newspapers were in the home. That percentage drops for Gen Z; just 27% said growing up newspapers were in the home "all or most of the time." While dinner with TV news was less prevalent than the presence of newspapers, for Millennials (40%) and older generations (33%), it was more customary than for Gen Z (23%).

Table 3.1 The Presence of News in the Homes of Gen Z, Millennials, and Older Generations While Growing Up

	Gen Z	Millennials	Older Generations
Raised to believe being informed about news is important	57%	68%	69%
Grew up in home in which news was around all or most of the time	32%	43%	39%
Grew up in home in which there were discussions about news all or most of the time	29%	33%	19%
Growing up newspapers were in the home all or most of the time	27%	46%	64%
Growing up TV news was on at dinner time all or most of the time	23%	40%	33%

When it came to news discussions, this was an activity more likely to be found in Millennial and Gen Z homes than the homes of older generations. Thirty-three percent of Millennials and 29% of Gen Z discussed news at home but only 19% of older generations did.

Passing on the Importance of News Engagement

News engagement socialization, of course, was not limited to the *presence* of print newspapers, TV news, or news discussions at home. As can be seen in Table 3.2, there were explicit efforts to pass on the importance of being informed to the next generation. Four-fifths (79%) of Gen Z could recall someone telling them that being informed about news was important. That percentage drops to a still significant 73% for Millennials. However, for older generations, only 55% recalled someone advising them that it was important to be informed about news.

At a time when disinformation pollutes the digital news landscape, advice doesn't stop with saying being informed is important. Table 3.2 also shows that 78% of Gen Z and 68% of Millennials said someone told them that the news

Table 3.2 Advice and School News Engagement Socialization

	% Saying Yes		
	Gen Z	Millennials	Older Generations
Advice			
Recall someone say being informed about news is important	79%	73%	55%
Recall someone say the news engaged with should be accurate	78%	68%	57%
School			
Teacher included news in elementary, middle school or high school classroom at least once a week	66%	52%	44%
Took a class in middle school, high school or college about news and journalism's principles and process	51%	47%	33%

they engage with should be accurate. For older generations, almost three-fifths (57%) recalled someone telling them to engage with accurate news.

The Classroom is Important for News Engagement Socialization Too

Traditionally, news engagement socialization began in the home with modeling—children observing their parents reading print newspapers and watching TV news—but there were also explicit efforts outside of the home to encourage news engagement. These explicit news engagement socialization efforts could be found in elementary, middle school, high school, and college classrooms. According to Table 3.2, 66% of Gen Z, 52% of Millennials, and 44% of older generations recalled a teacher including news in their elementary, middle school, or high school classroom at least once a week. And approximately half of Gen Z (51%) and Millennials (47%) took a class in middle school, high school, or college that focused on news and the process and principles of journalism. Only one-third of the Older Generations group recalled a middle school, high school, or college class that focused on journalism's process and principles.

The role of schools in news engagement socialization is not just apparent in Table 3.2, it's also documented in more than four decades of research, particularly the inclusion and impact of print newspapers in classrooms through newspaper-sponsored Newspaper in Education (NIE) programs (DeRoche, 1981; DeRoche & Skover, 1983; Grusin & Stone, 1993; Poindexter, 2018).

Disruption of News Engagement Socialization as We Knew It

The embrace of social media platforms for news and rejection of legacy print newspapers as documented in Chapter 2 as well as the Pew Research Center's 2023 study, "Audiences are declining for traditional news media in the U.S.—with some exceptions" (Lipka & Shearer, 2023) affirms the concern I expressed in the second edition of *Millennials, News, and Social Media: Is News Engagement a Thing of the Past?* I said:

> Reaching Generation Z will be even more challenging than reaching Millennials because this generation is growing up when smartphones and social media are the norm. In fact, 98% of homes with children eight or under have a mobile device and on average, children ages 0 to 8 "spend 48 minutes a day using mobile devices" (The Common sense census, 2017). Plus, because socializing kids into future news consumers is part teaching by example, it's more challenging to teach by example when engaging with news on a smartphone screen.
>
> When parents read print newspapers and the TV is tuned to news during the dinner hour, the importance of news could be telegraphed without saying a word. But today when parents are getting news from smartphones, they could be reading news but they could also be posting on Facebook, shopping, banking, or reading email or a book. The short-term and long-term effects of parents reading newspapers and discussing news that were found by journalism scholars will likely not be as effective in homes where eyes are glued to the mobile screens that fingers are tapping (York & Scholl, 2015). (Poindexter, 2018, p. 111)

So, while historically a variety of factors have contributed to whether news is engaged with, we cannot ignore the role smartphones may have played in the news engagement socialization process as they replaced print newspapers and television as the primary entryway to news that could be observed by anyone in the room, including kids. Did smartphones disrupt the news engagement socialization process as we knew it?

To begin understanding the role of smartphones in the news engagement socialization process, two questions were asked of the 84% of Gen Z survey participants who recalled a parent using a smartphone while growing up. First, Gen Z was asked if a parent engaged with news on their smartphone, followed by the question: "While growing up, did a parent ever tell you they were engaging with news on their smartphone?" While 62% said a parent engaged with news on a smartphone and 14% said a parent did not engage with news, 24% admitted they did not know.

It turns out the more insightful question to begin understanding the role of smartphones in the news engagement socialization process was the most direct: "While growing up, did a parent ever tell you they were engaging with news on their smartphone?" Forty-six percent of Gen Z said "Yes;" one-third (33%) responded "No;" and 21% admitted they did not remember. In other words, while 46% of Gen Z said a parent explicitly told them they were engaging with news on the smartphone, 54% said a parent had not told them they were engaging with news or they didn't remember. If a child is unaware that a parent is engaging with news on a smartphone, what does that mean for news engagement socialization? While more research needs to be done, one study of 12-to-17-year-olds and their parents who used mobile devices to engage with news were studied, researchers found that "parental modeling remains an important factor in socializing news consumption, even when modeling takes place via mobile devices" (Edgerly et al., 2018, pp. 1263–1264).

Still, the social media-smartphone news landscape has continued to change since the publication of the 2018 parental modeling-mobile device study. In fact, a recent Pew Research Center study found that "Americans are following the news less closely than they used to" (Forman-Katz, 2023). Is the decline in news engagement due to the disruption of the socialization process at home, young people having their own mobile devices at a younger and younger age or something else?

Impact of News Avoiders in the News Landscape

That something else that's contributing to declining news engagement, according to recent research, may be news avoiders. While only four percent of participants in The National Gen Z, Social Media & News Engagement Survey can be classified as news avoiders because in an average week, they never engage with news, that doesn't mean news avoidance is irrelevant.

In fact, news avoidance is not only more relevant than ever, but in a digital-mobile news landscape in the third decade of the twenty-first century, news avoidance today has some characteristics that differ from news avoidance in the twentieth century when news was delivered to homes through print newspapers or broadcast on TV at designated times. To get a handle on the disparate news avoidances that had been identified in over a quarter century of news audience studies, Poindexter (2008, p. 40) created a "news avoidance typology" to address what she called a "growing news avoider problem." The typology was comprised of four categories and each category included specific examples of news avoidance that had been identified in previous studies:

> **Other medium preferred or used**—TV, Internet, magazines, radio
> **Perceived constraints**—lack of time, time consuming, lack of usefulness
> **Real constraints**—time deficit, time conflict, health problems, language barriers, cost, circulation problems, not proficient using Internet, do not use Internet
> **Rejection of medium or news**—dislike content, format, structure, presentation, unattractiveness, purposelessness, and amount of detail; dislike bias; distrust, disinterested; dislike reading (Poindexter, 2008, p. 40)

To put the "news avoidance typology" in the context of the news landscape of 2008, the Pew Research Center reported that yesterday newspaper readership had declined from 58% in 1993 to 34% in 2008; regular nightly network news watching had declined from 60% to 29% during the same period, and getting news online three or more days a week, had increased from 0% in 1993 to 37%, 15 years later (Key News Audiences, 2008).

Although it's hard to avoid news today because it's not just everywhere, it's literally in our hands on our smartphones. Still, four percent or 57 of the participants in the National Gen Z, Social Media & News Survey were classified as "News Avoiders" because when asked how many days they get news in an average week, they responded "0 days." Asked "What is the main reason you don't get news?," 16 of the 57 "News Avoiders" said they were not interested in, didn't care about, or didn't like the news. These responses fit with "Rejection of medium or news" in the "News Avoidance Typology." Twelve "News Avoiders" said the news was depressing, "hurt their mental health," was too negative, bad, or it increased their "daily anxiety." While the 2008 News Avoidance Typology did not include a category that addressed negative mental health effects, The Reuters Institute Digital News Reports conducted in 2022 and 2023 identified news avoidances related to negative effects on mental health (Newman et al., 2022, 2023).

Lack of trust in the news and false news were the reasons that six survey participants avoided news. Lack of trust fits with the "Rejection of Medium or News" avoidance in the typology; additionally, the lack of trust news avoidance was identified in the 2022 and 2023 Reuters Institute reports on digital news (Newman et al., 2022, 2023). Finally, the remaining four "News Avoiders" responded with assorted reasons for avoiding news, including "don't know why," "not relevant" to their life, and "same stuff."

While different studies and reports may use different methods to identify "News Avoiders" and the reasons they avoid news, it's important to keep in mind that News Avoiders have always been a part of the news landscape and will likely increase with each generation until we strengthen news engagement socialization as well as identify innovative, common sense approaches to make engaging with news integral to the lives people live. One of these common-sense approaches, according to Table 3.3, may be as simple as having a news engagement routine.

News Engagement Routine Defined

If "routine," as defined by Collins Dictionary is "the usual *series* of things that you do at a *particular* time" and "the practice of regularly doing things in a *fixed* order," (Collins Dictionary, n.d.), "news engagement routine" would be defined as regularly reading, watching, listening to, sharing, discussing, commenting on news, etc., at a particular time, in a certain order, and in a familiar space.

A news engagement routine may be conscious or unconscious, formal or informal, or even simple or elaborate. When survey participants were asked if they had a routine when they get news, over half (54%) said they did. And according to Table 3.3, having a news engagement routine is related to significantly higher levels of engagement with news.

Table 3.3 Relationship Between News Engagement Routine and Engaging with News

	Doesn't Have News Engagement Routine	Has News Engagement Routine
Get news 7 days/week	39%	60%
Seek news 7 days/week	23%	45%
Get news 3 times or more during 24-hour period	41%	63%

Table 3.4 News Engagement Routine in the Lives of Gen Z, Millennials, and Older Generations

	Gen Z	Millennials	Older Generations (Gen X, Baby Boomers & Silent)
Has News Engagement Routine	40%	57%	59%
Lacks News Engagement Routine	60%	43%	41%

Whether getting or seeking news seven days a week or three times or more during a 24-hour period, survey participants who have a routine engage with news significantly more than those who don't have a routine. According to Table 3.3, 39% of survey participants who don't have a news engagement routine get news seven days a week; that percentage increases 21 percentage points to 60% for those with a routine. When it comes to *seeking* news, those with a news engagement routine are almost twice as likely as those without a routine (45% vs. 23%) to *seek* news seven days a week. And having a routine matters in how many times news is gotten during a 24-hour period: 41% of those without a news engagement routine get news three times or more during a 24-hour period; that number jumps to 63% for those with a news engagement routine.

Whether or not someone has a news engagement routine is related to the generation in which they were born, according to Table 3.4. Gen Z is least likely to have a routine when engaging with news: Two-fifths (40%) of Gen Z said they had a news engagement routine, which is significantly less than Millennials (57%) and the Older Generations group (59%) that combined Generation X, Baby Boomers, and the Silent Generation.

What Does a News Engagement Routine Look Like?

To ascertain what a news engagement routine looks like, survey participants who had a routine were asked to briefly describe it. The following prompt was given to get them started: "You might begin with the time of day that you first get news and the first place you check for news."

Since the emergence of social media, journalism and communication scholars have theorized about a passive "News Finds Me" (Gil de Zúñiga,

Figure 3.1 News Engagement Routines in Gen Z's Own Words

1.	"7:00 in the morning I go on YouTube to get the news."
2.	"After work I listen to people's reviews on TikTok."
3.	"As soon as I get news I have to do a Google search & look at multiple different websites to confirm or get more details."
4.	"Get notifications and check it"
5.	"I always start watching the news at 4 pm-7 pm. I will check my news stories on my phone early but don't spend much time unless an article or story looks interesting and then I will click on it"
6.	"I check my phone for new podcasts, browse my news apps"
7.	"I check the news after I eat breakfast. I get my news from CNN"
8.	"I check the news on my mobile telephone every morning, then I scroll through all social media. I will do this several times throughout the day into the night"
9.	"I check TikTok I check Instagram I check Youtube I check neighborhood apps I watch the news I talk to friends and family"
10.	"I do research to see if the stories are accurate"
11.	"I first check the news when I wake up around 4 am, then I read/watch the news with my morning coffee for about an hour"
12.	"I first get news while I'm working out at the gym"
13.	"I get a notification on my phone then I turn on the news"
14.	"I get my coffee sit down around 7 am and turn on Fox News."
15.	"I get my news when I'm watching and eating breakfast in the morning"
16.	"I get news starting 5 in the morning"
17.	"I get news when I'm driving to work on the radio and I also see it on my computer. I then call people who would be interested and talk about the news"
18.	"I google it"
19.	"I just set my news app for two notifications a day"
20.	"I like to check socials and what's trending for the day followed by news I currently am following closely"
21.	"I look at my phone and usually receive a notification from twitter when news stories become known. I get emails, and I only open the news stories if they are of interesting topics to me. I usually will open a browser if me and friends or family are all talking about a news story too."
22.	"I look it up when I get notified"
23.	"I look on the internet for news and sometimes Instagram"
24.	"I make sure to sit down and read the news with my coffee before work"
25.	"I mostly get my news in the morning when I get to work, and in the evening too"
26.	"I normally check the news while I eat breakfast in the morning each day"
27.	"I often watch the news in the morning with a cup of coffee and in the evening"
28.	"I use google search engine to seek day to day life news"

(continued)

Figure 3.1 Continued

29.	"I usually check news at night when I know something is going on. I usually google it"
30.	"I usually find news when I unlock my phone and slide my home screen over for Google News. I check when I wake up to see what's going on, and throughout the day when I get bored."
31.	"I usually get it on social media at night because that is when I scroll through there a lot. I will check certain people I follow for news at night as well."
32.	"I usually get news a few times in the morning a few times during the evening and several times at night"
33.	"I usually have it streaming on the Roku while eating my breakfast."
34.	"I usually wake up and get on my phone to check the news on YouTube or any other social media."
35.	"I usually will check the weather in the morning or look on social media to see about events."
36.	"I wake up and check my news app and see what news happened then tell my family and friends about it"
37.	"I wake up in the morning and watch it as I'm getting ready for work"
38.	"I watch the news in the morning before school, sometimes in the afternoon, and around dinner time"
39.	"Sit on my couch to watch news before breakfast"
40.	"The first place I check is usually Instagram"
41.	"The first place I check for news is BBC"

et al., 2017) approach to engaging with news but these data suggest at least two-fifths of Gen Z are not passively waiting for news to find them. Not only are they intentionally seeking news, they have a news engagement routine they follow regularly. Most of their routines are simple; some are elaborate, and according to Figure 3.1, a few are unique. Most importantly, the descriptions are in Gen Z's own words.

News Engagement Routines in the Digital News Landscape are Personalized

When in 1964, two journalism scholars called reading a daily newspaper a "thoroughly institutionalized behavior," newspaper reading routines didn't vary much. Reading the newspaper may have been accompanied by a cup of coffee and started with the front page above the fold. Or reading the paper may have begun with the sports section.

Today, although there appears to be unlimited variety in how, where, and when Gen Z engages with news, it's apparent the routines are not just intentional but when Gen Z goes to bed at night, they know where they'll first get news when they wake up in the morning. It might be from YouTube at 7:00 a.m. in the morning (#1); CNN after eating breakfast (#7); listening to the radio while driving to work (#17); working out at the gym (#12); checking the news app upon waking up (#36).

And while Gen Z may get news from multiple platforms, the first place they go for news, where and how they interact with it, underscores that news engagement routines are distinct and personalized. And the descriptions in Figure 3.1 appear to fit my definition of news engagement routine: "Regularly reading, watching, listening to, sharing, discussing, commenting on news, etc., at a particular time, in a certain order, and in a familiar space."

Because survey participants who had a news engagement routine were asked to describe it beginning with the time of day they first get news, the "familiar space" was home. However, a couple of participants said their news engagement routine began in the car while driving to work or in the gym while working out. No doubt if the prompt had been open-ended, more familiar spaces would have been described.

With the disruption of news engagement socialization as we knew it as well as the variety of platforms where news can be found, news engagement routines have an important role to play in helping Gen Z become more informed about news.

Questions and Reflections

1. Do you remember observing your parents or grandparents reading a print newspaper or watching news on TV? If yes, what specifically do you remember?
2. If you have a news engagement routine, how would you describe it?
3. What do you think are the benefits of a news engagement routine?

References

Bandura, A. (2001). Social cognitive theory of mass communication. *Media Psychology*, 3(3), 265–299.

Collins Dictionary. (n.d.). https://www.collinsdictionary.com/dictionary/english-word/routine

The common sense census: Media use by kids age zero to eight. (2017). https://www.commonsensemedia.org/sites/default/files/research/report/csm_zerotoeight_fullreport_release_2.pdf

DeRoche, E. F. (1981). Newspapers in education: What we know. *Newspaper Research Journal, 2*(3), 59–63.

DeRoche, E. F., & Skover, L. B. (1983). Newspapers for teaching and learning reading. *Newspaper Research Journal, 4*(2), 23–30.

Edgerly, S., Thorson, K., Thorson, E., Vraga, E. K., & Bode, L. (2018). Do parents still model news consumption? Socializing news use among adolescents in a multi-device world. *New Media & Society 2018, 20*(4), 1263–1281.

Forman-Katz, N. (2023). *Americans are following the news less closely than they used to.* https://www.pewresearch.org/short-reads/2023/10/24/americans-are-following-the-news-less-closely-than-they-used-to/

Gil de Zúñiga, H., Weeks, B., & Ardèvol-Abreu, A. (2017). Effects of the news-finds-me perception in communication: Social media use implications for news seeking and learning about politics. *Journal of Computer-Mediated Communication, 22,* 105–123.

Grusin, E. K., & Stone, G. C. (1993). The Newspaper in education and new readers: Hooking kids on newspapers through classroom experiences. *Journalism Monographs, 141,* 1–39.

Key news audiences now blend online and traditional sources. (2008). https://www.pewresearch.org/politics/2008/08/17/key-news-audiences-now-blend-online-and-traditional-sources/

Lipka, M., & Shearer, E. (2023). *Audiences are declining for traditional news media in the U.S.—with some exceptions.* https://www.pewresearch.org/short-reads/2023/11/28/audiences-are-declining-for-traditional-news-media-in-the-us-with-some-exceptions/?utm_source=Pew+Research+Center&utm_campaign=c48b8e6080-Weekly_12-2-23&utm_medium=email&utm_term=0_-c48b8e6080-%5BLIST_EMAIL_ID%5D

Maccormick, H. A. (2021). *Stanford psychology professor Albert Bandura has died.* https://news.stanford.edu/2021/07/30/psychology-professor-albert-bandura-dead-95/#:~:text=Bandura%20is%20internationally%20recognized%20as,of%20learning%20by%20observing%20others

Newman, N., Fletcher, R., Eddy, K. E., Robertson, C. T., & Nielsen, R. K. (2022). *Reuters Institute Digital News Report 2022.* https://reutersinstitute.politics.ox.ac.uk/sites/default/files/2022-06/Digital_News-Report_2022.pdf

Newman, N., Fletcher, R., Eddy, K. E., Robertson, C. T., & Nielsen, R. K. (2023). *Reuters Institute Digital News Report 2023.* https://reutersinstitute.politics.ox.ac.uk/sites/default/files/2023-06/Digital_News_Report_2023.pdf

Poindexter, P. (2008). When women ignore the news. In P. Poindexter, S. Meraz, & A. S. Weiss (Eds.), *Women, men, and news: Divided and disconnected in the news landscape.* Routledge.

Poindexter, P. M. (2018). *Millennials, news, and social media: Is news engagement a thing of the past?* (2nd ed.). Peter Lang.

Poindexter, P. M., & McCombs, M. E. (2001). Revisiting the civic duty to keep informed in the new media environment. *Journalism & Mass Communication Quarterly, 78*(1), 113–126.

Westley, B. H., & Severin, W. J. (1964). A profile of the daily newspaper non-reader. *Journalism Quarterly, 41*(1), 45–50, 156.

Wright, C. R. (1986). *Mass communication: A sociological perspective* (3rd ed.). Random House.
York, C., & Scholl, R. M. (2015). Youth antecedents to news media consumption: Parent and youth newspaper use, news discussion, and long-term news behavior. *Journalism & Mass Communication Quarterly, 92*(3), 681–699.

· 4 ·

GEN Z REPORT CARD ON NEWS, JOURNALISM, COVERAGE OF THEIR GENERATION

The relationship between Gen Z and news is not limited to the platforms this generation uses or their news engagement socialization and routines. That relationship is also a reflection of Gen Z's knowledge, perceptions, and expectations of the role and performance of the press in the United States as well as their own responsibilities and obligations in this democratic society.

One of five freedoms in the First Amendment to the U.S. Constitution, press freedom in the United States is not just unique; it is extraordinary when compared to other countries such as Russia, China, and Saudi Arabia that are not democracies (Reporters without borders, n.d.). In the United States, the First Amendment is the press' superpower, enabling independent organizations and individuals, regardless of their location on the political spectrum, to report news and share opinions about issues in the news without government interference. This same First Amendment also allows disinformation, intentionally inaccurate information that pollutes the news landscape and weakens democracy.

So what does Gen Z think of this institution that is included in and protected by the First Amendment to the U.S. Constitution? This chapter answers that important question that has implications for today and the future of journalism, the United States, and American democracy. To provide

Table 4.1 Generations Grade News Media on Their News Coverage

Grade	Gen Z	Millennials	Older Generations
A	11%	18%	11%
B	35%	35%	33%
C	42%	32%	29%
D	8%	11%	15%
F	4%	5%	12%

insight into how survey participants think about the press and how well it performs its U.S. Constitution-protected responsibility, in The National Gen Z, Social Media & News Engagement Survey, participants were asked: "In general, what grade, from A to F, would you give the news media for its news coverage?"

The follow-up question was: "What is the main reason for your grade?" Survey participants were also asked to grade the news coverage of their generation, from A to F, and the reason for the grade. News and news coverage were not defined for survey participants so their grades and the reasons for their grades were based on their perceptions of what news is and what news coverage should be.

Table 4.1 shows that Millennials (18%) were more likely than Gen Z (11%) and the Older Generations group (11%) that included Generation X, Baby Boomers, and Silent to give the news media a grade of A on their news coverage. A larger percentage of Gen Z (42%) assigned a grade of C to the news coverage compared to Millennials (32%) and Older Generations (29%). However, when it came to assigning a failing or near failing grade, a larger percentage of the Older Generation Group (27%) gave the news media a grade of D or F compared to Millennials (16%) and Gen Z (12%).

Reasons for Gen Z's News Coverage Grades

Many of the reasons behind Gen Z's grades of news coverage are listed in Figures 4.1 and 4.2. The reasons for the grades were thoughtful. Some were sophisticated. And most were a reminder that everyone has an opinion about news and journalism even if they're not familiar with the process and principles. And when the opinion is inconsistent with how journalism actually works in the United States, it can erode trust and confidence in the institution

Figure 4.1 In Gen Z's Own Words: Reasons for Giving a High Grade to News Media Coverage

1. "Because it's so important for the people"
2. "Because it gives me everything I need from beginning to end"
3. "Because it's really great and helps a lot"
4. "Because it's cool"
5. "Because they are a great source of information"
6. "Because they do a great job keeping up to date on what is going on in the world"
7. "Because they give legit news"
8. "Because they keep us informed"
9. "It is detailed and reliable"
10. "It is knowledgeable and typically from a credited source"
11. "Most of the health news is accurate"
12. "It's pretty trustworthy"

that is central to a functioning democracy. Figure 4.1 lists reasons for Gen Z's higher grades on news coverage in general.

Gen Z also assigned low grades to the news media's coverage. The reasons for the low grades are listed in Figure 4.2.

Figure 4.2 In Gen Z's Own Words: Reasons for Giving a Low Grade to News Media Coverage

1. "90% of it is depressing news and half of it is biased"
2. "Not real news, meant to mislead and make their audience misunderstand"
3. "A lot of news coverage that is accessible is very opinionated and focused on getting reactions, rather than delivering facts"
4. "All news outlets are biased"
5. "A lot of journalists don't tell the truth"
6. "I don't always find it trustworthy"
7. "I think some channels focus more on opinions than facts about stories or events"
8. "I think the news is a large reason why the country is so partisan"
9. "I think, overall, there's too much opinion in the reporting, too much bias"
10. "It doesn't always cover important and relevant issues"
11. "Media feels the incessant need to create false equivalencies for the sake of appearing unbiased"
12. "It sucks sometimes"

Grading News Coverage of Their Generation

In addition to asking for grades in general, Gen Z, Millennials, and the Older Generations (Generation X, Baby Boomers, and Silent) were asked what grade they would give news coverage about their generation. The grades are displayed in Table 4.2.

Table 4.2 shows that Millennials (21%) were significantly more likely than Gen Z (12%) or the Older Generations group (12%) to give an A grade to coverage of their generation. When general news coverage grades in Table 4.1 are compared with how generations graded coverage of their respective generations in Table 4.2, it's clear that Gen Z is far more critical about news of their generation than general news coverage. In fact, Gen Z is almost twice as likely to assign a grade of D or F to coverage about their generation than news coverage in general (23% vs. 12%).

The reasons Gen Z gave the news media lower and failing grades for coverage of their generation can be sorted into four themed categories: (A) little or no coverage about Gen Z; (B) failure to cover stories *important* to Gen Z; (C) journalists are represented by older generations and don't understand Gen Z; and (D) news outlets are biased against Gen Z/portray Gen Z negatively and inaccurately.

The four themed categories are not just a window into Gen Z thinking about news media coverage of their generation; it is another piece in the puzzle that represents the relationship between Gen Z and the news media, especially legacy news organizations. Since Gen Z explains their thinking best, their own words are displayed in Figure 4.3 for each of the four categories.

Table 4.2 Grading Their Generation's News Coverage

Grade	Gen Z	Millennials	Older Generations
A	12%	21%	12%
B	30%	33%	29%
C	34%	26%	34%
D	14%	12%	13%
F	9%	8%	12%

Figure 4.3 In Gen Z's Own Words: What Gen Z Thinks of News Coverage of Their Generation*

A. Little or No Coverage About Gen Z
1. "Don't really see anything involving my generation specifically"
2. "I could be wrong but I don't feel like there is much news out about people my age"
3. "I don't hear much about our generation"
4. "They don't really talk about our generation specifically that much but they do talk about it on rare occasions"
5. "They rarely have younger people on the news"
B. Failure to Cover Stories *Important* to Gen Z
1. "They cover news that is important to use but also sometimes they just skip over other things that are important to us"
2. "Need more mental health and climate change news"
3. "Not much to keep the younger generation interested"
C. Journalists are Represented by Older Generations and Don't Understand Gen Z
1. "A lot of the coverage is coming from those who are not part of our generation and therefore do not have the context for our behavior and our beliefs"
2. "It is older generations showing their personal opinions about younger generations"
3. "It's strange how older generations try to speak for us. We would never speak for them."
4. "Older generations simply don't understand and don't care to understand my generation"
D. News Outlets are Biased Against Gen Z/ Portray Gen Z Negatively and Inaccurately
1. "We are portrayed as lazy, not wanting to work, etc. But that's absolutely untrue."
2. "All negative news! No mention of the world that we are inheriting nor the previous generations that caused the problems we will have to face."
3. "I think a lot of media tries to blame young people for problems, when we were really born into a lot of these problems."
4. "I think the news is biased against my generation. I'm gen z and often the news is unfair/unkind to gen z."
5. "I think they make us out to be more wild than we are"
6. "It only shows the bad sides"
7. "My whole generation gets painted as very liberal and very extreme. but most of the people my age that i know are more moderate"
8. "News coverage makes my generation look like the villain when we're trying to restore the past's mistakes"

(continued)

Figure 4.3 Continued

9.	"Not enough focus on positive things. Too much of a spotlight on school shootings, violent crimes, and negative topics such as that"
10.	"The media portrays us as being overly-woke"
11.	"They tend to portray us like lazy good for nothings when in reality the people that usually write for these news organizations don't realize their generation is to blame for the bleak circumstances we are inheriting."
12.	"Too many stereotypes used"

*Quotes are verbatim. In rare cases, for clarification, a word was capitalized, punctuation was added or a misspelled word was corrected.

Gen Z's Perceptions and Expectations of the Press and the Press' Challenges

The overview of the Knight Foundation report "American Views 2022: Part 2, Trust, Media and Democracy" stated the obvious about why the press matters in a democracy and reminded us that when it comes to Gen Z, the press faces more than the two significant challenges that the overview singled out. The overview said: "Democracy in America relies on an independent press to inform citizens with accurate information. Yet today, two forces pose significant challenges to this function: the growing struggle of news organizations to maintain financial independence and the growing distrust of news among the public" (American Views, 2023).

Ironically and unfortunately, the Knight Foundation failed to identify what may well be the greatest challenge to the press in the third decade of the twenty-first century: The generation born 1997 through 2012.

If the press is to be prepared to meet the challenges it faces, it cannot ignore Gen Z. In 2030, the youngest of Gen Z will turn 18, graduating high school, perhaps heading to community or four-year colleges, starting their first full-time jobs, joining the military, etc., and on the path to replacing the oldest generations. In fact, when the youngest of Gen Z turn 18 in 2030, the youngest of the Silent Generation will turn 85 and Baby Boomers, will range in age from 66 to 84. As Gen Z replaces older generations what will their engagement with news be if little or no effort is made to encourage a life-long commitment to being informed and smart about news?

As the oldest generations are replaced by Millennials, Gen Z, and the generations yet to be born, will perceptions, expectations, and beliefs about the role, function, and performance of the press be more like the older or younger generations of today? While the future cannot be predicted there should at least be some insight into how challenging it will be to strengthen and enrich Gen Z's engagement with news in light of their feelings as displayed in Figure 4.3. If older generations that oversee and report the news disrespect Gen Z by excluding them from news coverage or portraying them inaccurately when they are included in the news, younger generations may turn away from news organizations permanently.

Table 4.3 provides hard data—not just heart-felt quotes—as to why, if news organizations ignore Gen Z, it will be at their own peril. Gen Z, Millennials, and the Older Generations group were asked their level of agreement with a series of statements that sought to capture perceptions, expectations, evaluations of the news media, and the role and responsibility of the press in society. On the measurement scale that ranged from 1 to 5, "1" stood for "Strongly *Disagree*" and "5" for "Strongly *Agree*." The "Strongly Agree" and "Agree" responses were combined, ranked, and compared for all three generational groups. Although there may be as much as a 21-percentage point generational gap between Gen Z and one of the generations born before 1997, the year the first of Gen Z was born, overall, the rankings were not that different.

The #1 ranked statement in Table 4.3 for Gen Z and Millennials is "All news on the Internet should be free to the public." Three-quarters of both Gen Z and Millennials agreed or strongly agreed with this assertion. A similar statement was asked of Millennials a half-decade before when the oldest Millennials were 37, and three-quarters also agreed with the statement (Poindexter, 2018). The #1 ranked statement for the Older Generations group was a tie between "An independent press is good for democracy" and "It's important for news media to be a watchdog of powerful people and the government" with 73% agreeing or strongly agreeing with these two statements.

The watchdog statement, which built on the national surveys of American journalists that have been conducted every decade since the 1970s (Willnat et al., 2022) as well as studies by Heider et al. (2005), Poindexter et al. (2006), and Poindexter (2018), was #5 for Gen Z with slightly more than half (52%) agreeing or strongly agreeing with this statement that speaks to the role of the press in society. Without this Constitution-protected watchdog role, some would argue there can be no democracy.

With two-thirds (66%) of Millennials agreeing or strongly agreeing with the press as watchdog statement, it ranked #3, tying with "News organizations are more concerned about being first than right." When the oldest Millennials were asked the same question in 2018, 62% agreed with the statement

(Poindexter, 2018). For Gen Z, however, fewer value the watchdog role which has implications for not just the press, but American democracy as a whole, since the press, by performing its watchdog role, journalism is able to fulfill its purpose which *The Elements of Journalism* said is "to provide people with the information they need to be free and self-governing" (Kovach & Rosenstiel, 2014). With 52% of Gen Z agreeing or strongly agreeing that it is "important for the news media to be a watchdog of powerful people and the government," the watchdog statement ranked #5 for Gen Z.

How Gen Z and journalists feel about journalism's watchdog role couldn't be more different. In the "Key Findings" of "The American Journalist Under Attack: Media, Trust & Democracy," 85% of journalists surveyed endorsed journalism's watchdog role (Willnat et al., 2022, p. 12) which is 33 percentage points higher than Gen Z's endorsement. From the perspective of journalists, being a watchdog is not just what they do; it's who they are. However, the Poindexter et al. (2006) study "Watchdog or good neighbor? The public's expectations of local news" found that the public would like for journalists to be the opposite of a watchdog; they wanted journalists to be more "helpful & caring" like a "good neighbor."

When participants in The National Gen Z, Social Media & News Engagement Survey were asked how they felt about the "good neighbor" concept, 58% of Gen Z, 70% of Millennials, and 65% of Older Generations agreed or strongly agreed they would like the news media to act like a "good neighbor" which ranked #3 for Gen Z and Older Generations and #2 for Millennials.

Five of the six lowest-ranked statements in Table 4.3 evaluated the news media's performance and reinforced Gen Z's dissatisfaction. Half (50%) of Gen Z agreed or strongly agreed with the statement: "The news media care little about people like you." Only one-third (34%) of Gen Z agreed or strongly agreed that news organizations "*protect* democracy more than *hurt* democracy." When asked if the news media accurately represent constituent groups in U.S. society or their generation, only one-third of Gen Z agreed or strongly agreed with the statements. And just over one quarter (26%) agreed or strongly agreed that "news organizations are willing to admit mistakes."

Two statements in Table 4.3 speak directly to the "growing struggle of news organizations to maintain financial independence" that the Gallup/Knight Foundation Survey (2023) referenced. If three-quarters (74%) of Gen Z agree or strongly agree that "All news on the Internet should be free to the public" and less than one-third (30%) agree or strongly agree that "paying for

Table 4.3 Agreement with Statements about News and the News Media

	% Saying Agree & Strongly Agree		
	Gen Z	Millennials	Older Generations
All news on the Internet should be free to the public**	74% (1)*	76% (1)	69% (2)
News organizations are more concerned about being first than right**	61% (2)	66% (3)	61% (4)
News media should be more helpful & caring like a good neighbor	58% (3)	70% (2)	65% (3)
An independent press is good for democracy	53% (4)	65% (4)	73% (1)
Important for news media to be watchdog of powerful people & government	52% (5)	66% (3)	73% (1)
The news media care little about people like you	50% (6)	56% (5)	43% (5)
News organizations protect democracy more than hurt democracy	34% (7)	47% (6)	38% (7)
News projects accurate representation of constituent groups in U.S. society	32% (8)	44% (8)	28% (8)
News projects accurate representation of your generation	32% (8)	44% (8)	28% (8)
Paying for a news subscription helps support an independent press	30% (9)	46% (7)	39% (6)
News organizations are willing to admit mistakes	26% (10)	43% (9)	22% (9)

*Rank Order
**Difference is not statistically significant

a news subscription helps support an independent press," the future financial independence of news organizations will be even more challenging as the generation born 1997 through 2012 comes of age and replaces older generations.

Whether news coverage grades, perceptions, expectations, and evaluations of press performance, the survey results reported in this chapter underscore that Gen Z cannot be ignored as the news media have ignored younger generations in the past (Poindexter, 2012, 2018). If Gen Z's perceptions and expectations of the press are inconsistent with the needs of the press and the press' views of its role in society, the press is in danger of losing the readers, viewers, and listeners it needs to both survive and thrive. Similarly, if the press' perceptions of its own role are inconsistent with the perceptions of Gen Z and the generations that follow, the challenges that the Knight Foundation identified are in danger of increasing exponentially.

Questions and Reflections

1. Figure 4.3 lists four different categories of complaints about the news media's coverage of Gen Z. What category, if any, do you agree with? What complaint, if any, would you add and why?
2. What do you think is the most important finding in Table 4.3? What are at least three reasons you think that statistic is the most important?

References

American views 2022: Part 2 trust, media and democracy. (2023). https://knightfoundation.org/reports/american-views-2023-part-2/

Heider, D., McCombs, M., & Poindexter, P. M. (2005). What the public expects of local news: Views on public and traditional journalism. *Journalism & Mass Communication Quarterly, 82*, 952–967.

Kovach, B. (2014). *The elements of journalism: What newspeople should know and the public should expect* (T. Rosenstiel, Trans.). Three Rivers Press.

Poindexter, P. M. (2018). *Millennials, news, and social media: Is news engagement a thing of the past?* (2nd ed.). Peter Lang.

Poindexter, P. M. (2012). *Millennials, news, and social media: Is news engagement a thing of the past?* Peter Lang.

Poindexter, P. M., Heider, D., & McCombs, M. (2006). Watchdog or good neighbor? The public's expectations of local news. *Press/Politics, 11*(1), 77–88.

Reporters without Borders Index. (n.d.). https://rsf.org/en/index

Willnat, L., Weaver, D., & Wilhoit, C. (2022). *The American journalist under attack: Media, trust & democracy. Key Findings 2022.* https://www.theamericanjournalist.org/_files/ugd/46a507_4fe1c4d6ec6d4c229895282965258a7a.pdf

· 5 ·

THE GEN Z VOTER

The first presidential election in the United States that Gen Z was old enough to vote in was 2016. In that historic presidential election, a major political party nominated a woman for the first time. The Democratic Party's nominee Hillary Clinton, a former First Lady, a former U.S. senator, and a former secretary of state, lost to Republican Party nominee Donald Trump, a reality TV star and billionaire real estate mogul. Although Hillary Clinton won the popular vote (65,853,625 to 62,985,106), Donald Trump won the vote that mattered—the Electoral College vote (304 to 227) (2016 Presidential election results, n.d.). As specified in Article II, Section 1 (n.d.) of the Constitution of the United States of America, the Electoral College vote—not the popular vote—has the final say on who is elected President of the United States.

By the time the 2024 presidential election season was underway, the oldest members of Gen Z had already experienced two presidential election cycles—2016 and 2020. Just as the 2016 presidential election was historic, so was the presidential election of 2020 but for a vastly different reason: For the first time in the history of the United States of America, the peaceful transfer of power from an incumbent president to a newly elected president was disrupted by a violent insurrection.

CHAPTER 5

After losing the popular vote (81,284,666 to 74,224,319) and the Electoral College vote (306 to 232) to the Democratic Party's nominee former Vice President Joe Biden, then-President Donald Trump, the Republican Party's nominee, refused to concede and he claimed the election was stolen from him. On January 6, 2021, the day Congress met at the U.S. Capitol to officially count the Electoral College votes and certify former Vice President Biden's presidential election victory, supporters of Donald Trump, violently stormed the Capitol building, attacking the police, damaging property, and causing chaos and fear in order to stop the counting of the Electoral College votes so that defeated 45th President Donald Trump could hold on to the job that he had lost (Presidential election results: Biden wins, n.d.; Select January 6th Committee Final Report, 2022).

For his role in the Jan. 6 insurrection, former President Donald Trump was indicted by a federal grand jury. Special Counsel Jack Smith whom Attorney General Merrick Garland picked to prosecute the former president, announced the indictment, saying: "Today, an indictment was unsealed charging Donald J. Trump with conspiring to defraud the United States, conspiring to disenfranchise voters, and conspiring and attempting to obstruct an official proceeding. The indictment was issued by a grand jury of citizens here in the District of Columbia and sets forth the crimes charged in detail" (Special counsel Jack Smith, 2023).

The Special Counsel went on to say: "The attack on our nation's capital on January 6, 2021, was an unprecedented assault on the seat of American democracy. As described in the indictment, it was fueled by lies. Lies by the defendant targeted at obstructing a bedrock function of the U.S. government, the nation's process of collecting, counting, and certifying the results of the presidential election" (Special counsel Jack Smith, 2023).

The indictment, which described former President Trump's alleged role in the Jan. 6 insurrection that precipitated his being indicted, said:

1. The Defendant, **DONALD J. TRUMP**, was the forty-fifth President of the United States and a candidate for re-election in 2020. The Defendant lost the 2020 presidential election.
2. Despite having lost, the Defendant was determined to remain in power. So for more than two months following election day on November 3, 2020, the Defendant spread lies that there had been outcome-determinative fraud in the election and that he had actually won. These claims were false, and the Defendant knew that they were false. But the Defendant repeated and widely disseminated them anyway—to make his knowingly false claims appear legitimate, create an intense national atmosphere of mistrust and anger, and erode public faith in the administration of the election.

Although the criminal trial of Donald Trump for his role in the Jan. 6 insurrection was initially scheduled to begin long before Election Day 2024, months of appeals, hearings, and court rulings delayed the trial's start, making it impossible to predict if there would be a trial and verdict before voters cast their ballots in the 2024 presidential election. Meanwhile, Donald Trump won the Republican Party's primary election and Joe Biden won the primary for the Democratic Party making the former president and current president the presumptive nominees of their respective political parties.

The rematch between the former president who was now 78 and the current president who was now 81 would make this election a contest between two of the oldest candidates in U.S. history. But there were other activities that would be recorded in the history books when historians wrote about the 2024 presidential election. (1) The presumptive Republican nominee had been indicted in four different locales: Washington D.C., Georgia, Florida, and New York City (Keeping track, 2024). At the conclusion of the New York City trial, former president and criminal defendant Donald Trump was convicted by a jury of his peers "on all 34 felony counts of falsifying business records to commit or conceal another crime. The criminal case centered around allegations that he attempted to cover up a $130,000 hush-money payment to an adult film actress so that it wouldn't hurt his prospects in the 2016 presidential election" (Waddick, 2024). The former president's sentence, to be determined by the judge, "could put Mr. Trump behind bars for up to four years, but the former president could receive probation instead, and may never see the inside of a prison cell" (Protess et al., 2024).

Despite the former president now being a convicted felon, the polls showed the Republican and Democratic presidential candidates being statistically tied even though news reports were often framed as the former president being ahead even though the one-or-two-point difference in the poll results was statistically insignificant.

Unprecedented Events Upend the 2024 Presidential Election

Perhaps, to shake up the race, the Biden campaign proposed two unusually early presidential debates which former President Trump immediately agreed to. The first debate, held Thursday, June 27, 2024, and watched by 51 million people (Gold, H., 2024) showcased a former president who "made more than 30 false claims" (Trump, 2024) and a current president who performed so poorly that members of his own party (Klein et al., 2024), donors (Goldmacher & Schleifer, 2024), and the *New York Times* Editorial Board (2024) called on him to step aside. The *Times* Editorial Board, which is separate from the newsroom, is "a group of opinion journalists whose views are informed by expertise, research, debate and certain longstanding values" (Editorial Board, 2024). The Editorial Board wrote:

> At Thursday's debate, the president needed to convince the American public that he was equal to the formidable demands of the office he is seeking to hold for another term. Voters, however, cannot be expected to ignore what was instead plain to see: Mr. Biden is not the man he was four years ago. (Editorial Board, 2024)

Ignoring calls to step aside, President Biden continued his quest for re-election, sitting for network TV news interviews with ABC and NBC (Peoples, 2024; Williams & Klein, 2024) as well as Black radio stations (Paybarah, 2024), and he ramped up rallies with voters. Plus, he held a news conference after hosting world leaders for the 75th anniversary of the NATO alliance. During the hourlong post-NATO Summit news conference, President Biden answered questions on international affairs as well as whether or not he had the "strength and stamina" to campaign and serve another term (Boak & Riccardi, 2024).

Meanwhile, former President Trump kept the public guessing about his VP pick. And he held one of his popular outdoor rallies in rural Pennsylvania, the Saturday evening before the start of the Republican National Convention in Milwaukee. Shortly after walking to the podium and beginning his remarks, a 20-year-old white male on a rooftop fired an "AR-15-style semiautomatic rifle" at former President Trump (Gold, M. et al., 2024).

The bullet, the former President later said in an online post, had "pierced the upper part" of his ear (Gold, M., et al., 2024). News video of the shooting showed former President Trump grab his ear and drop down behind the podium. As Secret Service tried to shield the former President, the blood smeared on his right ear and face was visible. Once it was clear the would-be-assassin no longer posed a threat, having been shot and killed by a member of the Secret Service's elite Counter Sniper Team (Finley & Santana, 2024), the Secret Service helped the former President stand up. On his feet, former President Trump raised his fist in what looked like defiance against the would-be assassin and in solidarity with his supporters, said: "Fight!"

Although bedlam had ensued, reporters on the scene soon reported that former President Trump had been whisked off to a local hospital; one rally-goer on the stage had been shot and killed; two others had been seriously wounded

(Gomez et al., 2024). The assassination attempt on former President Trump shocked the country and the world and for a brief time brought everyone together, regardless of political party and other differences. Weeks later, Secret Service still did not know why the 22-year-old had tried to assassinate the former president.

On Monday, the Republican National Convention convened as planned in Milwaukee, and former President Trump announced his VP pick: JD Vance, the junior senator from Ohio and author of *The New York Times* best seller *Hillbilly Elegy*. The former president with a large white bandage covering his injured right ear, sat with his family during prime-time convention entertainment and speeches. On the final night of the convention, the 45th president of the United States still wearing the white bandage on his right ear accepted the Republican Party's nomination to be the 47th president of the United States. Former President Trump began his 90-minute nomination acceptance speech describing what happened when a would-be assassin's bullet came within an ear of succeeding (Read the transcript, 2024).

Meanwhile, President Biden cut his campaigning short in Las Vegas after testing positive for COVID-19 and flew home to Delaware (Madhani, 2024). While isolating at his Delaware home, President Biden posted several times that he would soon return to the campaign trail. And then on Sunday afternoon, July 21, 2024, the President released a statement on Joseph R. Biden, Jr. stationery that in three sentences expressed his gratitude and intentions:

> It has been the greatest honor of my life to serve as your President. And while it has been my intention to seek reelection, I believe it is in the best interest of my party and the country for me to stand down and to focus solely on fulfilling my duties as President for the remainder of my term. I will speak to the Nation later this week in more detail about my decision. (Joseph., 2024).

Minutes later, President Biden posted on X:

> My fellow Democrats, I have decided not to accept the nomination and to focus all my energies on my duties as President for the remainder of my term. My very first decision as the party nominee in 2020 was to pick Kamala Harris as my Vice President. And it's been the best decision I've made. Today I want to offer my full support and endorsement for Kamala to be the nominee of our party this year. Democrats—it's time to come together and beat Trump. Let's do this. (Biden, 2024)

The back-to-back announcements upended the 2024 presidential race and fired up the Democratic party with excitement, enthusiasm, and energy. It was a new campaign for the Democratic Party and a new presidential election!

On August 2, Friday afternoon, Vice President Kamala Harris received "the majority of votes—at least 2,350—from her party's delegates during a virtual vote" (Morin & Garrison, 2024). When she accepted the nomination three weeks later Thursday evening, August 22, 2024, at the Democratic National Convention in Chicago, Kamala Harris made history again. This time as the first woman of color—Black and South Asian—to be the presidential nominee of a major political party in the United States (Morin & Garrison, 2024). In her acceptance speech, she said:

> Every day in the courtroom, I stood proudly before a judge and I said five words: 'Kamala Harris for the people.' My entire career, I only had one client: the people." "And so, on behalf of the people; on behalf of every American, regardless of party, race, gender or the language your grandmother speaks; on behalf of my mother and everyone who has ever set out on their own unlikely journey; on behalf of Americans like the people I grew up with, people who work hard, chase their dreams and look out for one another; on behalf of everyone whose story could only be written in the greatest nation on Earth, I accept your nomination to be president of the United States of America. (Korecki & Allen, 2024)

Gen Z Opportunity to Participate in Third History-Making Presidential Election

In 2016, the first presidential election that Gen Z was old enough to vote in was a unique experience because for the first time in U.S. history, a woman was the nominee for a major political party. Voting for the first time in the 2020 presidential election was also unique for first-time Gen Z voters but for a different reason. First-time Gen Z voters would vote in a deadly pandemic and the first vaccine wouldn't be authorized for another five weeks (FDA Takes Key Action, 2020).

After President Biden endorsed his vice president, Kamala Harris, a former prosecutor, a former attorney general, a former senator and the Vice President of the United States of America to take his place at the top of the Democratic Party's presidential ticket, first-time Gen Z voters had the opportunity to make history in the 2024 presidential election regardless of which candidate they voted for or the election's outcome. With her father from Jamaica and mother from India, the 2024 presidential election would be the first time a woman of color was a major political party's nominee for president. First-time Gen Z voters would, therefore, join voters regardless of generation or political party, in participating in a history-making presidential election in which one of the major party candidates was a Black and South Asian woman. It turned out more history was made during the 2024 presidential election when the votes were counted. First, Donald Trump, the 45th President of the United States, defeated Vice President Kamala Harris and made history by becoming the 47th U.S. president—only the second time in U.S. history a president was elected to two nonconsecutive terms. In 1884, Grover Cleveland was elected to serve as the 22nd U.S. president and in 1892, he was elected again—this time to serve as the 24th U.S. president (Hajela, 2024). Youth turnout in the 2024 presidential election was also history-making but not because it was high as in 2020. In 2024, young voter turnout "dropped notably" (Medina et al., 2025).

The Gen Z Voter's Political Profile

The 2016 and 2020 first-time Gen Z voters participated in history-making presidential elections and the first-time voters in 2024 would also make history. But what else do we know about Gen Z voters? And are they distinctly different from Millennials and the Older Generations group? The National Gen Z, Social Media & News Engagement Survey has answers to those questions.

According to Table 5.1, Gen Z is more likely to identify as a Democrat (36%) and less likely to identify as a Republican (23%). One-third (33%) of Gen Z also identifies as an Independent. When compared with Millennials, according to Table 5.1, Gen Z's political identity is distinct. Gen Z is less likely than Millennials to say they are a Democrat (36% vs. 44%) and more likely than Millennials to identify as an Independent (33% vs. 24%). Overall, the Older Generations group, which is comprised of Generation X, Baby Boomers, and the Silent Generation, the parents and grandparents of Gen Z and Millennials, is more likely than the two younger generations to identify as Republicans.

The ideological spectrum, from Left Leaning to Right Leaning, in Table 5.1 was created from the answers to the question: "Do you consider yourself: Very Conservative, Conservative, Moderately Conservative, Middle of the Road, Moderately Liberal, Liberal, Very Liberal or Progressive, Other"? The three conservative groups were combined and labeled "Right Leaning" while the three liberal groups were combined and labeled "Left Leaning." "Middle of the Road" is labeled "Middle" in Table 5.1.

When it comes to "Left Leaning," 36% of Gen Z and Millennials embraced that ideology. However, Gen Z (30%) is less likely than Millennials (38%)

Table 5.1 Gen Z's Political Affiliations, Ideological Leanings, and Beliefs About the Importance of Voting

	Gen Z	Millennials	Older Generations (Gen X, Baby Boomers & Silent)
Political Affiliation			
Democrat	36%	44%	38%
Republican	23%	25%	32%
Independent	33%	24%	26%
Other	8%	6%	3%
Ideological Spectrum			
Left Leaning	36%	36%	27%
Middle	27%	24%	30%
Right Leaning	30%	38%	40%
Other	8%	5%	2%
Importance of Voting in Elections			
Very Important	38%	45%	66%
Important	31%	31%	22%
Somewhat Important	24%	15%	8%
Not Important	7%	8%	4%

and the Older Generations group (40%) to identify as "Right Leaning." Approximately one quarter of Gen Z (27%) and Millennials (24%) identified with the "Middle" compared to 30% of the Older Generations group.

Perhaps, the data in Table 5.1 that are most insightful about Gen Z's political profile speak to beliefs about the importance of voting in elections—a right of citizenship that is not just enshrined in the 15th, 19th, 24th, and 26th Amendments to the U.S. Constitution but is a behavior that is essential to a functioning and healthy democracy.[1] Inspired by a Pew Research Center study, participants in The National Gen Z, Social Media & News Engagement

---

[1] "The 15th Amendment gave African American men the right to vote in 1870. But many weren't able to exercise this right. Some states used literacy tests and other barriers to make it harder to vote. The 19th Amendment, ratified in 1920, gave American women the right to vote. The 24th Amendment, ratified in 1964, eliminated poll taxes. The tax had been used in some states to keep African Americans from voting in federal elections. The 26th Amendment, ratified in 1971, lowered the voting age for all elections to 18" (Voting rights laws and constitutional amendments, n.d.).

Survey were asked about the importance of voting to them. Specifically, they were asked: "Thinking about what it means to be a good citizen," how important is it to "vote in elections?" with the response choices, "Very Important," "Important," "Somewhat Important," and "Not Important" (Gramlich, 2019).

According to Table 5.1, Gen Z, Millennials, and the Older Generations group could not be more different when it comes to their beliefs about the importance of voting in elections. For Gen Z, 38% said it was very important to vote in elections while 45% of Millennials and 66% of the Older Generations group said voting in elections was very important.

Relationship Between Gen Z's Beliefs About Voting's Importance and Voting Activity

If more than two-thirds (69%) of Gen Z believe voting is very important or important, does that mean at least the same percentage voted in the 2020 presidential election? No. Gen Z's short voting history displayed in Table 5.2 does not match their beliefs about the importance of voting reported in Table 5.1. In other words, 69% of Gen Z said voting was "very important" or "important" but only 56% of Gen Z voted in the 2020 presidential election. Gen Z was also significantly less likely than older generations to vote in 2020—73% of Millennials and 86% of the Older Generations group voted in the 2020 presidential election.

Table 5.2 Presidential Election Voting and Registration: How Gen Z Compares with Millennials and Older Generations

	Gen Z	Millennials	Older Generations (Gen X, Baby Boomers & Silent)
Voted in 2020 Presidential Election	56%*	73%	86%
Definitely Intend to Vote in 2024 Presidential Election	51%	63%	78%
Probably Will Vote in 2024 Presidential Election	30%	18%	13%
Currently Registered to Vote	79%	84%	91%

*Survey participants born 2003 through 2005, approximately 5% of Gen Z would have been too young to vote in 2020.

Gen Z also lagged behind Millennials and the Older Generations group in their 2024 voting intentions, according to Table 5.2. Over half (51%) of Gen Z *definitely* intended to vote in the 2024 presidential election which was less than Millennials (63%) and the Older Generations group (78%). When *probably* intends to vote is compared, Gen Z was more likely than the older generations to say they *probably* would vote in 2024. In fact, 30% of Gen Z said they would probably vote compared to 18% of Millennials and 13% of the Older Generations group. These differences in the "Definitely Intend" to vote vs. "Probably Will Vote" suggest that Millennials and the Older Generations group were more committed than Gen Z to voting in the 2024 presidential election.

With states requiring that citizens register prior to voting, survey participants were also asked about their current voter registration status. Although almost four out of five members of Gen Z said they were registered to vote, Gen Z lagged behind Millennials and the Older Generations group in voter registration: 79% of Gen Z said they were registered which means 21% were

Figure 5.1 Why Gen Z is not Registered to Vote

1. Believe Vote Won't Count
"I do not believe the public's vote counts"
"Cause elections don't matter"
2. Not Knowledgeable about Registering to Vote
"I don't know the process to register myself to vote"
3. No Interest in Voting; Don't Care
"I have little interest in participating in the voting process"
"Don't care what happens to this country as long as I survive it"
"I have no respect for democracy"
4. Don't Follow Politics; Don't Like Politics
"I am not educated enough in politics to vote"
"I don't follow politics very closely so I don't feel like I should vote"
5. Don't Have Time; Too Busy
"Because I have no time"
"Have not had the time to do so"
6. Voter Registration Requirements and Structural Barriers
"Just turned 18"
"I moved to a new city and have not gotten around to it"
"DMV issues with changing ID"
"Was registered until last general election when my signature apparently didn't match the one on record so they unregistered me ☹"

not registered voters. Eighty-four percent of Millennials and 91% of the Older Generations group reported they were registered voters.

Survey participants who were *not* registered to vote were asked the follow-up question: "What is the main reason you are not registered to vote?" Gen Z's reasons for not being registered to vote were reviewed and sorted into categories that ranged from beliefs about voting and knowledge about registering to vote to disinterest, time constraints, and registration issues. Figure 5.1 displays the categories and select Gen Z quotes to illustrate the reasons some in this generation were not registered to vote.

Most Important Issue Facing Gen Z Provides Additional Insight. When asked during the survey, "What is the most important issue facing your generation?" Gen Z responded with answers that were qualitatively sorted into 12 categories which are displayed in Figure 5.2. Gen Z's specific words that represent the 12 categories were not identical, but the meaning was consistent with 11 different issues plus "Other." To qualify as a category, at least five survey participants had to identify the same issue which were abortion rights, climate change, gun control/gun violence, economic insecurity, inflation, jobs, mental health, racism, social media, women's rights, and generation criticism. "Other" includes issues that although mentioned only one or two times, were important to be included in this category.

The issues displayed in Figure 5.2 that Gen Z identified align with many events and issues identified in Chapter 1 that have contributed to defining this generation born during the years 1997 through 2012. Additionally, these

Figure 5.2 Most Important Issues Facing Gen Z

Abortion Rights
Climate Change
Gun Control/Gun Violence
Economic Insecurity
Inflation
Jobs
Mental Health
Racism
Social Media
Women's Rights
Generation Criticism
Other (Student loans, bullying, crime, transgender rights, immigration, don't know)

issues correlate with some of the top 10 news topics described in Chapter 2 that Gen Z engages with. These news topics include restrictions on abortion rights, gun violence, and climate change. Student loan debt, crime, and immigration listed in the "Other" category in Figure 5.2 are also among Gen Z's top news topics.

With so many personal criticisms of their own generation, the "Generation Criticism" category was created to capture Gen Z's self-critique. Gen Z criticized their generation for laziness, apathy, lack of common sense, lack of human compassion, lack of a work ethic, lack of self-esteem, and lack of self-confidence.

Barriers to Vote Despite Intentions to Vote

In the United States, before you can vote, you are required to register to vote. While registering can be a barrier to voting, registering to vote is not a guarantee that a U.S. citizen will vote (Poindexter, 2022, p. 4).[2] Other barriers to voting, according to University of Virginia professor John Holbein (2020), include locating and traveling to polling locations, navigating long lines, and even finding time to vote. And according to a guide to voting in the 2022 midterm elections written exclusively for Gen Z, level of interest and awareness can also be voting barriers. "Some eligible citizens may not be interested in voting and others may not be aware of an upcoming election until it's too late to register" (Poindexter, 2022, p. 5).[2]

> But the biggest impediment to voting for some first-time voters may be as simple as not knowing what's required to vote or how, when, and where to vote. It's also the case that because some are not informed about the candidates and issues and are unsure about where to find information they can trust, they decide not to vote, even though they're registered. (Poindexter, 2022, p. 5)[2]

Despite voting impediments, according to Table 5.2, 51% of Gen Z said they *definitely* intend to vote and another 30% said they probably will vote when asked: "Do you intend to vote in the 2024 Presidential Election?" In a follow-up question, survey participants were asked: "What is the main reason you definitely or probably will vote in the 2024 Presidential Election?"

---

2 See Appendix for Poindexter, P. M. (2022). *Voting & engaging with news about the 2022 midterm elections: A guide for Gen Z voters.*

Figure 5.3 Themes That Reflect Main Reasons Gen Z Will Vote in the 2024 Presidential Election

Candidate Related
Democracy Related, including Obligation, Duty, Important, Privilege, Right
Want Voice to Be Heard
For the Voting Experience
First Vote
Issues
Lose Right to Complain
To Have Impact on the Future and Feel a Part of the Community
Unconventional and Inspirational
Other

Answers from the 355 Gen Z survey participants were reviewed and sorted into 10 themed categories which are displayed in Figure 5.3.

The largest group of answers fit a candidate-related theme with Gen Z saying they planned to vote in the 2024 presidential election to either support the incumbent president or return the former president to the White House. Democracy-related answers were the second largest group of reasons. Some examples of Gen Z's democracy-related reasons were: "Voting is essential to maintaining democracy" and "Voting is important and your civic duty. I always vote." "It's important for every citizen to vote." "It is important as an American right."

Distinct from candidate and democracy-related reasons, voting was framed as your vote is your voice: "I believe it is important to vote so that my voice is heard." "It's important to have a voice in who becomes president of the United States." A few Gen Z participants even connected voting to the right to complain, saying "If you don't vote, you lose the right to complain."

And because a handful of reasons stood out for being unconventional or inspirational, a separate category was created for them. Examples include: (1) "By not voting, you are voting so you might as well vote"' (2) "It's the best part of America"; (3) "I enjoy voting"; (4) "To be a part of my community"; (5) "This is the most important election that I will be eligible to be a part of."

Engaging with Election News is a Prerequisite to Casting an Informed Vote

If the 2024 presidential election were the "most important election" Gen Z would be "eligible to be a part of" and the issues identified in Figure 5.2 mattered as Gen Z said, one would expect that Gen Z would engage with presidential election news to cast an informed vote. Although informing oneself before an election is more than paying attention to news about a specific election, less than a quarter (23%) of Gen Z engaged with presidential election news often, according to Table 2.7 in Chapter 2. In comparison, one-third (32%) of Millennials and 42% of the Older Generations group reported engaging with presidential election news often.

Not engaging with news regularly decreases the chances of casting an informed vote and risks voting against what one cares about most. Unfortunately, in today's social media and news landscape that is polluted with disinformation, clicking on a social media or a digital news platform is no guarantee that the news can be trusted. Therefore, for Gen Z voters to have the impact they're voting for, they must not only make engaging with news a routine, they must have some knowledge about how journalism works in order to detect the disinformation that lurks in the social media-news landscape pretending to be news in order to misinform and mislead. Disinformation and other barriers to becoming smart about news will be explored in Chapter 6.

Questions and Reflections

1. What are three things you learned in this chapter that you did not know?
2. How did your answers on the questionnaire for *The National Gen Z, Social Media & News Engagement Survey* compare with results in Table 5.2?
3. Search for and read through the following analyses of the 2024 presidential election results: (1) AP VoteCast: How America voted in 2024 (Lodhi et al., n.d.); (2) *Young people and the 2024 election: Struggling, disconnected, and dissatisfied* (Medina, 2025). Based on what you've learned so far about Gen Z, Millennials, and older generations and know from your personal experiences, what surprises, if any, were there in these analyses of the 2024 election results and why were you

surprised? What else, if anything, would you like to know about Gen Z and the 2024 presidential election?
4. "Voting & Engaging with News about the 2022 Midterm Elections: A Guide for Gen Z Voters," which is in the Appendix, has advice for Gen Z voters that would apply to any election. Based on that guide as well as this chapter and your own experience, what advice would you give a Gen Z voter who is voting for the first time?

References

2016 Presidential election results. (n.d.). https://www.nytimes.com/elections/2016/results/president

Article II, Section 1, Clause 2. (n.d.). https://constitution.congress.gov/browse/essay/artII-S1-C2-1/ALDE_00013798/

Biden, J. (2024). My fellow Democrats. https://x.com/JoeBiden/status/1815087772216303933

Boak, J., & Riccardi, N. (2024). Key takeaways from Biden's news conference: Insistence on staying in the race and flubbed names. https://apnews.com/article/biden-news-conference-reelection-age-0d9f4936484ff71295e2b088e5c525dd

CDC Covid Timeline. (n.d.). https://www.cdc.gov/museum/timeline/covid19.html

Donald Trump, felon. (2024). https://www.nytimes.com/2024/05/30/opinion/trump-trial-guilty-felony.html?pgtype=Article&action=click&module=RelatedLinks

Editorial Board. (2024). To serve his country, President Biden should leave the race. https://www.nytimes.com/2024/06/28/opinion/biden-election-debate-trump.html?smid=nytcore-ios-share&referringSource=articleShare&sgrp=c-cb

FDA takes key action in fight against COVID-19 by issuing emergency use authorization for first COVID-19 vaccine. (2020). https://www.fda.gov/news-events/press-announcements/fda-takes-key-action-fight-against-covid-19-issuing-emergency-use-authorization-first-covid-19

Final report: Select committee to investigate the January 6th attack on the United States Capitol December 22, 2022 117th Congress Second Session House Report 117-663. (2022). https://www.govinfo.gov/content/pkg/GPO-J6-REPORT/pdf/GPO-J6-REPORT.pdf

Finley, B., & Santana, R. (2024). What to know about the Secret Service's Counter Sniper Team. https://apnews.com/article/trump-shooting-secret-service-counter-sniper-team-4b37fd13def3199f5235518b41a02909

Gold, H. (2024). 51 million viewers tuned in to CNN's presidential debate with Biden and Trump. https://www.cnn.com/2024/06/28/media/ratings-debate-trump-biden-cnn?cid=ios_app

Gold, M., Barnes, J., E., & Levien, S. J. (2024). Trump is safe after assassination attempt; suspected gunman is dead. https://www.nytimes.com/live/2024/07/13/us/biden-trump-election?campaign_id=60&emc=edit_na_20240714&instance_id=0&nl=breaking-news&ref=cta&regi_id=39911568&segment_id=172119&user_id=14a904208c0f435fd6fe63243eadd0d2

Goldmacher, S., & Schleifer, T. (2024). *Donors to Pro-Biden Super PAC are said to withhold roughly $90 million.* https://www.nytimes.com/2024/07/12/us/politics/biden-donors-money.html?smid=nytcore-ios-share&referringSource=articleShare&sgrp=c-cb

Gomez, J., Kochi, S., Rosica, J., & Moorwood, V. (2024). *Trump rally shooting victims: Pennsylvania firefighter killed, 2 local residents wounded.* https://www.usatoday.com/story/news/politics/elections/2024/07/14/who-are-trump-rally-shooting-victims/74399786007/

Gramlich, J. (2019). *What makes a good citizen? Voting, paying taxes, following the law top list.* https://www.pewresearch.org/short-reads/2019/07/02/what-makes-a-good-citizen-voting-paying-taxes-following-the-law-top-list/

Grover Cleveland set precedent of nonconsecutive presidential terms. https://apnews.com/article/grover-cleveland-president-nonconsecutive-terms-7ea2c92c72911462ccb1bc2e7352fa23

Hajela, D. (2024). *Trump isn't first to be second: Grover Cleveland set precedent of nonconsecutive presidential terms.* https://apnews.com/article/grover-cleveland-president-nonconsecutive-terms-7ea2c92c72911462ccb1bc2e7352fa23

Holbein, J. (2020). *Why so few young Americans vote.* https://theconversation.com/why-so-few-young-americans-vote-132649

Joseph R. Biden, Jr. (2024). https://static01.nyt.com/newsgraphics/documenttools/5c749e32c65e55c0/37384880-full.pdf

Keeping track of the Trump criminal cases. (2024). https://www.nytimes.com/interactive/2023/us/trump-investigations-charges-indictments.html

Klein, B., Hunt, K., Lee, M., Fox, L., & Tausche, K. (2024). *Biden's debate performance sets off alarm bells for Democrats.* https://www.cnn.com/2024/06/28/politics/joe-biden-debate-performance-panic/index.html

Korecki, N., & Allen, J. (2024). *Harris weaves her life story into a vision for America as she accepts Democratic nomination.* https://www.nbcnews.com/politics/2024-election/kamala-harris-accepts-democratic-nomination-life-story-vision-america-rcna165260

Lodhi, H., Cheng, S., Kaufmann, P., Urenda, P. B., & Fox, E. (n.d.). *AP VoteCast: How America voted in 2024.* https://apnews.com/projects/election-results-2024/votecast/

Madhani, A. (2024). *President Joe Biden tests positive for COVID-19 while campaigning in Las Vegas, has 'mild symptoms'.* https://apnews.com/article/biden-covid-las-vegas-ff29bb071f18b993d20dedccbe2c8fbf

Medina, A., Siegel-Stechler, K., & Suzuki, S. (2025). *Young people and the 2024 election: Struggling, disconnected, and dissatisfied.* https://circle.tufts.edu/latest-research/2024-poll-barriers-issues-economy

Morin, R., & Garrison, J. (2024). *Harris makes history as first Black woman, Asian American presidential nominee.* https://www.usatoday.com/story/news/politics/elections/2024/08/02/kamala-harris-democrat-presidential-candidate/74631136007/

Paybarah, A. (2024). *Radio station parts ways with host who interviewed Biden with questions from his aides.* https://www.washingtonpost.com/politics/2024/07/07/biden-interview-wurd-campaign/

Peoples, S. (2024). *Biden faced a low bar in his first post-debate interview. It's not certain he cleared it.* https://apnews.com/article/biden-interview-democrat-debate-abc-81d82d10698973be7e801abc16f93030

Poindexter, P. M. (2022). *Voting & Engaging with News about the 2022 Midterm Elections: A Guide for Gen Z Voters* (see Appendix).

Presidential election results: Biden wins. (n.d.). https://www.nytimes.com/interactive/2020/11/03/us/elections/results-president.html

Presidential election results: Trump wins. (2025). https://www.nytimes.com/interactive/2024/11/05/us/elections/results-president.html

Protess, B., Bromwich, J. E., Haberman, M., Christobek, K., McKinley, J., & Rashbaum, W. K. (2024). *Trump convicted on all counts to become America's first felon president.* https://www.nytimes.com/2024/05/30/nyregion/trump-convicted-hush-money-trial.html?smid=nytcore-ios-share&referringSource=articleShare&sgrp=c-cb

Read the transcript of Donald J. Trump's convention speech. (2024). https://www.nytimes.com/2024/07/19/us/politics/trump-rnc-speech-transcript.html?smid=nytcore-ios-share&referringSource=articleShare&sgrp=c-cb

Select January 6th Committee Final Report and Supporting Materials Collection. (2022). https://www.govinfo.gov/collection/january-6th-committee-final-report?path=/GPO/January%206th%20Committee%20Final%20Report%20and%20Supporting%20Materials%20Collection

Special counsel Jack Smith delivers statement. (2023). https://www.justice.gov/sco-smith/speech/special-counsel-jack-smith-delivers-statement-0

Trump made more than 30 false claims during CNN's presidential debate—far more than Biden. (2024). https://www.cnn.com/2024/06/27/politics/fact-checking-the-cnn-presidential-debate?cid=ios_app

Voting rights laws and constitutional amendments. (n.d.). https://www.usa.gov/voting-rights

Waddick, K. (2024). *How Donald Trump's criminal conviction is already rewriting American history.* https://www.usatoday.com/story/news/politics/2024/06/01/trump-verdict-conviction-american-history-impact/73785567007/

Williams, M., & Klein, B. (2024). *Takeaways from Biden's interview with NBC News.* https://amp.cnn.com/cnn/2024/07/15/politics/joe-biden-nbc-interview

· 6 ·

BARRIERS TO A NEWS SMART GEN Z

Why does it matter if Gen Z or any generation is informed?

If "the purpose of journalism is to provide people with the information they need to be free and self-governing" as Bill Kovach and Tom Rosenstiel, authors of *The Elements of Journalism*, assert, how can Gen Z or any generation be free and self-governing without knowing the news and information that journalists report (Kovach & Rosenstiel, 2014, p. 9)? Can an uninformed person truly be free? Can uninformed citizens protect our democratic system of government that is founded on "We the People"—not a king or dictator?

With press freedom enshrined in the First Amendment to the U.S. Constitution, journalism's purpose is elevated to a responsibility that the 1947 Commission on Freedom of the Press, known as the Hutchins Commission after the commission chairman Robert Hutchins, chancellor of the University of Chicago, declared the "first requirement" a "free society" should demand is "the media should be accurate. They should not lie" (A free and responsible press, 1947, p. 21).

The national commission, funded by *Time* magazine founder Henry Luce, described the process that journalism must employ to report news if the public is to trust it, saying: "the first link in the chain of responsibility is the reporter at the source of the news" (p. 21). The Commission continued, adding that the reporter "must be careful and competent;" "estimate correctly which sources are most authoritative," and "prefer firsthand observation to hearsay" (p. 21). Additionally, according to the Hutchins Commission, the reporter "must know what questions to ask, what things to observe, and which items to report" (p. 21). Just as important as "reportorial accuracy," the Hutchins Commission report said is "the identification of fact as fact and opinion as opinion, and their separation, so far as possible" (A free and responsible press, 1947, p. 22).

Reporter Accuracy Does Not Guarantee an Informed Public

Although it's unknown *why* someone, perhaps, a parent, a grandparent, an aunt, a teacher, a sibling, a friend, or a neighbor, said to Gen Z that it is important to be informed, it is known from Table 3.2 that an overwhelming majority (79%) of Gen Z could recall someone saying "being informed about news is important." Unfortunately, according to Figure 6.1 there are nine barriers that may prevent Gen Z from becoming informed and some barriers may be insurmountable.

The nine barriers to becoming informed, which will be examined individually, represent a synthesis of the results of The National Gen Z, Social Media & News Engagement Survey as well as published research literature, news audience-focused papers presented at annual conferences of the Association for Education in Journalism and Mass Communication (AEJMC), news stories, opinion columns, reports, and books about journalists, journalism, the news

Figure 6.1 Barriers to a News Smart Gen Z

Weakening News Engagement Socialization
Tenuous Civic Duty to Keep Informed
Limited Supplemental News Engagement Benefits
Excessive Amount of Time Spent on Social Media
Marginal Use of Apps for News
Lack of a News Engagement Routine
Inability to Distinguish News That Can Be Trusted from Disinformation
Gen Z isn't into Paying for News
Minimal Attention Paid to News about Presidential Elections, Democracy, the White House, Congress, the Supreme Court, and the Federal Government at Work

media, social media, disinformation, artificial intelligence (AI), and democracy as well as studies from the Pew Research Center, the Harvard Youth Poll, Institute of Politics (IOP) at the Harvard Kennedy School, CIRCLE at Tufts University plus lessons I've learned from working in the news media, teaching, conducting research, and advocating for engaging with credible news.

1. *Weakening News Engagement Socialization.* Engagement with news is not automatic like breathing; news engagement is learned. As discussed in Chapter 3, in the pre-digital landscape, children learned the importance of being informed by observing their parents read a print newspaper or watch local and network news on TV. As smartphones and other personal mobile devices replaced print newspapers and TV as go-to places for news whenever you wanted it and wherever you might be, opportunities to learn that it was important to be informed by observing parents read newspapers and watch TV news declined, weakening news engagement socialization. Without robust news engagement socialization during the formative years, the chances of growing into an adult who embraces engaging with news decline.

2. *Tenuous Civic Duty to Keep Informed.* Weak news engagement socialization can make the civic duty to keep informed more tenuous by not reinforcing the belief that connects following the news with civic responsibility. Results of a study conducted in the pre-social media-digital news age not only documented the existence of a civic duty to keep informed, the study's authors found that adults who believe they have a civic duty to keep informed were more likely to read a daily newspaper and watch news on network and local TV and cable (Poindexter & McCombs, 2001). However, with today's lukewarm relationship between older generations and legacy news media, especially newspapers, as documented in Chapter 2's Table 2.5, the civic duty to keep informed, which will be examined further in Chapter 7, may have deteriorated.

3. *Limited Supplemental News Engagement Benefits.* Is engaging with news enjoyable? Is engaging with news empowering? Does news help with daily life? While the primary reason to engage with news is to inform oneself, there are supplemental benefits to engaging with news that have been identified in previous studies. However, Gen Z does not appear to be receiving these benefits. According to Table 6.1, only a small percentage of Gen Z strongly agrees that engaging with news is enjoyable (15%), is empowering (15%), or helps with daily life (13%).

These very modest supplemental news engagement benefits for Gen Z are a sharp contrast to mid-twentieth century and early twenty-first-century audience research from the "uses and gratifications" tradition that found psychological and practical benefits connected readers to the newspaper (Berelson, 1949; Katz et al., 1974; Lee, 2013). For example, a 1945 newspaper strike in New York City provided researchers with an opportunity to learn what the newspaper meant to readers when the strike prevented the newspaper from being delivered. The study found that for its readers, the newspaper provided "relief from boredom," a "tool for daily life," and a means to "overcome insecurity when you didn't know what was going on" (Berelson, 1949).

More than two and a half decades later in a report cited in Poindexter (2008a, p. 26), gratifications for women and men were found to be mostly similar but women were more likely than men to read newspapers to "obtain useful information for daily life." And in a study published in the *Journal of Broadcasting & Electronic Media*, Lee (2013) found that "entertainment and social motivations" were keys to younger adults' engagement with news.

If, as Table 6.1 shows, only 13%–15% of Gen Z enjoy getting news, feel empowered or are helped by news, the benefits that motivated and gratified older generations in a print newspaper world are significantly less effective with Gen Z in today's social media-digital news world. As a result, another barrier to Gen Z becoming informed is erected.

4. *Excessive Amount of Time Spent on Social Media.* Of 10 social media and video-sharing platforms in the United States, YouTube and Facebook are the most popular, according to the Pew Research Center (Gottfried, 2024). Eighty-three percent of U.S. adults use YouTube and 68% are on Facebook. "Additionally, roughly half of U.S. adults (47%) say they use Instagram." Although the other social media platforms are not as popular, still "27% to 35% of U.S. adults use Pinterest, TikTok, LinkedIn, WhatsApp and Snapchat. "About one-in-five say they use Twitter" (renamed "X" after being purchased by billionaire Elon Musk), "and Reddit" (Gottfried, 2024).

Table 6.1 Supplemental News Engagement Benefits

	% Saying Strongly Agree		
	Gen Z	Millennials	Older Generations (Gen X, Baby Boomers & Silent)
Enjoyment	15%	33%	34%
Empowerment	15%	28%	22%
Help with Daily Life	13%	22%	17%

Does social media time facilitate or obstruct engaging with news? When the focus is on the time spent on social media and how that time is being used, Table 6.2 suggests social media platforms are more a barrier than bridge to Gen Z's news engagement.

According to Table 6.2, 64% of Gen Z are on social media seven days per week. Plus, 32% of Gen Z devote three to four hours per day on social media, and 25% spend five or more hours per day. In other words, almost three-fifths of Gen Z (57%) are on social media at least three hours a day.

If a significant percentage of Gen Z used their time on social media to engage with news, these platforms would be perceived as a bridge to news engagement. But with only 10% spending "a lot" of time engaging with news, social media appear to be taking Gen Z away from news rather than toward it.

5. *Marginal Use of Apps for News.* Apps produced by news organizations such as the *New York Times*, NPR, *USA Today*, NBC, the *Washington Post*, CNN, the *Los Angeles Times*, and the Associated Press (AP) are among the digital platforms where trusted news can be found. Unfortunately, according to Table 2.4 in Chapter 2, only 30% of Gen Z uses apps which means 70% of this generation is ignoring a news platform that is not just credible but is as easy to use as social media.

News on apps is organized, crisply written, and regularly updated. In addition to news, on apps that are digital extensions of legacy newspapers such as the *New York Times*, *Washington Post*, and the *Los Angeles Times*, there are

Table 6.2 Time Spent on Social Media

	Gen Z	Millennials	Older Generations (Gen X, Baby Boomers & Silent)
On Social Media 7 Days/Week	64%	63%	50%
Spend 3 to 4 Hours Per Day on Social Media	32%	32%	18%
Spend 5 or More Hours Per Day on Social Media	25%	19%	7%
Spend A lot of Time Engaging with News on Social Media	10%	19%`	10%

opinion essays, including editorials and opinion columns written by staff editors and columnists, that are clearly labeled so the opinion is not mistaken for news.

Separate from opinion written by the news organization's staff, are opinion essays written by guests with expertise on topics in the news from politics and public health to economics and education. The guest opinion essays may also focus on changing trends or interesting topics that readers may not be familiar with.

Apps can also alert users when news is breaking, that is, if the notification is activated. News apps don't just inform users with trusted news; they also can contribute to strengthening the civic duty to keep informed, enhancing one of the responsibilities that accompanies living in a democracy, that is, being an informed citizen.

Whether disinterest, lack of awareness or some other reason is keeping Gen Z from using apps, the result is the same: By not using news apps that are updated 24/7 with trusted news by known news organizations, Gen Z may be unknowingly erecting a barrier to becoming smart about news.

6. *Lack of a News Engagement Routine.* Seventy-five years of research literature about the news audience have identified a variety of factors that have contributed to reading, watching, and listening to legacy news platforms, including print newspapers and news magazines, TV, radio, and cable and more recently digital platforms from social media to apps and podcasts, created during the first two decades of the twenty-first century (Poindexter, 2018). These news engagement-related factors include demographics—age, education, income, gender, race, ethnicity, and generation—as well as sociopsychological variables, from socialization and uses and gratifications to the civic duty to keep informed. Additionally, research has identified news avoidances, that is, reasons the public has avoided engaging with news (Newman et al., 2022, 2023; Poindexter, 2008b).

The one factor that has contributed to increased news engagement that has not been examined in detail, until now, is news engagement routine. Explored in Chapter 3, news engagement routine was defined as "regularly reading, watching, listening to, sharing, discussing, commenting on news, etc., at a particular time, in a certain order, and in a familiar space." The National Gen Z, Social Media & News Engagement Survey found that having a news engagement routine matters and it can play a role in overcoming barriers to becoming informed.

According to Chapter 3's Table 3.3, survey participants who have a news engagement routine were significantly more likely than those without a routine to get news seven days a week (60% vs. 39%). Those with a routine were also twice as likely as those without a routine to seek news daily (45% vs. 23%). And 63% of those with a routine reported getting news three times or more during a 24-hour period compared to the 41% without a routine. The results underscore that the absence of a routine can be a barrier to engaging with news and becoming informed.

7. *Inability to Distinguish News That Can Be Trusted from Disinformation.* In today's social media-digital news landscape, the ability to distinguish between news that can be trusted and disinformation is a necessity. Merriam-Webster (n.d.) defines disinformation, which some news organizations call misinformation, as "false information deliberately and often covertly spread (as by the planting of rumors) in order to influence public opinion or obscure the truth." It should be noted that while some dictionaries, researchers, academic centers, and other groups distinguish misinformation from disinformation by focusing on whether the inaccurate information was intentional, it's not unusual for some news organizations to use the terms misinformation and disinformation interchangeably.[1]

Disinformation is not limited to text; it can also be a photo, a video, or audio which are called deepfakes and defined as "an image or recording that has been convincingly altered and manipulated to misrepresent someone as doing or saying something that was not actually done or said" (Merriam-Webster, n.d.). While disinformation has been used to push lies dressed up as news, deepfakes have been used to spread election deceptions such as pretending a candidate said something to mislead voters in robocalls or give the false impression that a popular celebrity endorsed a candidate when there was no evidence of an endorsement (Bond, 2024; Rosenzweig-Ziff, 2024).

Fearing the harm that disinformation supercharged by artificial intelligence (AI) could cause the 2024 U.S. presidential election, academics at Stanford, the University of Chicago, and Columbia University released a White Paper for "voters, journalists, civil society, tech leaders, and other stakeholders"

---

[1] Examples of journalists and news organizations using "misinformation" and "disinformation:" interchangeably: "The rise of AI fake news is creating a 'misinformation superspreader'" in the *Washington Post* (Verma, 2023); ProPublica's "How Verified Accounts on X Thrive While Spreading Misinformation About the Israel-Hamas Conflict" (Kao & Bengani, 2023); CNN's "OpenAI sets rules to combat election misinformation. It's been tried before" (Fung, 2024b).

(Bueno de Mesquita, et al., n.d.). Titled "Preparing for Generative AI in the 2024 Election: Recommendations and Best Practices Based on Academic Research," the White Paper explained the "risk and promise of AI for electoral democracy" and it made recommendations to combat AI (Bueno de Mesquita et al., n.d.).

The AI risk to elections was real which is why the Federal Communications Commission (FCC) acted swiftly after news reports said AI-enhanced robocalls, impersonating President Joe Biden, "called New Hampshire voters and urged them not to participate in the state's primary" (Fung, 2024a). Voting unanimously, the FCC, outlawed "scam robocalls featuring fake, artificial intelligence-created voices" that experts said "could undermine election security or supercharge fraud" (Fung, 2024a). Elaborating in a statement, the chair of the FCC Jessica Rosenworcel said: "Bad actors are using AI-generated voices in unsolicited robocalls to extort vulnerable family members, imitate celebrities, and misinform voters" (Fung, 2024a).

In addition to the academic White Paper and a new FCC law, at least 37 state legislatures introduced or enacted laws to regulate "A.I.-generated images, audio, or video depicting a candidate saying or doing things they never did to damage that candidate's reputation and deceive voters" (Tracker, n.d.). According to the non profit, non-partisan Public Citizen that tracked state legislation that sought to regulate deepfakes, "without regulation, deepfakes are likely to further confuse voters and undermine confidence in elections. A deepfake video could be released days or hours before an election with no time to debunk it—misleading voters and altering the outcome of the election" (Tracker, n.d.).

The News Literacy Project (n.d.), a non-partisan education non-profit founded in 2008, to "ensure all students are skilled in news literacy before they graduate high school" also tracked disinformation pushed during the 2024 election. Accessible to educators, journalists, disinformation scholars, campaigns, and the public as a whole, the database was organized into five categories of disinformation: (1) candidate image ("falsehoods that mislead the public about a candidate's character, appearance or reputation"); (2) candidate popularity ("falsehoods that mislead the public about a candidate's endorsements and level of grassroots support"); (3) conspiracy ("falsehoods that mislead the public by pushing baseless conspiracy theories about the candidates, the election, the government and other topics"); (4) election integrity ("falsehoods that mislead the public about the function and security of the election system"); (5) platform and policy ("falsehoods that mislead the public about a candidate's record, policies and campaign promises") (Misinformation Dashboard, 2024).

While AI was used to create fake images, audio, and video, the risks of artificial intelligence were not limited to elections. In fact, Dr. Geoffrey Hinton, an AI pioneer, was so concerned about artificial intelligence that he "quit his job at Google" so he could "freely speak out" about the harm that AI can cause (Metz, 2023).

To establish a baseline for Gen Z's ability to distinguish trustworthy news from disinformation, participants in The National Gen Z, Social Media & News Engagement Survey were asked five questions from a Pew Research Center study on evaluating news for trustworthiness (Gramlich, 2021). Additionally, survey participants were asked about their familiarity with disinformation and if they had ever encountered it.

Table 6.3 rank orders the factors that Gen Z, Millennials, and the Older Generations group identified as "very important" when evaluating trustworthiness of news stories. What stands out is no one trustworthiness detector exceeds 50% and the rankings are similar across generations, suggesting there is a consensus as to what factors are "very important" when evaluating a news story's trustworthiness. In other words, Gen Z, Millennials, and the Older Generations group agree that the sources cited in a news story as well as the news organization that published the story matter most when evaluating trustworthiness.

The number of shares and comments a news story attracts ranked lowest for Gen Z, Millennials, and the Older Generations group as a very important

Table 6.3 How Gen Z Evaluates Trustworthiness of a News Story

	% Saying Very Important		
	Gen Z	Millennials	Older Generations (Gen X, Baby Boomers & Silent)
Sources Cited in Story	49% (1)	48% (1)	44% (2)
News Organization that Published Story	44% (2)	47% (2)	49% (1)
Specific Journalist who Reported Story	29% (3)	30% (3)	28% (3)
Person who Shares Story	25% (4)	30% (3)	28% (3)
Person has Lots of Shares and Comments	16% (5)	23% (4)	8% (4)

factor in evaluating a news story's trustworthiness. Still, Gen Z (16%) and Millennials (23%) valued shares and comments at least twice as much as the Older Generations group (8%).

In today's social media and digital news landscape, it's important to know what factors matter and which ones don't when evaluating the trustworthiness of news stories; it's also essential to be aware of the potential presence of disinformation that masquerades as legitimate news, pushing lies to an unsuspecting public eager to get the latest news.

According to Table 6.4, about two-thirds of Gen Z, Millennials, and the Older Generations group said they were "very familiar" or "familiar" with the term "disinformation" while about one-third said they were only "somewhat" or "not familiar." However, the level of familiarity with the term disinformation does not automatically translate into knowing that disinformation is a problem when getting news online, especially on social media. Consequently, these results should serve as a yellow flashing light that more education is needed to counter disinformation and the danger it poses, especially in election years like 2024 when around the globe, "billions of people voted" in what the *New York Times* called "one of the largest and most consequential democratic exercises in living memory" (Hsu et al., 2024).

Credible news organizations, of course, report legitimate election news, but that news may be overwhelmed by a tsunami of election disinformation. However, if the public is educated with the tools to detect and reject disinformation, the power of the false information, dressed up as news, that's pushed in the social media and digital news landscape will be greatly diminished and another barrier to Gen Z's being smart about news will have been removed.

In a follow-up question, Gen Z, Millennials, and the Older Generations group who had some level of familiarity with disinformation were asked if they

Table 6.4 Familiarity with Term "Disinformation"

	Gen Z	Millennials	Older Generations (Gen X, Baby Boomers & Silent)
Very Familiar	36%	39%	39%
Familiar	30%	26%	26%
Somewhat Familiar	24%	23%	21%
Not Familiar	10%	12%	13%

Table 6.5 Encountered Disinformation?

	Gen Z	Millennials	Older Generations (Gen X, Baby Boomers & Silent)
Yes	67%	62%	70%
No	13%	20%	10%
Don't Know	21%	18%	19%

had encountered this intentionally false information, the majority of Gen Z (67%), Millennials (62%), and the Older Generations Group (70%) said they had. About one-fifth of Gen Z, Millennials, and the Older Generations group said they didn't know if they had encountered disinformation, but that percentage probably underestimates the true percentage because disinformation is everywhere. And it can find you even if you don't recognize it.

8. *Gen Z isn't into Paying for News.* At the end of 2023, the *New York Times* had "10.36 million subscribers, 9.7 million of them digital-only" (Robertson, 2024). From the end of 2022 to the end of 2023, print subscribers to the *New York Times* declined by 70,000, from "730,000" to "660,000" (Robertson, 2024). If the *New York Times* and other legacy newspaper organizations are looking to Gen Z to increase paid subscriptions, they should look elsewhere. Gen Z isn't into paying for news.

To gauge Gen Z's attitudes about paying for news, questions were asked about news on the Internet as well as paid subscriptions for news and non-news content. As can be seen in Table 6.6, almost half of Gen Z (47%) strongly agrees that "all news on the Internet should be free to the public." While news on TV and radio has always been "free" to the public because broadcast programs are advertiser-supported, the business model for legacy newspapers traditionally was a combination of advertiser and subscriber revenue with the vast majority of a newspaper's revenues coming from display and classified advertising.

As the Internet, Gen Z, and social media came of age, free digital news not only became the norm, but it changed ideas about whether news should be free. And if the norm is that news should be free, it's not a surprise that a mere 10% of Gen Z "strongly agree" with the statement, "paying for a news subscription helps support an independent press" (see Table 6.6).

Table 6.7 reinforces the idea that Gen Z is not into paying for news. Participants in The National Gen Z, Social Media & News Engagement Survey were asked about subscribing to five different types of digital content: Movie/

Table 6.6 Attitudes About the Cost of News on the Internet and the Purpose of News Subscriptions

	% Strongly Agree		
	Gen Z	Millennials	Older Generations (Gen X, Baby Boomers & Silent)
All News on the Internet Should be Free to the Public	47%	45%	39%
Paying for a News Subscription Helps Support an Independent Press	10%	21%	16%

TV; Music; Other; Sports; and News. While Gen Z subscribes to five different types of digital content, news is at the bottom of the list.

As can be seen in Table 6.7, 78% of Gen Z subscribe to streaming movies and TV programs and 71% subscribe to streaming music. Only one-quarter (26%) of Gen Z subscribes to digital news. Digital news subscriptions ranked third for Millennials and the Older Generations group. In fact, a larger percentage of Millennials (36%) than Gen Z (26%) and the Older Generations group (24%) subscribed to digital news.

The fact that three-quarters of Gen Z do *not* subscribe to digital news and a whopping 90% does not understand the connection between financially supporting news and the existence of an independent press raises questions about whether this is an insurmountable problem or a barrier that can be overcome if Gen Z understood that digital news subscriptions support an

Table 6.7 Types of Digital Subscriptions Paid for By Gen Z

Type of Digital Subscription	Gen Z	Millennials	Older Generations (Gen X, Baby Boomers & Silent)
Movie/TV	78% (1)	83% (1)	67% (1)
Music	71% (2)	61% (2)	28% (2)
Other	33% (3)	26% (5)	17% (4)
Sports	30% (4)	34% (4)	16% (5)
News	26% (5)	36% (3)	24% (3)

independent press that is indispensable to becoming informed and essential to a healthy democracy.

9. *Minimal Attention Paid to News about Presidential Elections, Democracy, the White House, Congress, the Supreme Court and the Federal Government at Work.* When citizens in the United States turn 18, they're eligible to vote; however, eligibility does not guarantee voting. And eligibility does not mean the first vote cast will be informed. But when high schools prepared students to vote in their first election, it did have a positive impact on voting, according to the Harvard Youth Poll (2023). New voters who were taught about the importance of their vote, how to register to vote, when the voting deadlines were, and how to "research candidates and ballot issues" were more likely to say they would vote in the 2024 presidential election. Reminders about voting deadlines; conversations about voting with friends and family members; non-partisan voting guides; non-partisan how-to-vote training; meeting a candidate or official representative of the campaign in person also contributed to newly eligible voters casting their first votes.

While it's unknown how much of voter preparation emphasized the importance of following election news, we do know from The National Gen Z, Social Media & News Engagement Survey that less than a quarter (23%) of Gen Z followed news about the presidential election and Supreme Court rulings, according to Chapter 2's Table 2.7. And a smaller percentage engaged with news about the president (21%), voting (20%), politics (20%), democracy safeguards and threats (18%), and news about Congress (18%).

Based on the violent January 6, 2021 assault on the U.S. Capitol to halt the peaceful transfer of power to the democratically elected president Joe Biden, the July 1, 2024 Supreme Court ruling that presidents have absolute immunity for official acts, the 900-plus page conservative "blue print" known as "Project 2025" that the Heritage Foundation expected Donald Trump to implement to overhaul the Executive Branch, if he were re-elected, and former President Trump's call to "terminate the Constitution" as well as his assertion that he would be a dictator on Day 1 of a second term, might lead some to conclude that all was not well with U.S. democracy (Select January 6th Committee, 2022; Quinn & Rosen, 2024; Trump v. United States, 2024; Graham, 2023; Yen, 2022).

But how would Gen Z know if all were not well with U.S. democracy if the vast majority of this generation didn't follow news about the presidential election, Supreme Court rulings, the president, Congress, politics, voting, or threats to democracy?

As the 2024 presidential election drew closer, it was expected that a larger percentage of Gen Z (and older generations) would pay attention to news relevant to the election and the future of democracy. But that expectation may have been more hope than reality. Without intentionally incorporating presidential election- and democracy-related news from trusted sources into one's news engagement routine, the barrier to casting an informed vote during a presidential election will be a challenge for Gen Z and older generations to overcome.

Overcoming Barriers to a News Smart Gen Z

Chapter 6 began by asking: Why does it matter if Gen Z or any generation is informed? Can Gen Z or any generation be free and self-governing without knowing the news and information that journalists report? Can uninformed citizens protect our democratic system of government that is founded on "We the People"—not a king or dictator? An analysis of The National Gen Z, Social Media & News Engagement Survey identified nine barriers to Gen Z becoming informed. To overcome these barriers, Chapter 7 will propose ideas and actions that if implemented can help ensure that Gen Z as well as generations that follow will not just know why it's important to be informed, they will know how to inform themselves from news that can be trusted.

Questions and Reflections

1. Review the nine barriers to a news smart Gen Z in Figure 6.1. Which, if any, of the barriers do you *disagree* with? Explain why you disagree.
2. What barrier to a news smart Gen Z, if any, would you add? Explain why you added that barrier.
3. How do your questionnaire answers compare to the results in Table 6.3 about evaluating a news story's trustworthiness? What else, if anything, would you add to evaluating the trustworthiness of a news story and why?
4. With one-third of Gen Z saying in Table 6.5 that they had *not* encountered disinformation or didn't know if they had, what do you think is the most effective way to educate Gen Z and others about disinformation?
5. What do you think are the main reasons digital news subscriptions rank last for Gen Z?

6. What, if anything, would motivate Gen Z to pay for a digital news subscription?

References

A free and responsible press: A general report on mass communication: Newspapers, radio, motion pictures, magazines, and books. (1947). The University of Chicago.

Berelson, B. (1949). What "missing the newspaper" means. In P. F. Lazarsfeld & F. N. Stanton (Eds.), *Communication Research 1948–1949* (pp. 111–129). Harper & Brothers.

Bond, S. (2024). *AI fakes raise election risks as lawmakers and tech companies scramble to catch up.* https://www.npr.org/2024/02/08/1229641751/ai-deepfakes-election-risks-lawmakers-tech-companies-artificial-intelligence

Bueno de Mesquita, E., Canes-Wrone, B., Hall, A. B., Lum, K. L., Martin, G. J., & Velez, Y. R. (n.d.). *Preparing for generative AI in the 2024 election: Recommendations and best practices based on academic research.* https://www.gsb.stanford.edu/sites/default/files/publication/pdfs/white-paper-2023-ai-and-elections-best-practices_0.pdf

De Fleur, M. L., & Ball-Rokeach, S. (1975). *Theories of mass communication* (3rd ed.). David McKay Company.

Fung, B. (2024a). *FCC votes to ban scam robocalls that use AI-generated voices.* https://www.cnn.com/2024/02/08/tech/fcc-scam-robocalls-ai-generated-voices?cid=ios_app

Fung, B. (2024b). *OpenAI sets rules to combat election misinformation. It's been tried before.* https://www.cnn.com/2024/01/16/tech/openai-election-misinformation?cid=ios_app

Gottfried, J. (2024). *Americans' social media use.* https://www.pewresearch.org/internet/2024/01/31/americans-social-media-use/

Graham, D. A. (2023). *Trump says he'll be a dictator on "Day One" but not after that.* https://www.theatlantic.com/ideas/archive/2023/12/trump-says-hell-be-a-dictator-on-day-one/676247/

Gramlich, J. (2021). *What makes a news story trustworthy? Americans point to the outlet that publishes it, sources cited.* https://www.pewresearch.org/short-reads/2021/06/09/what-makes-a-news-story-trustworthy-americans-point-to-the-outlet-that-publishes-it-sources-cited/

Harvard Youth Poll. (2023). https://iop.harvard.edu/youth-poll/46th-edition-fall-2023

Hsu, T., Thompson, S. A., & Myers, S. L. (2024). *Elections and disinformation are colliding like never before in 2024.* https://www.nytimes.com/2024/01/09/business/media/election-disinformation-2024.html?smid=nytcore-ios-share&referringSource=articleShare

Kao, J., & Bengani, P. (2023). *How verified accounts on X thrive while spreading misinformation about the Israel-Hamas conflict.* https://www.propublica.org/article/x-verified-accounts-misinformation-israel-hamas-conflict?utm_source=sailthru&utm_medium=email&utm_campaign=majorinvestigations&utm_content=feature

Katz, E., Blumler, J. G., & Gurevitch, M. (1974). Utilization of mass communication by the individual. In J. G. Blumler & E. Katz (Eds.), *The uses of mass communications: Current perspectives on gratifications research* (pp. 19–32). Sage Publications.

Kovach, B., & Rosenstiel, T. (2014). *The elements of journalism: What newspeople should know and the public should expect*. Three Rivers Press.

Lee, A. M. (2013). News audiences revisited: Theorizing the link between audience motivations and news consumption. *Journal of Broadcasting & Electronic Media, 57*(3), 300–317.

Merriam-Webster. (n.d.). *Deepfake*. https://www.merriam-webster.com/dictionary/deepfake#:~:text=A%20deepfake%20is%20an%20image,transparent%3A%20deepfakes%20are%20not%20real

Merriam-Webster. (n.d.). *Disinformation*. https://www.merriam-webster.com/dictionary/disinformation#:~:text=%3A%20false%20information%20deliberately%20and%20often,opinion%20or%20obscure%20the%20truth

Metz, C. (2023). *"The Godfather of A.I." leaves google and warns of danger ahead*. https://www.nytimes.com/2023/05/01/technology/ai-google-chatbot-engineer-quits-hinton.html?smid=nytcore-ios-share&referringSource=articleShare&sgrp=c-cb

Misinformation Dashboard: Election 2024. (2024). https://misinfodashboard.newslit.org/

Newman, N., Fletcher, R., Eddy, K. E., Robertson, C. T., & Nielsen, R. K. (2022). *Reuters Institute Digital News Report 2022*. https://reutersinstitute.politics.ox.ac.uk/sites/default/files/2022-06/Digital_News-Report_2022.pdf

Newman, N., Fletcher, R., Eddy, K. E., Robertson, C. T., & Nielsen, R. K. (2023). *Reuters Institute Digital News Report 2023*. https://reutersinstitute.politics.ox.ac.uk/sites/default/files/2023-06/Digital_News_Report_2023.pdf

News Literacy Project, The. (n.d.). https://newslit.org/

Poindexter, P. (2008a). Factors contributing to the sex divide in newspapers and television news. In P. Poindexter, S. Meraz, & A. S. Weiss (Eds.), *Women, men, and news: Divided and disconnected in the news media landscape* (pp. 17–34). Routledge.

Poindexter, P. (2008b). When women ignore the news. In P. Poindexter, S. Meraz, & A. S. Weiss (Eds.), *Women, men, and news: Divided and disconnected in the news landscape*. Routledge.

Poindexter, P. M. (2018). *Millennials, news, and social media: Is news engagement a thing of the past?* (2nd ed.). Peter Lang.

Poindexter, P. M., & McCombs, M. E. (2001). Revisiting the civic duty to keep informed in the new media environment. *Journalism & Mass Communication Quarterly, 78*(1), 113–126.

Quinn, M., & Rosen, J. (2024). *What is Project 2025? What to know about the conservative blueprint for a second Trump administration*. https://www.cbsnews.com/amp/news/what-is-project-2025-trump-conservative-blueprint-heritage-foundation/

Robertson, K. (2024). *New York Times Co. adds 300,000 digital subscribers in quarter*. https://www.nytimes.com/2024/02/07/business/media/new-york-times-q4-earnings.html?smid=nytcore-ios-share&referringSource=articleShare&sgrp=c-cb

Rosenzweig-Ziff, D. (2024). *AI deepfakes of Taylor Swift spread on X. Here's what to know*. https://www.washingtonpost.com/technology/2024/01/26/ai-deepfakes-taylor-swift-nude/

Select January 6th Committee Final Report and Supporting Materials Collection. (2022). https://www.govinfo.gov/collection/january-6th-committee-final-report?path=/GPO/January%206th%20Committee%20Final%20Report%20and%20Supporting%20Materials%20Collection

Tracker: State legislation on deepfakes in elections. (n.d.). Public Citizen. https://www.citizen.org/article/tracker-legislation-on-deepfakes-in-elections/

Trump v. United States. (2024). https://www.supremecourt.gov/opinions/23pdf/23-939_e2pg.pdf

Verma, P. (2023). *The rise of AI fake news is creating a "misinformation superspreader."* https://www.washingtonpost.com/technology/2023/12/17/ai-fake-news-misinformation/

Yen, H. (2022). *Trump rebuked for call to "terminate" constitution over 2020 election results.* https://www.pbs.org/newshour/amp/politics/trump-rebuked-for-call-to-terminate-constitution-over-2020-election-results

· 7 ·

THE FUTURE OF JOURNALISM, THE UNITED STATES, AND DEMOCRACY DEPEND ON AN INFORMED GEN Z AND A NATIONWIDE BELIEF THAT BEING INFORMED IS ESSENTIAL AND A RESPONSIBILITY

When in 2019, the president of the Pew Research Center announced "where Millennials end and Generation Z begins" (Dimock, 2019), those of us who study generations finally had dates that defined the birth years of the first post-Millennial generation that we could agree on. Knowing Gen Z was born during the years 1997 through 2012 made it possible to identify events and issues as well as educational, social, political, economic, public health, scientific, cultural, entertainment, sports, social media, news, and technology trends associated with this generation.

Plus, Gen Z's birth years provided an opportunity to compare engagement with news, news engagement socialization, beliefs about the importance of being informed as well as news topic and platform preferences with Millennials. Most importantly, the start and end dates for the birth years of Gen Z opened the door to understanding social media's impact on news engagement and attitudes as well as the future of journalism, the United States, and democracy.

Through The National Gen Z, Social Media & News Engagement Survey, we learned how embedded social media is in the lives of Gen Z. And a Pew

Research Center report released in 2024 reinforced the grip that social media has not just on the lives of the youngest Americans but all Americans. While TV and print newspapers were entryways to news through the first decade of the twenty-first century, today a social media platform is where Gen Z, Millennials, and many in the Older Generations group start when they get news. But because social media cannot be trusted to consistently distribute credible news, a future informed public, thriving independent journalism, and healthy democracy cannot be guaranteed.

According to the 2024 Pew report, "half of all U.S. adults say they at least sometimes get news" from social media (Wang & Forman-Katz, 2024). Furthermore, those who get news on social media have a "variety of things they like about it, including convenience, speed and the element of social interaction" (Wang & Forman-Katz, 2024).

No doubt social media's convenience and speed as a place to go for news, disadvantage non-social media platforms where trusted news can be depended on. When Facebook emerged in 2004, it was rapidly adopted by Millennials as an innovative communication platform. As other social media platforms followed, they too, were adopted for the social—not news. When Twitter was founded two years after Facebook, there was also a recognition that social media platforms could be indispensable distributors of news reported by journalists and their news organizations.

Consequently, Millennials adopted Twitter as their go-to news source.[1] And it didn't take long for other social media platforms to be adopted as places to go for news because of their relative advantage over legacy news outlets. Relative advantage is one of five attributes that determine an innovation's "rate of adoption" or "relative speed with which an innovation is adopted by members of a social system" (Rogers, 2003, p. 221). "Compatibility, complexity, trialability, and observability" are the other four attributes that determine how rapidly an innovation is adopted (Rogers, 2003, p. 221).

Would social media have been adopted as rapidly for news if the iPhone had not been invented? Probably not—especially because 24/7 access to updated news was as close as the sleek, all-purpose smart device that was small enough to hold in one hand. Plus, there was no more waiting for the newspaper

---

1 Founded in 2006, Twitter was purchased in 2022 by Elon Musk who first changed the rules, then changed the name to X (Vanian, 2022). Under Musk, Twitter's blue bird logo was replaced with "X" and the language of "tweets" and "tweeting" no longer applied. In 2018, 27% of Millennials were on Twitter, 23% read news on Twitter daily, and 8% tweeted a news story often (Poindexter, 2018, pp. 60–61).

to be delivered or the news to be broadcast at a designated time. And with a smartphone, you didn't have to be at home. You could be anywhere!

The 2024 Pew report also revealed some of what users disliked about news posted on social media platforms: inaccuracy, low quality, and political bias. In fact, "the share who say inaccuracy is the aspect they dislike most has increased from 31% to 40% in the past five years" (Wang & Forman-Katz, 2024).

Social media's grip on where Gen Z gets news is likely not going to change for the oldest of this generation but there's time to have some influence on the youngest who are in middle school and high school. And for Gen Z's oldest who voted in their second or third presidential election in 2024, it's not too late to encourage diversity in news platforms, make them smarter about which news to trust, and remind them that while on social media, they should exhibit a journalist's skepticism before clicking on a link that may or may not be news. And it's important to underscore that one should always be alert to the possibility of encountering disinformation. And if disinformation is encountered, it should not be shared.

Today's social media-dominant news landscape could not have been envisioned in 1964 when "A Profile of the Daily Newspaper Non-Reader" was published in *Journalism Quarterly*, later renamed *Journalism and Mass Communication Quarterly*, the preeminent journal of the Association for Education in Journalism and Mass Communication (AEJMC). The article's authors asserted that "reading the daily newspaper was one of the most thoroughly institutionalized behaviors of Americans" (Westley & Severin, 1964, p. 45). The journalism scholars added that "despite the inroads made by television, the newspaper continues to be the chief source of information for most of us" (Westley & Severin, 1964, p. 45).

By the early 1990s, newspaper reading and network TV news watching were about neck and neck with approximately three-fifths of the public reading newspapers and watching network TV news (Key news audiences, 2008). However, local TV attracted a larger audience with about four-fifths of the public watching local TV news broadcasts (Key news audiences, 2008).

By 2008, according to the Pew Research Center, only 34% of the public read newspapers, which meant reading a daily newspaper was no longer a "thoroughly institutionalized behavior" as Westley & Severin (1964, p. 45) proclaimed 44 years before. Network and local TV news viewing had also declined; in 2008, only 29% watched network TV news and 52% watched local TV news (Key news audiences, 2008).

And for the first time, getting news online surpassed reading a print newspaper; 37% went online to get news at least three days a week compared to 34% who read a newspaper yesterday. In 2008, social media platforms were so new that the Pew Research Center had not yet asked about them as a place to get news. But 16 years later when Gen Z was coming of age, "half of all U.S. adults" would get news from social media "at least sometimes" (Wang & Forman-Katz, 2024).

But it was 2012 when I published *Millennials, News, and Social Media: Is News Engagement a Thing of the Past?* that I became concerned that our future as an informed society was in doubt. That's why I called for a "national 'Engage with News' Day" to be held the first Tuesday of October (Poindexter, 2012, p. 131). As the 2013–2014 president of the Association for Education in Journalism and Mass Communication (AEJMC), the largest association of journalism and communication educators, professionals, and graduate students, I made my "Engage with News Day" idea a reality and founded News Engagement Day.

Sponsored by AEJMC and always held on the first Tuesday in October, approximately one month before Election Day in November, we celebrated the 10th year of News Engagement Day (n.d.) in 2023. As I wrote in the souvenir program, "Celebrating 10 Years of News Engagement Day," for a special session held at the annual AEJMC conference in Washington D.C., there was more work to do:

> Since News Engagement Day was founded in 2014, a new generation, Gen Z, born 1997 through 2012, has come of age as disinformation has been vigorously pushed on social media, cable TV, and other platforms to purposely misinform the public about facts, history, and news, including the results of the 2020 presidential election. Today in our social media-smartphone news landscape, polluted with disinformation, News Engagement Day is more important than ever but we have to do more. We have to ensure the public is also equipped to distinguish credible news from made-up information pretending to be news in order to trick the public into believing lies over verified fact-based news reported by journalists and news organizations guided by the highest ethical principles. (Celebrating, 2023)[2,3]

---

2 The "Celebrating 10 Years of News Engagement Day" souvenir program is in the Appendix.
3 News Engagement Day, proposed in 2012 and initially called National News Engagement Day, was launched at the National Press Club in Washington D.C., Tues., September 23, 2014. The news conference is posted on YouTube: https://www.youtube.com/watch?v=a-tM9UuHtZ4

Figure 7.1 Select Constituent Groups that Have an Opportunity and Responsibility to Ensure Gen Z and Future Generations Are Informed, an Independent Press Thrives, and Democracy Is Protected

Parents
Elementary-through-College Educators and Librarians
News Outlets, Associations, and Journalists, including Student Journalists
News Literacy, Civic Education, and Journalism Groups, Non-Profits, Foundations, and Centers

A 2023 Pew Research Center study reaffirmed that more had to be done because news engagement was going in the wrong direction. "Although the decline was smaller among adults 18 to 29, their share was relatively low to begin with: 27 percent said they followed the news closely in 2016, and this fell to 19 percent in 2022. The recent decline in Americans' attention to the news has occurred across demographic lines, including education, gender, race, ethnicity and political party affiliation" (Forman-Katz, 2023).

The responsibility to reverse these declining news engagement trends is on all of us; however, the constituent groups listed in Figure 7.1, have the potential to produce the greatest sustained impact during the shortest time period. Without the attention and effort of these groups, whether or not Gen Z and future generations will be informed, whether or not we will have a thriving independent press, and whether or not our democracy can be protected by an informed public is uncertain. The constituent groups include parents, elementary-through-college educators and librarians, news outlets, associations, and journalists, including student journalists, and news literacy, civic education, journalism groups, non-profits, foundations, and centers.

Parents Are Not Just a Child's First Teacher

Traditionally, parents were the ones, whom by example, taught their children that news, whether reading it in print newspapers or watching it on TV, was important. Today, parents are still a child's first teacher but how they teach their children that news is important must be in harmony with how news is accessed today and the variety of digital platforms where news can be found, including social media and news apps.

During the pre-social media-smartphone era when parents read print newspapers and watched news on TV, Bandura's "social learning theory"

(Bandura, 2001; Severin & Tankard, 2001) helped explain that children were observing their parents and learning that news was important to keep up with. But if a parent is reading news on a smartphone and the child has no idea what their parent is doing, how can the child learn the lesson about the importance of keeping up with news?

Today, when parents engage with news on their smartphones, it's important to show their child the news on their screen and explain that they're learning the latest news so they're up-to-date on what's going on. How much is said about the news would, of course, depend on the age of the child. The important thing is that just as parents teach their children to say "please" and "thank you," share, and use a fork and not fingers when eating mashed potatoes and other non-finger foods, parents can help their children learn that engaging with news on the phone is important but they have to explicitly show and tell them.

From time to time, parents may also share real kid-friendly news stories like a *USA Today* story about a baby calf with the headline: "'In the moooood for love': Calf with heart-shaped mark on forehead melts hearts online" (Shafiq, 2024). The photo caption said: "A nearly 2-month-old calf who has a heart-shaped mark on her forehead has been melting hearts all the way from her little farm in Oklahoma" (Shafiq, 2024).

The first paragraph reported the calf had been "named Cupid by adoring fans" and "was born on Dec. 27 at Merchen Farms, a small family-owned operation in Wanette, Oklahoma, about 60 miles from Oklahoma City" (Shafiq, 2024).

Parents can also watch a kids' TV news program with their children. *NBC Nightly News: Kids Edition* (n.d.), which is hosted by *NBC Nightly News* anchor Lester Holt, and is available on YouTube and some local NBC-affiliated TV stations "is a digest of the top headlines, broken down for kids to best understand the world today." The newscast description for the March 21, 2024 broadcast made it clear that the program explores topics of interest to kids and adults:

> We take a look at the science behind extreme weather, more specifically, twisters! We teach you about how tornadoes form and how you can keep you and your family safe. Then, it's allergy season. We explain what allergies are and everything you need to know about how to combat them this spring. Also, what's on your mind? We answer your questions about why you may have jet lag when traveling to different countries with time differences. And, pass the bricks! This California teen is inspiring creativity and paying it forward by sharing his love for LEGOs. Here's how he's building something big with LEGOs! (*Nightly News: Kids Edition*, 2024)

The news magazine *Time for Kids* offers news for four grade levels: K-1, 2, 3–4, and 5–6. One *Time for Kids* news article, written for grade level 5–6, reported on the Endangered Species Act, its history, and impact. The article began:

"In December, the Endangered Species Act (ESA) turned 50. It has rescued hundreds of animals and plants from going extinct. The ESA was passed in 1973. It directed the U.S. Fish and Wildlife Service and the National Marine Fisheries Service to list endangered and threatened species of plants and animals. Harming or collecting these species became illegal" (Martin, 2024). Whether a digital newspaper or TV newscast or magazine created for kids, there are a variety of ways to introduce kids to news and encourage lifelong news engagement.

Elementary-Through-College Educators and Librarians are the Best Constituent Group to Ensure a Future News Literate Public

For elementary-through-college educators and librarians, to make a significant news literacy difference, there must be an agreed-upon understanding of what constitutes news literacy so that lesson plans and syllabus learning objectives as well as library resources are working toward a mutual goal: Educating students today to produce an informed public for tomorrow.

It took conducting and publishing many research studies on the news audience, developing and implementing programs and activities for K-12 classrooms in Los Angeles and Austin, founding News Engagement Day in 2014 as president of the Association for Education in Journalism and Mass Communication (AEJMC), and creating and teaching the courses, "Journalism, Society, and the Citizen Journalist" and "News Literacy for a Digital Age" in the School of Journalism and Media at the University of Texas at Austin for me to develop a real-world definition of news literacy and identify the factors that are essential to achieving it.

Over time I refined my multi-part real-world definition of news literacy as: (1) one of several subfields of media literacy with other subfields being TV, advertising, radio, film, photography, social media, etc. that (2) enhances knowledge of and critical thinking about news, journalists, journalism practice, principles, ethics, news organizations, and news platforms; (3) distinguishes news from opinion, advertising, and disinformation; (4) increases understanding about the history and role of the press in the United States, including its First Amendment roots; and (5) raises awareness about the strengths and weaknesses of different platforms where news can be found.

A news literate person is therefore (1) informed about the news, from local to global and can compare and critique news media coverage, including its deficiencies; (2) has at least some fundamental knowledge about journalists, news reporting, news organizations, and ethical principles that guide the reporting of trustworthy news; (3) has the tools to distinguish credible news from non-news, including opinion, advertising, disinformation; (4) values the importance of being informed from news that can be trusted (Choose your news, n.d.), which is essential to a healthy democracy.

While news literacy education needs to be age-appropriate, it's never too early to introduce a child to news, bring news into the classroom, or use real news as examples in the lessons being taught. Reading news articles will help students become more proficient in reading, strengthen their vocabulary, enable them to learn about different parts of the world, and boost their confidence.[4]

And if news is included in civic education, students will be better prepared to be "democracy participants" when they're old enough to vote. In fact, a Harvard Institute of Politics (2023) youth poll found that even though "active high school civic education is linked to a higher propensity for voting," "most young Americans do not believe that their high school education taught and prepared them to understand practical aspects of voting and civic education," including their vote's importance, how to register to vote, the deadlines for voting, and how to research candidates and issues. Since much of this election information is reported by local news outlets and is available on their websites, high school teachers can show their students where to find the information and how to navigate it.

---

4 *Millennials and news: What kids say about the news.* (n.d.). https://vimeo.com/49395735 The video, produced by Paula Poindexter, shows confident kids thoughtfully discussing the news after participating in mynews@school, a 10-week, news-in-the-classroom program that Poindexter developed with the *Austin American-Statesman*. In addition to access to the e-replica edition of the *Statesman*, which Poindexter paid for, the program included weekly lesson plans about the purpose, principles, and process of journalism that Poindexter developed. Plus, Poindexter visited the participating classrooms and she sponsored a pizza party for each participating class. At the conclusion of mynews@school, students and teachers completed a post-program survey. Participating students received certificates and each teacher received a cash gift of $50.

For college students, the Harvard Institute of Politics (2023) youth poll also found that "deadline reminders, non-partisan voting guides, how-to-vote training, and conversations with friends and family" were effective in turning out the vote. Voting guides provide helpful information about registering to vote, how, when, and where to vote and even information about the candidates. The guide, "Voting & Engaging with News about the 2022 Midterm Elections: A Guide for Gen Z Voters" (Poindexter, 2022)[5] which connected News Engagement Day (n.d.) with the 2022 Midterm Elections was unique in its emphasis on casting an informed vote by engaging with credible news *prior* to voting.

Status of Media Literacy Education Laws

According to the Media Literacy Now report, *U.S. Media Literacy: A State-by-State Status of Media Literacy Education Laws for K-12 Schools*, at least 18 states have passed laws that require the teaching of media literacy (U.S. media literacy, 2023). A review of the laws reveals there's no common goal that states are trying to achieve. Furthermore, the focus of the state laws appears to be on media literacy as a whole—not news literacy specifically.

Still, if educators include news in their lesson plans and students have the opportunity to read and discuss news, compare news about specific topics as reported by different news outlets and platforms, students can improve their vocabulary and reading proficiency, enhance their critical thinking skills, and have a head start on the path to becoming news literate. Plus, educators can encourage students to develop a news engagement routine. As we learned in Chapter 3, news engagement routines can have a positive impact on following news regularly.

Evaluating a News Story's Credibility Is a Necessary Individual Task that Cannot Be Skipped and It Can't Take Too Long

The amount of effort that has focused on helping the public, including the youngest members, distinguish credible news from disinformation that

---

5 A copy of "Voting & Engaging with News about the 2022 Midterm Elections: A Guide for Gen Z Voters" can be found in the Appendix.

Figure 7.2 Gen Z's News Credibility Quick Check

1. Scan/read/watch/listen to two or three platforms that report news. Examples of free news outlets that report credible news are NPR, Associated Press (AP), and the evening network news broadcasts, NBC, ABC, CBS, and PBS.
2. Evaluate the credibility of news with knowledge of three journalism principles: (a) credible news is verified from multiple sources; (b) on-the-record sources are preferred over anonymous sources but when anonymous sources are used, the report must explain why; (c) credible news outlets do not pay sources for news.
3. Click on or Google the reporter of a news story to evaluate their reporting experience and expertise in the story's topic.
4. Opinion is *not* news and should always be labeled as opinion.

pretends to be news is admirable. Some of these efforts which require multiple steps to decipher a news story's credibility are time-consuming. How much time will Gen Z invest in trying to decipher a specific story's trustworthiness? Based on their news engagement habits and attitudes about news and their beliefs about the importance of following news, it's doubtful they will invest a significant amount of time. However, Gen Z might spend some time evaluating a news story's credibility if it doesn't take too long. Gen Z's News Credibility Quick Check in Figure 7.2 doesn't take too long.

To increase proficiency in evaluating news credibility, download the app for at least one of the news outlets and activate the notification that will send breaking news headlines. Clicking on the breaking news headline will take you to the story to read and evaluate.

The principles that journalists use to report the news should also be applied to content creators/influencers on social media as well as hosts on cable news programs who share their opinions which may or may not be anchored in fact. Gen Z's News Credibility Quick Check is a good place to start in evaluating them too, so you're not fooled by "likes," "comments," or ratings.

News Outlets, Associations, and Journalists, Including Student Journalists, Have a Responsibility to Be Part of the Solution

In the first edition of my book *Millennials, News, and Social Media: Is News Engagement a Thing of the Past?*, published in 2012, I proposed 26 "Best Practices" for the news industry to improve its coverage of Millennials (Poindexter, 2012, pp. 122–123). Born 1981 through 1996, Millennials were

Table 7.1 Grading News Media Coverage of Their Generation: Millennials in 2012* vs. Gen Z in 2023

Grade	Millennials in 2012*	Gen Z in 2023
A	6%	12%
B	26%	30%
C	44%	34%
D	18%	14%
F	6%	9%

*Poindexter (2012, p. 44).

not happy that news coverage about their generation was generally negative if they were covered at all. "For 68% of Millennials surveyed for the 2012 book, the news media's grade did not rise above a C. While 44% assigned a grade of C, one quarter gave D or F grades to news coverage of their age group" (Poindexter, 2012, pp. 43–44).

In Table 7.1's comparison between Millennials' 2012 grades and Gen Z's 2023 news coverage grades, Millennial news coverage grades were worse than Gen Z grades in 2023.

Although a larger percentage of Gen Z's news coverage grades were higher than Millennial grades, Gen Z still gave news coverage more C, D, and F grades than grades of A and B.

The reasons behind Gen Z's grades of news media coverage of their generation can be explained by organizing their answers into four themed categories (see Figure 4.3, Chapter 4). First, Gen Z articulated there was little or no coverage about them. Second, Gen Z said the news media failed to cover stories that were important to their generation. Third, Gen Z expressed that because journalists represent older generations, they don't understand them. Fourth, Gen Z asserted that news outlets are biased against Gen Z and portray them negatively and inaccurately. Finally, when given the opportunity to weigh in on whether or not news outlets care about them, as reported in Chapter 4, Table 4.3, half of Gen Z agreed or strongly agreed with the statement, "the news media care little about people like you."

In recognition of dissatisfaction with news media coverage by another generation of young adults, I combined the 2018 "Best Practices for Covering and Engaging the Millennial Generation" in the second edition of *Millennials, News, and Social Media: Is News Engagement a Thing of the Past* (Poindexter,

2018, pp 135–136) that still apply today with updated recommendations inspired by Gen Z's concerns about their news coverage or lack of news coverage expressed in The National Gen Z, Social Media & News Engagement Survey. The result is a "News Media Action Plan for Covering and Engaging Gen Z," which is described in Figure 7.3.

Figure 7.3 News Media Action Plan for Covering and Engaging Gen Z

1.	Regularly include Gen Z stories in news coverage.
2.	Include Gen Z as sources in general news and trend stories that impact Gen Z and are of interest to them.
3.	Explicit Gen Z stories should include Gen Z sources and these Gen Z sources should be among the first quoted. Whether Gen Z explicit or implicit, care must be taken to include direct Gen Z quotes and not just paraphrased Gen Z voices.
4.	Generational rites of passage, including getting a driver's license, graduating high school, voting for the first time, going to college, first job, etc., are important events that can generate ideas for Gen Z stories. These rites-of-passage stories should be handled with sensitivity and from the Gen Z point of view—not the perspective of journalists, parents, or employers.
5.	Appoint a Gen Z advisory panel for consultation and regular feedback on Gen Z news coverage. Respect the feedback and use it to improve Gen Z coverage.
6.	Gen Z digital subscription fees should be discounted beginning in high school and continue through college, and for at least two years after college. As reported in Table 6.7, Chapter 6, at least 70% of Gen Z pays for Movie/TV and music digital subscriptions but only 26% pay for news subscriptions. Plus, almost half of Gen Z says news on the Internet should be free. If digital news subscriptions were discounted, Gen Z might try one and become a devoted subscriber.
7.	Post a video Q&A, customized for the platform, on the news organization's social media, website, news app, and on YouTube to educate Gen Z about the news reporting process and principles that guide the reporting of news that can be trusted. "The American Journalist" survey (Willnat et al., 2022), the ethics code of the Society of Professional Journalists (SPJ, n.d.), and The Trust Project (n.d.) can be referenced to understand and apply journalists' guiding principles.
8.	During election seasons, especially presidential and midterm elections, produce and distribute election guides that contribute to informed democracy participation. Include a section exclusively for the first-time Gen Z voter. As discussed in Chapter 5, the information needs of a first-time voter differ from experienced voters and the election guide should include the fundamentals of registering and voting that experienced voters take for granted.

Figure 7.3 Continued

9.	Journalists who report on presidential elections should be acquainted with Gen Z's criticisms of news coverage, so they don't continue to exclude and stereotype this generation. Remember, Gen Z votes too and they should be included and quoted in the election coverage and represented in photographs like older voters and so should the issues that matter to them.
10.	News organizations not only have a responsibility to include Gen Z in news coverage, they have a responsibility to ensure news coverage about Gen Z is accurate. News outlets may not be able to conduct their own research on Gen Z but they can read credible studies to become more knowledgeable about this generation. In addition to Gen Z data reported in this book, journalists can read the following Gen Z-focused reports: Northwestern's "News Socialization Study on Teens' News Engagement" conducted by the Medill School at Northwestern University (Reger, 2023); Pew Research Center studies on teens and social media and technology, including YouTube, TikTok, Snapchat, and Instagram (Anderson et al., 2023); and polls of Gen Z voters conducted by the Harvard Institute of Politics (2023) and CIRCLE at Tufts University (Booth, 2023).
11.	As one of two generations with the most racial and ethnic diversity, news stories about Gen Z should reflect that diversity. Additionally, everyday activities as well as official & expert sources and private citizen sources must be diverse. To avoid stereotyping, journalists must educate themselves about the 18 different ways news outlets have historically stereotyped African Americans/ Black people, Latinos/ Hispanics, Asian Americans, Native Americans, and other people of color (Poindexter, 2011, pp. 109). Journalists would also benefit from regularly consulting style guides and handbooks produced by journalism associations of color, including the National Association of Black Journalists (NABJ, n.d.); National Association of Hispanic Journalists (NAHJ cultural competence, 2020); Asian American Journalists Association (Guidances and resources, n.d.); and the Indigenous Journalists Association (Reporting and indigenous, n.d.).
12.	With three percent of Gen Z describing their gender as non-binary and one-fourth self-identifying as bisexual, gay, lesbian or transgender as reported in Table 2.1 in Chapter 2, journalists must also be mindful of including LGBTQ+ voices in news stories. And just as journalists should consult style guides for reporting on people of color, they should familiarize themselves with and consult The Stylebook on LGBTQ+ (n.d.) as well as The Trans Journalists Association's Stylebook and Coverage Guide (n.d.).
13.	Although produced by the Institute for Social Policy and Understanding (ISPU)— not journalists—this non-profit publishes "Covering American Muslims objectively + creatively" (n.d.), a guide that would be useful to journalists who report on the Muslim American community.

(continued)

Figure 7.3 Continued

14. In the spirit of NIE (Newspapers in Education)—pre-Facebook and pre-iPhone—when "over 950 news organizations delivered newspapers and educational programs to nearly 40 per cent of all public school students in the United States" (Poindexter, 2018, p. 113), it is recommended that today's news organizations provide discounted classroom digital subscriptions to elementary-through high school and college classrooms and re-think and re-brand NIE as "Digital News in Education" to make it relevant to the digital news landscape that Gen Z is familiar with.

While some news organizations once sponsored news-in-education type programs but no longer do because they can no longer afford them, it's essential to remember that these programs are investments in the future of news organizations, their communities, the schools, and democracy.

Although the *New York Times* has always had its own unique brand of news-in-the-schools program, their commitment has never wavered. Their commitment to middle school and high school students and teachers is evident in The Learning Network which provides free resources, including lesson plans, for teachers and free access to the newspaper (The Learning Network, n.d.).

And no doubt, the *New York Times*' commitment to education and making discounted subscriptions available to college educators and students has played a role in record digital news subscriptions and revenue in 2024 (Robertson, 2024). The *New York Times* is not facing declining subscriptions and revenue, and it is not laying off employees as the *Washington Post* and *Los Angeles Times*, some of the 20th Century's largest and most influential newspapers, have been forced to do (Grynbaum et al., 2024).

Additionally, community newspapers are dying: "An average of five local newspapers are closing every two weeks, according to Northwestern University's Medill School, with more than half of all American counties now so-called news deserts with limited access to news about their hometowns" (Grynbaum et al., 2024).

News Literacy and Civic Education Groups as well as Journalism Groups, Non-Profits, Foundations, and Centers Must Work Together If Engaging with Credible News Is to Be Embraced as Essential and a Responsibility in a Democracy

Dozens of groups are working toward the same goal of ensuring the public is informed and has the knowledge and skills to distinguish credible news from non-news, including opinion, advertising, and disinformation. The work of the individual groups should not only continue, it should be accelerated because more needs to be done; more can be done; and more must be done to ensure that the public is informed in the future.

A synergistic first step might be for the dozens of news literacy, civic education, journalism groups, non-profits, foundations, and centers, including the Center for News Literacy founded by Howard Schneider at Stony Brook University, to join together and promote the importance of being informed on News Engagement Day (n.d.) and during National News Literacy Week (n.d.). News Engagement Day, sponsored by the Association for Education in Journalism and Mass Communication (n.d.), the largest association of journalism and communication educators, professionals, and graduate students in the U.S., is held every year on the first Tuesday of October. National News Literacy Week is sponsored by the News Literacy Project (n.d.) which was founded by former *Los Angeles Times* investigative reporter Alan C. Miller.

The Future of News Engagement, Journalism, the United States, and Democracy Is *Not* Independent of What Happens Globally

Although the future of journalism, the United States, and democracy depend on an informed Gen Z and a nationwide belief that being informed is essential and a responsibility, the belief in the importance of a news literate public is not limited to the United States. In an ideal world, citizens in every country across the globe would not only have access to independent, credible news but they would engage with it regularly.

Table 7.2 Select Rankings from Reporters Without Borders Index*

Rank	Country	Score
1	Norway	95.18
2	Ireland	89.91
3	Denmark	89.48
15	Canada	85.53
21	Germany	81.91
23	Costa Rica	80.20
24	France	78.72
25	South Africa	78.6
27	Australia	78.24
32	Jamaica	75.89
35	Taiwan	75.54
45	United States	71.22
47	South Korea	70.83
68	Japan	63.95
79	Ukraine	61.19
83	Chile	60.09
92	Brazil	58.67
97	Israel	57.57
123	Nigeria	49.56
128	Mexico	47.98
161	India	36.62
164	Russia	34.77
170	Saudi Arabia	32.43
172	Cuba	29.0
177	Iran	24.81
179	China	22.97
180	North Korea	21.72

*Reporters without borders index (n.d.).

Unfortunately, the ideal of a news-literate global public is not the reality. In fact, according to the press freedom index of Reporters without Borders (n.d.), citizens in many countries, including democracies, do not have access to independent news that can be trusted. In a ranking of 180 countries based on an analysis of the country's "media landscape," "legal framework," "journalists' safety" as well as the economic, political, and socio-cultural environment, Norway ranked #1 with a score of 95.18.

Table 7.2 displays select countries, from democracies to autocracies, and their Reporters without Borders ranks and scores that represent both journalists' freedom to report news and citizens' freedom to access independent news that can be trusted as well as journalists' lack of freedom to report and citizens' lack of freedom to access news that can be trusted.

Reporters without Borders assigned a rank of 45 and a score of 71.22 to the United States and explained why the United States was ranked lower than what some may have expected. The description said: "While the mainstream media in the United States generally operate free from government interference, many popular news outlets are owned by a handful of wealthy individuals. In a diverse global media landscape, local news has declined significantly in recent years. A growing interest in partisan media threatens their objectivity, while public confidence in the media has fallen dangerously" (Reporters without Borders n.d.).

Additionally, the Reporters without Borders Index emphasized that following four years of former President Trump "denigrating the press," calling it "fake" news and "the enemy of the American people," President Biden sought to reclaim the United States as a "model" for "freedom of expression" (Reporters, n.d.; Grynbaum, 2017).

However, Reporters without Borders (n.d.) concluded: "Despite these efforts, many of the underlying, chronic issues impacting journalists remain unaddressed by the authorities—including the disappearance of local news, the polarisation of the media or the weakening of journalism and democracy caused by digital platforms and social networks."

While the Index description of the U.S. news landscape portrayed a watchdog press losing some of its bark, the description of what was happening in authoritarian countries made it clear that not only does the press in authoritarian countries "report" what the government dictates, access to independent news that we take for granted in the United States, is blocked in Russia, Saudi Arabia, Cuba, Iran, China, and North Korea.

For example, since Russia, which has a rank of 164 and 34.77 score, invaded Ukraine, "almost all independent media have been banned, blocked and/or declared 'foreign agents' or 'undesirable organisations.' All others are subject to military censorship" (Russia, n.d.).

Access to independent news that can be trusted is not just important in daily life, it is essential to being "free and self-governing" as the authors of *The Elements of Journalism* asserted. Additionally, voting rights for all citizens, convenient methods and venues for citizens to vote, fair elections, and the peaceful transfer of presidential power as well as the "principle" that no one—not even the president of the United States—is above the law are not just indispensable rights and principles, they separate democracies from autocracies.

Access to Independent, Trusted News was Especially Relevant in 2024 when "Billions of People" Voted in "Major Elections"

According to the *New York Times*, in 2024 "around half of the global population" would vote "in one of the largest and most consequential democratic exercises in living memory" (Hsu et al., 2024). But would the votes that citizens cast be informed?

The answer to that question depended on where voters lived. Citizens who voted in countries with low rankings on the Reporters Without Borders Index would not have access to independent, credible news. And if they lived in Russia, not only would access to independent, credible news be unavailable, according to the news producer for CNN Digital Worldwide, the winner of Russia's presidential election would be known before the first vote was cast (Picheta, 2024).

With half the global population voting in 2024, that meant half the global population would be dealing with the "global menace" of "false narratives and conspiracy theories;" "baseless claims of election fraud" that have "battered trust in democracy;" A.I.-supercharged disinformation; and the scaling back of election safeguards by major social media companies (Hsu et al., 2024).

From the vantage point of Brookings Institution senior fellow Darrell M. West, "almost every democracy" was "under stress, independent of technology." Plus, West said, adding "disinformation on top of that" created "many opportunities for mischief" (Hsu et al., 2024).

Global Perception of Social Media's Impact on Democracy

But despite the scaling back of social media safeguards and the stress that democracy was under, a Pew Research Center study found social media was seen as "good for democracy" by "majorities in most countries surveyed"—except in the United States (Gubbala & Austin, 2024). When survey participants in the United States were asked: "Overall, when you consider all the advantages and disadvantages of social media, would you say social media has been more of a good thing or more of a bad thing for democracy in the U.S.,"

64% across all age groups said social media was a *bad* thing for democracy and only 34% said social media had been good for democracy.

Asked about the relationship between the press and democracy in The National Gen Z, Social Media & News Engagement Survey, Gen Z wasn't that positive. As reported in Table 4.3 of Chapter 4, only one-third (34%) strongly agreed or agreed that news organizations protect democracy more than hurt democracy. And when Gen Z was asked if an independent press was good for democracy, only 53% agreed or strongly agreed even though an independent press is essential to democracy as the Reporters Without Borders Index made clear.

Not only does Gen Z fail to provide a strong endorsement of the press' protection of our democracy or even being good for democracy, when Gen Z was asked in The National Gen Z, Social Media, and News Survey about the importance of four activities (volunteering, voting, jury duty, following news) that were associated with being a good citizen, following news ranked last—only 23% said following the news was very important to being a good citizen[6] (Thinking about, 2020).

Table 7.3 Civic Activities and Beliefs Perceived to Be Important to Being a Good Citizen

	Gen Z	Millennials	Older Generations (Generation X, Baby Boomers, Silent)
% Saying Very Important			
Volunteer to Help Others	45% (1)*	49% (1)	42% (3)
Vote in Elections	38% (2)	45% (2)	66% (1)
Serve Jury Duty if called	33% (3)	38% (3)	52% (2)
Follow what is happening in the news	23% (4)	31% (4)	32% (4)
% Saying Strongly Agree	Gen Z	Millennials	Older Generations (Generation X, Baby Boomers, Silent)
We have a <u>duty</u> to keep informed about news & current events	24%	34%	39%

*Rank order

6 Questions were inspired by 2019 Pew Research Center study, What makes a good citizen (Gramlich, 2019).

And when Gen Z was asked if there were a duty to keep informed about news and current events, only one-fourth (24%) strongly agreed there was. That belief was 10 percentage points lower than Millennials and 15 percentage points less than the Older Generations Group, according to Table 7.3.

Inflection Point? Tipping Point? Point of No Return?

Gen Z, Social Media, and News: Implications for the Future of News Engagement, Journalism, the U.S., and Democracy began by identifying 22 events and issues that Gen Z has personally experienced, seen reported in the news, shared on social media, or discussed with family and friends. These 22 events and issues were singled out because they have contributed to defining and understanding this generation born 1997 through 2012.

For example, Gen Z is the only generation that active shooter drills have been a required part of their kindergarten, elementary, middle school, and high school education. Unfortunately, research now shows that participation in these active shooter drills is related to depression, stress, and anxiety (The Impact of Active Shooter Drills, 2023).

And while Gen Z, just like the rest of the world, experienced the once-in-a-century deadly COVID-19 pandemic, those who were graduating high school or going to college missed out on memory-making experiences such as senior prom and graduation that they can never get back. There are no photos of senior prom or graduation because these end-of-the-year celebratory events were canceled. And the excitement and even nervousness of walking into your first college class was not to be for the high school class of 2020. Because of the pandemic, colleges and universities shut down and moved classes online which meant freshmen "attended" their first college class from home, perhaps, in their bedroom or at their kitchen table, where they logged onto Zoom.

In addition to the events and issues that contributed to defining Gen Z, this generation was also defined demographically as well as by their engagement with social media and news. Not surprisingly Gen Z spends a significant amount of time on social media but only 10% are spending a lot of time engaging with news while on social media. And we learned about Gen Z's news engagement socialization, voter profile, news topic preferences, and attitudes about news.

Gen Z's attitudes about news are noteworthy and concerning: Overall, Gen Z is more negative than positive toward news despite having grown up with someone telling them that it is important to be informed. And just as Millennials were not happy with how the news media covered their generation, Gen Z is also unhappy with how they are covered. Additionally, Gen Z says the news media doesn't care about them and they receive few supplemental benefits from engaging with news. They don't feel empowered and they don't think news helps with daily life. Furthermore, only one-third of Gen Z as reported in Chapter 4's Table 4.3 agrees or strongly agrees news organizations protect democracy more than hurt democracy. And when they're asked about four activities that one would expect a "good citizen" to embrace—volunteering, voting, serving on a jury, and following the news—following news is not only at the bottom of the list but only 23% of Gen Z says following the news is very important to being a good citizen. Similarly, only 24% strongly agree that we have a duty to keep informed about news and current events.

So, when it comes to Gen Z's relationship with news, are we at: an Inflection Point? a Tipping Point? a Point of No Return? The amount of time Gen Z spends on social media, the minimal time spent seeking news, the negative attitudes toward the news media, and the failure to embrace keeping informed as a responsibility suggest that the inflection point that some of us feared has arrived, and it's tipping in the wrong direction. And without an intervention to strengthen news engagement, develop news credibility evaluation skills, and improve attitudes about news and the outlets that report it, we could reach a point of no return which would be detrimental to the future of journalism, the United States, and democracy but also Gen Z and the generations that follow.

With so much at stake, doing nothing is not an option. Furthermore, we all have a responsibility to ensure Gen Z and future generations are informed, an independent press thrives, and democracy is protected so parents, elementary-through-college educators and librarians, news outlets, associations, and journalists, including student journalists, news literacy, civic education, and journalism groups, non-profits, foundations, and centers, it's past time to get to work.

Questions and Reflections

1. Review the list of constituent groups in Figure 7.1. Which constituent group matters most in ensuring Gen Z and future generations are informed, an independent press thrives, and democracy is protected?
2. Review and test out Gen Z's News Credibility Quick Check in Figure 7.2. What news outlet and news story did you test it on? What was your conclusion about the news story's credibility and what was your evaluation based on? What would you add or change about the News Credibility Quick Check?
3. The News Media Action Plan for Covering and Engaging Gen Z in Figure 7.3 has recommendations. What three recommendations do you think would have the most constructive impact on including and reporting on Gen Z? What, if any, recommendation would you add?
4. Find a country in Table 7.2—Select Rankings from Reporters Without Borders Index—that interests you, perhaps, because you've traveled there, would like to travel there in the future or you have a family connection. Go to the Reporters without Borders Index at rsf.org/en/index, click on the country to learn about the media landscape as well as the political, economic, and socio-cultural context for journalism. What did you learn and how does that country's media landscape compare with the United States?
5. Imagine 2030. How old will the youngest and oldest of Gen Z be? What will news engagement, journalism, the United States, and/or democracy be like in 2030? Why is that your vision for 2030?

References

Anderson, M., Faverio, M., & Gottfried, J. (2023). *Teens, social media and technology 2023.* https://www.pewresearch.org/internet/2023/12/11/teens-social-media-and-technology-2023/

Asian American Journalists Association guidances & resources. (n.d.). https://www.aaja.org/news-and-resources/guidances/

Association for Education in Journalism and Mass Communication. (n.d.). https://www.aejmc.org/

Bandura, A. (2001). Social cognitive theory of mass communication. *Media Psychology, 3*(3), 265–299.

Booth, R. B. (2023). *Gen Z, aware of its power, wants to have impact on a wide range of issues.* https://circle.tufts.edu/latest-research/gen-z-aware-its-power-wants-have-impact-wide-range-issues

Celebrating 10 Years of News Engagement Day! (2023). See Appendix.

Center for News Literacy. (n.d.). https://centerfornewsliteracy.org/

Choose your news with confidence: Learn the Trust Indicators® and easily identify reliable, ethical journalism. (n.d.). https://thetrustproject.org/trust-indicators/

Covering American Muslims objectively + creatively: A guide for media professionals. (n.d.). https://www.ispu.org/journalists/

Dimock, M. (2019). *Defining generations: Where Millennials end and Generation Z begins.* https://www.pewresearch.org/fact-tank/2019/01/17/where-millennials-end-and-generation-z-begins

Edgerly, S., Thorson, K., Thorson, E., Vraga, E. K., & Bode, L. (2018). Do parents still model news consumption? Socializing news use among adolescents in a multi-device world. *New Media & Society, 20*(4), 1263–1281.

Forman-Katz, N. (2023). *Americans are following the news less closely than they used to.* https://www.pewresearch.org/short-reads/2023/10/24/americans-are-following-the-news-less-closely-than-they-used-to/

Gramlich, J. (2019). *What makes a good citizen? Voting, paying taxes, following the law top list.* https://www.pewresearch.org/short-reads/2019/07/02/what-makes-a-good-citizen-voting-paying-taxes-following-the-law-top-list/

Grynbaum, M. M. (2017). *Trump calls the news media the "enemy of the American people."* https://www.nytimes.com/2017/02/17/business/trump-calls-the-news-media-the-enemy-of-the-people.html?smid=nytcore-ios-share&referringSource=articleShare&sgrp=c-cb

Grynbaum, M. M., Koblin, J., Mullin, B., & Robertson, K. (2024). *The news about the news business is getting grimmer.* https://www.nytimes.com/2024/01/24/business/media/media-industry-layoffs-decline.html

Gubbala, S., & Austin, S. (2024). *Majorities in most countries surveyed say social media is good for democracy.* https://www.pewresearch.org/short-reads/2024/02/23/majorities-in-most-countries-surveyed-say-social-media-is-good-for-democracy/

Harvard Institute of Politics youth poll. (2023). https://iop.harvard.edu/youth-poll/46th-edition-fall-2023

Hsu, T., Thompson, S. A., & Myers, S. L. (2024). *Elections and disinformation are colliding like never before in 2024.* https://www.nytimes.com/2024/01/09/business/media/election-disinformation-2024.html?smid=nytcore-ios-share&referringSource=articleShare

The Impact of Active Shooter Drills in Schools: Time to Rethink Reactive School Safety Strategies. (2023). Everytown. https://everytownresearch.org/report/the-impact-of-active-shooter-drills-in-schools/#intro

Key news audiences now blend online and traditional sources: Audience segments in a changing news environment. (2008). https://www.pewresearch.org/politics/2008/08/17/key-news-audiences-now-blend-online-and-traditional-sources/

Learning Network, The. (n.d.). https://www.nytimes.com/section/learning

Martin, L. J. (2024). *Animal action*. https://www.timeforkids.com/g56/animal-action-g5/?rl=en-910

Millennials and news: What kids say about the news. (n.d.). https://vimeo.com/49395735

NAHJ cultural competence handbook. (2020). https://nahj.org/wp-content/uploads/2020/08/NAHJ-Cultural-Competence-Handbook.pdf

NABJ style guide. (n.d.). https://nabjonline.org/news-media-center/styleguide/

NBC nightly news: Kids edition. (n.d.). https://www.nbcnews.com/nightlykids

Newman, N., Fletcher, R., Schulz, A., Andi, S., Robertson, C. T., & Nielsen, R. K. (2021). *Reuters Institute Digital News Report 2021*. https://reutersinstitute.politics.ox.ac.uk/sites/default/files/2021-06/Digital_News_Report_2021_FINAL.pdf

News Engagement Day. (n.d.). https://www.aejmc.com/home/events/newsengagementday/

News Engagement Day Press Conference. (2014). https://www.youtube.com/watch?v=atM9UuHtZ4

News Literacy Project. (n.d.). https://newslit.org/

Nightly news: Kids edition (March 21, 2024). (2024). https://www.nbcnews.com/video/nightly-news-kids-edition-march-21-2024-207440965592

Picheta, R. (2024). *Russia's presidential election is nearing. We already know who the winner will be.* https://amp.cnn.com/cnn/2024/02/25/europe/russia-presidential-election-explainer-putin-intl/index.html

Poindexter, P. M. (2022). *Voting & engaging with news about the 2022 midterm elections: A guide for Gen Z voters* (see Appendix).

Poindexter, P. M. (2018). *Millennials, news, and social media: Is news engagement a thing of the past?* (2nd ed.). Peter Lang.

Poindexter, P. M. (2012). *Millennials, news, and social media: Is news engagement a thing of the past?* Peter Lang.

Poindexter, P. M. (2011). African-American images in the news: Understanding the past to improve future portrayals. In S. D. Ross & P. M. Lester (Eds.), *Images that injure: Pictorial stereotypes in the media* (3rd ed., pp. 107–120). Praeger.

Presidential election results: Biden wins. (n.d.). https://www.nytimes.com/interactive/2020/11/03/us/elections/results-president.html

Reger, R. (2023). *Teens tuning in: New Medill survey shows higher-than-expected news engagement among young people*. https://localnewsinitiative.northwestern.edu/posts/2023/09/06/medill-teen-news-engagement-survey/index.html

Reporters without Borders Index. (n.d.). https://rsf.org/en/index

Reporting and indigenous terminology. (n.d.). https://indigenousjournalists.org/wp-content/uploads/2023/06/NAJA_Reporting_and_Indigenous_Terminology_Guide.pdf

Robertson, K. (2024). *New York Times Co. adds 300,000 digital subscribers in quarter*. https://www.nytimes.com/2024/02/07/business/media/new-york-times-q4-earnings.html?smid=nytcore-ios-share&referringSource=articleShare&sgrp=c-cb

Rogers, E. M. (2003). *Diffusion of innovations* (5th ed.). Free Press.

Russia. (n.d.). https://rsf.org/en/country/russia

Select January 6th Committee Final Report and supporting materials collection. (2022). https://www.govinfo.gov/collection/january-6th-committee-final-report?path=/GPO/January%206th%20Committee%20Final%20Report%20and%20Supporting%20Materials%20Collection

Severin, W. J., & Tankard Jr., J. W. (2001). *Communication theories: Origins, methods, and uses in the mass media* (5th ed.). Longman.

Shafiq, S. (2024). *"In the moooood for love": Calf with heart-shaped mark on forehead melts hearts online.* https://www.usatoday.com/story/life/animalkind/2024/02/15/merchen-farms-wanette-oklahoma-calf/72615279007/

SPJ Code of Ethics. (n.d.). https://www.spj.org/ethicscode.asp

The stylebook on LGBTQ+ terminology. (n.d.). https://www.nlgja.org/stylebook-on-lgbtq-terminology/

Thinking about what it means to be a good citizen, how important is it to. (2020). https://www.journalism.org/wp-content/uploads/sites/8/2020/12/PJ_2020.12.08_News-Consumption_Survey-Toplines.pdf

The trans journalists association's stylebook and coverage guide. (n.d.). https://styleguide.transjournalists.org/?ref=transjournalists.org

The Trust Project. (n.d.). https://thetrustproject.org/trust-indicators/

U.S. media literacy: A state-by-state status of media literacy education laws for K-12 schools. (2023). https://medialiteracynow.org/wp-content/uploads/2023/05/MediaLiteracyPolicyReport2022.pdf

Vanian, J. (2022). *Twitter is now owned by Elon Musk—here's a brief history from the app's founding in 2006 to the present.* https://www.cnbc.com/amp/2022/10/29/a-brief-history-of-twitter-from-its-founding-in-2006-to-musk-takeover.html

Wang, L., & Forman-Katz, N. (2024). *Many Americans find value in getting news on social media, but concerns about inaccuracy have risen.* https://www.pewresearch.org/short-reads/2024/02/07/many-americans-find-value-in-getting-news-on-social-media-but-concerns-about-inaccuracy-have-risen/

Westley, B. H., & Severin, W. J. (1964). A profile of the daily newspaper non-reader *Journalism Quarterly, 41*(1), 45–50, 156.

Willnat, L., Weaver, D., & Wilhoit, C. (2022). *The American journalist under attack: Media, trust & democracy: key findings 2022.* https://www.theamericanjournalist.org/_files/ugd/46a507_4fe1c4d6ec6d4c229895282965258a7a.pdf

York, C., & Schol, R. M. (2015). Youth antecedents to news media consumption: Parent and youth newspaper use, news discussion, and long-term news behavior. *Journalism & Mass Communication Quarterly, 92*(3), 681–699.

· Appendix A ·

LIST OF END-OF-CHAPTER QUESTIONS AND REFLECTIONS

End-of-Chapter 1 Questions and Reflections

1. Review the 22 events and issues described in Chapter 1. What event or issue do you think has most contributed to defining Gen Z? Why did you select that event or issue?
2. What event or issue would you add to defining Gen Z? Explain your rationale for adding that event or issue.

End-of-Chapter 2 Questions and Reflections

1. The questionnaire for The National Gen Z, Social Media & News Engagement Survey is in the Appendix. Make a copy of the questionnaire, then fill it out.
2. Compare your answers to the Gen Z responses reported in Tables 2.4, 2.5, and 2.7. If any of your questionnaire answers differ from Gen Z responses in the three tables, reflect on the reasons for the differences.

End-of-Chapter 3 Questions and Reflections

1. Do you remember observing your parents or grandparents reading a print newspaper or watching news on TV? If yes, what specifically do you remember?
2. If you have a news engagement routine, how would you describe it?
3. What do you think are the benefits of a news engagement routine?

End-of-Chapter 4 Questions and Reflections

1. Figure 4.3 lists four different categories of complaints about the news media's coverage of Gen Z. What category, if any, do you agree with? What complaint, if any, would you add and why?
2. What do you think is the most important finding in Table. 4.3? What are at least three reasons you think that finding is the most important?

End-of-Chapter 5 Questions and Reflections

1. What are three things you learned in this chapter that you did not know?
2. How did your answers on the questionnaire for The National Gen Z, Social Media & News Engagement Survey compare with results in Table 5.2?
3. "Voting & Engaging with News about the 2022 Midterm Elections: A Guide for Gen Z Voters," which is in the Appendix, has advice for Gen Z voters that would apply to any election. Based on that guide as well as this chapter and your own experience, what advice would you give a Gen Z voter who is voting for the first time?

End-of-Chapter 6 Questions and Reflections

1. Review the nine barriers to a news smart Gen Z in Figure 6.1. Which, if any, of the barriers do you *disagree* with? Explain why you disagree.
2. What barrier to a news smart Gen Z, if any, would you add? Explain why you added that barrier.
3. How do your questionnaire answers compare to the results in Table 6.3 about evaluating a news story's trustworthiness? What

else, if anything, would you add to evaluating the trustworthiness of a news story and why?
4. With one-third of Gen Z saying in Table 6.5 that they had *not* encountered disinformation or didn't know if they had, what do you think is the most effective way to educate Gen Z and others about disinformation?
5. What do you think are the main reasons digital news subscriptions rank last for Gen Z?
6. What, if anything, would motivate Gen Z to pay for a digital news subscription?

End-of-Chapter 7 Questions and Reflections

1. Review the list of constituent groups in Figure 7.1. Which constituent group matters most in ensuring Gen Z and future generations are informed, an independent press thrives, and democracy is protected?
2. Review and test out Gen Z's News Credibility Quick Check in Figure 7.2. What news outlet and news story did you test it on? What was your conclusion about the news story's credibility and what was your evaluation based on? What would you add or change about the News Credibility Quick Check?
3. The News Media Action Plan for Covering and Engaging Gen Z in Figure 7.3 has recommendations. What three recommendations do you think would have the most constructive impact on including and reporting on Gen Z? What, if any, recommendation would you add?
4. Find a country in Table 7.2—Select Rankings from Reporters Without Borders Index—that interests you, perhaps, because you've traveled there, would like to travel there in the future or you have a family connection. Go to the Reporters without Borders Index at rsf.org/en/index, click on the country to learn about the media landscape as well as the political, economic, and socio-cultural context for journalism. What did you learn and how does that country's media landscape compare with the United States?
5. Imagine 2030. How old will the youngest and oldest of Gen Z be? What will news engagement, journalism, the United States, and/or democracy be like in 2030? Why is that your vision for 2030?

· Appendix B ·

HOW THE NATIONAL GEN Z, SOCIAL MEDIA & NEWS ENGAGEMENT SURVEY WAS CONDUCTED

The National Gen Z, Social Media & News Engagement Survey was conducted in August 2023 with an online panel of 1,504 U.S. adults, 18 years and older. The online panel was recruited by Dynata, an international research firm that is a leader in recruiting online panel participants and conducting online research (Dynata, n.d.; Panel Book, n.d.).

The survey questionnaire included 84 closed-ended and open-ended questions. Six questions were written in a format with multiple questions so technically there were more than 84 questions. For example, question 39 asked about 26 different types of news categories and topics. On average, participants completed the questionnaire in 10 to 15 minutes.

Immediately after the study's proposal and questionnaire were approved by the University of Texas at Austin's Institutional Review Board (IRB) (Human Research, n.d.), the survey was launched with Dynata managing the fieldwork and entering the collected data from the 1,504 completed questionnaires into the statistical software, IBM SPSS (n.d.).

The first step in the analysis was to create a generational variable that would be the primary independent variable. Using question #46, "What year were you born?," I sorted all survey participants into five generations as defined by the Pew Research Center (Dimock, 2019): Gen Z (1997 through

2012); Millennials (1981 through 1996); Generation X (1965–1980); Baby Boomers (1946–1964); Silent Generation (1928–1945). Of the 1,504 survey participants, 24% were Gen Z and 24% were Millennials. The three oldest generations Gen X (22%), Baby Boomers (23%), and Silent (6%) were combined into a single group labeled Older Generations, which after rounding was 52% of survey participants.

Combining the three oldest generations into one group was not only because of the years they were born; the growing up and young adult experiences of Generation X, Baby Boomers, and Silent were more similar to each other than to Millennials and Gen Z. Plus, there was little variety in news sources when the older generations grew up and at the time, the Internet, Facebook, and smartphones would have been unimaginable.

A significant amount of the generational analysis compares Gen Z, Millennials, and the Older Generations Group. Some analyses compare Gen Z only with Millennials and for other analyses, Gen Z is the exclusive focus.

So that this book is accessible to everyone, from Gen Z and K-to-College Educators to journalists, public opinion researchers, political strategists, and the public as a whole, crosstabulations and frequencies are the primary analytical tools. The differences reported in the crosstabulation tables are overwhelmingly statistically significant unless specified as non-significant. Qualitative analysis is primarily used for the open-ended questions in which Gen Z participants expressed their opinions. While the responses are generally sorted into thematic categories, verbatim quotes—not percentages—are reported so Gen Z's own words speak for Gen Z.

Even though online panel participants were recruited, the goal was still to represent U.S. demographics as determined by the census. The chart provides online panel statistics and census data when questions were asked in a similar manner, such as for race/ethnicity and gender. The race/ethnicity data for the online panel was compiled from questions 70 and 71 of the questionnaire.

Question 70 asked survey participants to indicate their race or ethnic group and the follow-up Question 71 asked: "Are you of Hispanic or Latino origin, such as Latin American, Mexican, Puerto Rican or Cuban?" Those who answered "Yes" to Hispanic or Latino origin and had selected Caucasian or White, African American or Black, etc. in Question 70 were moved to the Hispanic or Latino category. As can be seen from the chart, the U.S. Census also distinguishes non-Hispanic White from Hispanic/Latino.

Comparison of Online Panel and U.S. Census on Select Demographic Variables

	Online Panel	U.S. Census (Quick Facts, n.d.)
Race and Ethnicity		
White (Non-Hispanic/Latino)	61%	59%
Hispanic/Latino	13%	19%
African American/Black	15%	14%
Asian American	6%	6%
Native American	2%	1%
Two or More Races	2%	3%
Other	2%	---
Gender		
Male	49%	50%
Female	50%	50%
Non-Binary/Other	1%	---
Education		
Some High School	3%	---
High School Degree	22%	---
Some College/Technical School Degree	28%	---
College Degree	30%	---
Graduate/Professional School Degree	13%	---

Instead of limiting gender to male or female as the U.S. Census does, Question 67 which asked participants how they described themselves (Male, Female, Non-binary, Other) followed by Q68 which provided six categories they could pick from. These response choices are based on response choices on Gallup Polls (Jones, 2023).

Since The National Survey of Gen Z, Social Media, and News Engagement Survey questionnaire differed from the Census in asking about education and income, the chart only includes education statistics from the survey. The census data for H.S. Graduate and Bachelor's Degree or higher were only for ages 25 and older, which excludes the majority of Gen Z.

The U.S. Census reported a median household income of $75,149. Because the household income question on the survey asked about income ranges, the income results on the survey cannot be compared with the census. Still, it's important to note that just over half (54%) of survey participants had a household income of $50,000 to $59,999.

References

Dimock, M. (2019). *Defining generations: Where Millennials end and Generation Z begins.* https://www.pewresearch.org/fact-tank/2019/01/17/where-millennials-end-and-generation-z-begins

Dynata. (n.d.). https://www.dynata.com/

Human Research and the IRB. (n.d.). https://research.utexas.edu/ors/human-subjects/

IBM SPSS Statistics. (n.d.). https://www.ibm.com/products/spss-statistics

Jones, J. M. (2023). *U.S. LGBT Identification Steady at 7.2%* https://news.gallup.com/poll/470708/lgbt-identification-steady.aspx

Panel Book. (n.d.). https://www.dynata.com/content/Panel-Book.pdf

Quick Facts United States. (n.d.). https://www.census.gov/quickfacts/fact/table/US/PST045223

· Appendix C ·

QUESTIONNAIRE FOR THE NATIONAL GEN Z, SOCIAL MEDIA & NEWS ENGAGEMENT SURVEY

Thank you for agreeing to participate in this study about news, social media, and issues in the public sphere. Your answers to the questionnaire will provide insight into engaging with news and social media and public life. It is important to read each question carefully and answer each question as best you can. Answers to the questionnaire, which cannot be connected to individual study participants, will be analyzed as a whole. You may begin answering the questions now.

1. Yes, I do agree with the terms and conditions above
2. No, I don't agree with the terms and conditions above → **TERMINATE**
    S1. Are you 18 or older?
       1. Yes
       2. No [Terminate]

    S2. Do you live in the US?
       1. Yes
       2. No [Terminate]

1. Approximately how many days in an average week do you get news?
    1. 0 days ⟶(Skip to Q7.)
    2. 1 day

3. 2 days
4. 3 days
5. 4 days
6. 5 days
7. 6 days
8. 7 days

2. Some people purposely seek news; others get news while doing something else. How many days in an average week do you <u>purposely seek</u> news?
   1. 0 days
   2. 1 day
   3. 2 days
   4. 3 days
   5. 4 days
   6. 5 days
   7. 6 days
   8. 7 days

3. Do you get news from the following platforms often, sometimes, or seldom/never?

	Often	Sometimes	Seldom/Never
A. Social Media	1	2	3
B. News Apps	1	2	3
C. YouTube	1	2	3
D. Podcasts	1	2	3
E. Cable	1	2	3
F. Local TV	1	2	3
G. Network TV	1	2	3
H. Print Newspapers	1	2	3
I. Print Magazines	1	2	3
J. Radio	1	2	3
K. Family	1	2	3
L. Friends	1	2	3
M. Notifications you activate on your smartphone	1	2	3
N. Google or other search engines	1	2	3

O. Newsletters	1	2	3
P. Smart Speaker	1	2	3
Q. Other (Please specify):_____	1	2	3

4. Approximately, how many different times during a 24-hour period do you get news?
   1. 0 times
   2. 1 or 2 times
   3. 3 to 5 times
   4. 6 to 9 times
   5. 10 times or more
5. Some people have a routine when they get news while others don't. In general, do you have a routine when you get news?
   1. Yes
   2. No (Skip to Q8.)
6. If you have a routine for getting news, please briefly describe your routine when you get news. You might begin with the time of day that you first get news and the first place you check for news.
   _____

(Skip to Q8.)

7. What is the main reason you don't get news?
   _____

These questions are about growing up with the news.

8. Some people grew up in a home with news around them and others did not. Was news around you all or most of the time, some of the time, occasionally, or never in the home you grew up in?
   1. All or most of the time
   2. Some of the time
   3. Occasionally
   4. Never
   5. Can't remember

9. Growing up, how often was the TV tuned to the news around dinner time?
   1. All or most of the time
   2. Some of the time
   3. Occasionally
   4. Never
   5. Can't remember
10. How often were newspapers around in the home you grew up in?
    1. All or most of the time
    2. Some of the time
    3. Occasionally
    4. Never
    5. Can't remember
11. How often were there discussions about something in the news in the home you grew up in?
    1. All or most of the time
    2. Some of the time
    3. Occasionally
    4. Never
    5. Can't remember
12. Can you recall anyone ever telling you that being informed about news is important?
    1. Yes
    2. No (Skip to Q14.)
    3. Can't remember (Skip to Q14.)

13. Who was the person who said to you that being informed about the news is important?
    _____

14. Have you ever told anyone that being informed about news is important?
    1. Yes
    2. No (Skip to Q16.)
    3. Can't remember (Skip to Q16.)

15. Who was the person you told that being informed is important?
    1. Parent
    2. Other relative (Please specify:_____)
    3. Friend
    4. Other (Please specify:_____)
16. Can you recall anyone telling you that the news you engage with should be accurate?
    1. Yes
    2. No (Skip to Q18.)
17. Who was the person who said that the news you engage with should be accurate?
    _____

18. Growing up, how often did you discuss the news with your friends?
    1. Often
    2. Sometimes
    3. Occasionally
    4. Never
    5. Can't remember
19. Did you have a teacher who included news in your elementary, middle school, or high school classroom at least once a week?
    1. Yes
    2. No
    3. Can't remember
20. Did you take a class in middle school, high school or college in which you learned about news and journalism, including the principles and process of news and journalism?
    1. Yes
    2. No
    3. Can't remember

These questions are about your engagement with social media.

21. Approximately how many days in an average week are you on social media?
    1. 0 days ———————————→(Skip to Q28.)
    2. 1 day
    3. 2 days
    4. 3 days
    5. 4 days
    6. 5 days
    7. 6 days
    8. 7 days
22. Approximately, how much time do you spend on social media per day?
    1. Less than 1 hour
    2. 1 to 2 hours
    3. 3 to 4 hours
    4. 5 hours or more
23. What social media platform do you spend the most time on?
    _____

24. How much of your social media time is spent engaging with news?
    1. None (Skip to Q29.)
    2. A little
    3. Some
    4. A lot
25. Which social media platform do you primarily use for engaging with news?
    _____

26. What do you like <u>best</u> about engaging with news on social media?
    _____

27. What do you like <u>least</u> about engaging with news on social media?
    _____

(Skip to Q30.)

28. What is the main reason you are <u>not</u> on social media?

_____

(Skip to Q30.)

29. What is the main reason you do not engage with news on social media?

_____

These questions are about using a smartphone for news.

30. Were you born in 1981 or later?
    1. Yes
    2. No (Skip to Q34.)
31. While growing up, do you recall at least one parent using a smartphone?
    1. Yes
    2. No (Skip to Q34.)
    3. Don't remember (Skip to Q34.)
32. While growing up, did a parent engage with news on their smartphone?
    1. Yes
    2. No
    3. Don't Know
33. While growing up, did a parent ever tell you they were engaging with news on their smartphone?
    1. Yes
    2. No
    3. Don't remember

The next two questions focus on issues.

34. What is the most important issue facing <u>this country</u>?

_____

35. What is the most important issue facing <u>your generation</u>?

_____

APPENDIX C

The following questions are about trustworthy qualities in a news story.

36. When you read, watch, or listen to a news story, how important is each of the following in deciding whether it is trustworthy?

	Very Important	Somewhat Important	Important	Not Important
A. The news organization that publishes the story.	1	2	3	4
B. The person, if any, who shares the story with you.	1	2	3	4
C. The story has a lot of shares, comments, or likes on social media.	1	2	3	4
D. The sources that are cited in the story.	1	2	3	4
E. The specific journalist who reported the story.	1	2	3	4

37. If you relied on only <u>one</u> factor to judge the trustworthiness of a news story, what would that factor be?

    _____

38. Where do you usually go to find trustworthy news stories to read, watch, or listen to?

    _____

The next questions ask how often you pay attention to various categories of news.

39. Do you often, sometimes, occasionally, or never pay attention to the following categories of news:

	Often	Sometimes	Occasionally	Never
A. International News	1	2	3	4
B. National News	1	2	3	4
C. State News	1	2	3	4
D. Local News	1	2	3	4
E. Breaking News	1	2	3	4
F. Presidential Election News	1	2	3	4
G. News about Voting	1	2	3	4
H. News about the President	1	2	3	4
I. News about Congress	1	2	3	4

J.	Supreme Court Cases and Rulings	1	2	3	4
K.	News about Democracy Safeguards & Threats	1	2	3	4
L.	Politics	1	2	3	4
M.	Crime News	1	2	3	4
N.	Sports News	1	2	3	4
O.	Weather News	1	2	3	4
P.	Business & Consumer News	1	2	3	4
Q.	Technology News	1	2	3	4
R.	Entertainment, Arts & Culture	1	2	3	4
S.	News about Climate Change	1	2	3	4
T.	News about Gun Violence	1	2	3	4
U.	Immigration News	1	2	3	4
V.	State Laws Restricting Teaching about Black History	1	2	3	4
W.	Restrictions on Abortion Rights	1	2	3	4
X.	News about Student Loan Debt	1	2	3	4
Y.	Health News	1	2	3	4

40. **(If you "Never" pay attention to Health News, please Skip to Q42.)** If you pay attention to health news at least occasionally, what type(s) of health news do you pay attention to most?
    _____

41. From where do you get most of your health news?
    _____

42. In general, what grade, from A to F, would you give the news media for its news coverage?
    1. A
    2. B
    3. C
    4. D
    5. F

43. What is the main reason for your grade?
    _____

44. In general, what grade, from A to F, would you give the news media for its news coverage of your generation?
   1. A
   2. B
   3. C
   4. D
   5. F

45. What is the main reason for your grade?
   _____

46. Here are some things that have been said about the news and journalism. Please indicate your level of agreement or disagreement with the statement with 1 being strongly disagree and 5 being strongly agree.

		Strongly Disagree				Strongly Agree
A.	You enjoy keeping up with the news.	1	2	3	4	5
B.	We all have a duty to keep ourselves informed about news and current events.	1	2	3	4	5
C.	It's important for the news media to be a watchdog of powerful people and the government.	1	2	3	4	5
D.	You were raised to believe being informed about the news is important.	1	2	3	4	5
E.	Paying for a news subscription helps support an independent press.	1	2	3	4	5
F.	Being informed about the news makes you feel empowered.	1	2	3	4	5
G.	The news media should be more helpful and caring like a good neighbor.	1	2	3	4	5
H.	All news on the Internet should be free to the public.	1	2	3	4	5
I.	The news media care little about people like you.	1	2	3	4	5
J.	Most of the people who are important to you value keeping up with the news.	1	2	3	4	5
K.	You depend on the news to help you	1	2	3	4	5

	with your daily life.				
L.	News organizations are more concerned about being first than being right.	1	2	3	4	5
M.	News organizations are willing to admit their mistakes.	1	2	3	4	5
N.	News organizations protect democracy more than hurt democracy.	1	2	3	4	5
O.	You depend on social media to help you with your daily life.	1	2	3	4	5
P.	The news projects an accurate representation of the constituent groups in U.S. society.	1	2	3	4	5
Q.	The news projects an accurate representation of your generation.	1	2	3	4	5
R.	An independent press is good for democracy.	1	2	3	4	5

The following questions are about disinformation.

47. How familiar are you with the term "disinformation"?
    1. Very familiar
    2. Familiar
    3. Somewhat Familiar
    4. Not Familiar (Skip to Q53.)
48. Briefly explain what the term "disinformation" means to you:
    _____
49. Have you ever encountered disinformation?
    1. Yes
    2. No (Skip to Q53.)
    3. Don't Know (Skip to Q53.)
50. Where have you mostly encountered disinformation?
    _____
51. What is an example of disinformation that you've encountered?
    _____
52. What do you usually do when you encounter disinformation?
    _____

The following questions are about being a good citizen.

53. Thinking about what it means to be a good citizen, how important is it to:

	Very Important	Important	Somewhat Important	Not Important
A. Follow what is happening in the news	1	2	3	4
B. Vote in elections	1	2	3	4
C. Serve jury duty if called	1	2	3	4
D. Volunteer to help others	1	2	3	4

The following questions are about your background and interests.

54. What issue, event or activity best characterizes your generation?
    _____

55. Which of the following <u>digital</u> subscriptions do you pay for?

	Yes	No
A. Music	1	2
B. Movies and/or TV	1	2
C. Sports	1	2
D. News	1	2
E. Other (Please specify:_____)	1	2

56. On average, how much do you spend on digital subscriptions per month?
    _____

57. Are you currently registered to vote?
    1. Yes ⟶ (Please skip to Q59.)
    2. No ⟶ (Please answer Q58.)

58. What is the main reason you are <u>not</u> registered to vote?
    _____

59. Did you vote in the 2020 U.S. Presidential Election?
    1. Yes (Please skip to Q61.)
    2. No ⟶ (Please answer Q60.)

60. What is the main reason you did <u>not</u> vote in the 2020 Presidential Election?

    _____

61. Do you intend to vote in the 2024 U.S. Presidential Election?
    1. Definitely will vote——→(Please answer Q62.)
    2. Probably will vote——→(Please answer Q62.)
    3. Probably will <u>not</u> vote (Please skip to Q63.)
    4. Definitely will <u>not</u> vote (Please skip to Q63.)
62. What is the main reason you definitely or probably <u>will</u> vote in the 2024 Presidential Election?

    _____

(After answering Q62, please skip to Q64.)

63. What is the main reason you probably or definitely will <u>not</u> vote in the 2024 Presidential Election?

    _____

64. Generally speaking, do you identify yourself as a:
    1. Democrat
    2. Republican
    3. Independent
    4. Other (Please specify:_____)
65. Do you consider yourself:
    1. Very Conservative
    2. Conservative
    3. Moderately Conservative
    4. Middle of the Road
    5. Moderately Liberal
    6. Liberal
    7. Very Liberal or Progressive
    8. Other (Please specify:_____)
66. What year were you born? _____
67. Do you describe yourself as?
    1. Male
    2. Female
    3. Non-binary

4. Other (Please specify:_____)
68. Which of the following do you consider yourself to be? You can select as many as apply.
    1. Straight or heterosexual
    2. Lesbian
    3. Gay
    4. Bisexual
    5. Transgender
    6. Other (Please specify: _____)
69. What is the highest level of education that you've completed?
    1. Some High School or Less
    2. High School Degree
    3. Some College or Technical School Degree
    4. College Graduate
    5. Some Graduate or Professional School
    6. Masters, M.D. or Doctorate
    7. Other (Please specify: _____)
70. What is your race or ethnic group?
    1. Caucasian or White
    2. African American or Black
    3. Hispanic or Latino
    4. Asian American (Please specify country/countries of origin:_____)
    5. Native American
    6. More than one race (Please specify races:_____)
    7. Other (Please specify:_____)
71. Are you of Hispanic or Latino origin, such as Latin American, Mexican, Puerto Rican, or Cuban?
    1. Yes
    2. No
72. Approximately, which is your household income?
    01. Under $20,000
    02. $20–$29,000
    03. $30–$39,000
    04. $40–$49,000
    05. $50–$59,000
    06. $60–$69,000
    07. $70–$79,000
    08. $80–$89,000

09. $90–$99,000
  10. $100,000–$124,000
  11. $125,000–$149,000
  12. $150,000–$174,000
  13. $175,000–$199,000
  14. $200,000 or more
73. In what state do you live?
  _____

74. Do you live in a city, the suburbs, a small town, or a rural area?
  1. City
  2. Suburbs
  3. Small town
  4. Rural area
  5. Other (Please specify:)_____
75. Do you:
  1. Own
  2. Rent
  3. Live with your parents
  4. Other (Please specify.) _____
76. Do you have children?
  1. Yes
  2. No (Please skip to Q78.)
77. What are the ages of your children?
  _____

78. Did you take out student loans for college, graduate school, or professional school?
  1. Yes
  2. No (Please skip to Q80.)
  3. Didn't go to college (Please skip to Q80.)
79. How much of your student loans have been paid back or canceled because of participation in the U.S. Government's Public Service Loan Forgiveness (PSLF) Program?
  1. All
  2. Most
  3. Some
  4. None

80. Which of the following are regular pastimes?

	Yes	No
A. Playing a sport	1	2
B. Playing a musical instrument	1	2
C. Playing online video games	1	2
D. Other (Please specify:_____)	1	2

81. If you play video games online, how often do you discuss news while playing?
   1. Often
   2. Sometimes
   3. Occasionally
   4. Never
   5. Don't play video games online
82. Do you own a gun?
   1. Yes
   2. No (Please skip to Q84.)
83. What is the main reason that you own a gun?
   _____

(After answering Q83, please skip Q84 and go to closing thank you.)

84. What is the main reason that you <u>do not</u> own a gun?
   _____

Thank you for participating in this study. Your participation will help us better understand news and social media engagement.

· Appendix D ·

CELEBRATING 10 YEARS OF NEWS ENGAGEMENT DAY! SOUVENIR PROGRAM

Used with Permission from Paula M. Poindexter

APPENDIX D

Celebrating 10 Years of News Engagement Day!

AEJMC & News Engagement Day Committee Panel

2:30 p.m. to 4 p.m., Mon., Aug. 7, 2023

AEJMC Annual Conference

Marriott Marquis

Washington D.C.

History of News Engagement Day

The first News Engagement Day, which was called National News Engagement Day, was announced at a news conference at the National Press Club in Washington D.C., Tues., September 23, 2014 and launched two weeks later, Tues., October 7. Sponsored by AEJMC, the Association for Education in Journalism and Mass Communication, the world's largest association of journalism and communication educators, professionals, and graduate students, News Engagement Day, which is always held the first Tuesday in October, began as an initiative of 2013–2014 AEJMC President Paula Poindexter.

Poindexter's idea for News Engagement Day came while writing *Millennials, News, and Social Media: Is News Engagement a Thing of the Past?* In the book, published in 2012 by Peter Lang, with a revised and updated second edition published in 2018, Poindexter proposed an "Engage with News" Day as a national campaign to help reverse the public's declining attention to news, lack of understanding about journalism, and waning trust in the news media. A journalism professor at the University of Texas at Austin, Poindexter felt that unless we were proactive in encouraging the public, especially Millennials, born 1981 through 1996, to engage with news that news engagement would continue its downward slide, and threaten the future of the news media, our democracy, and the public good.

Beginning on university campuses with journalism and communication programs, News Engagement Day has grown into a worldwide event, where people of all ages across the globe are encouraged to engage with news, whether reading, watching, listening to, posting, discussing, or sharing. And year round, journalists, educators at all levels and across all fields as well as leaders in the public and private sectors and from the neighborhood to the national levels are encouraged to understand the process and principles of journalism as well as the importance of a robust independent press and informed public to a healthy democracy.

Since News Engagement Day was founded in 2014, a new generation, Gen Z, born 1997 through 2012, has come of age as disinformation has been vigorously pushed on social media, cable TV, and other platforms to purposely misinform the public about facts, history, and news, including the results of the 2020 presidential election. Today in our social media-smartphone news landscape, polluted with disinformation, News Engagement Day is more important than ever but we have to do more. We have to ensure the public is also equipped to distinguish credible news from made-up information pretending to be news in order to trick the public into believing lies over verified fact-based news reported by journalists and news organizations guided by the highest ethical principles.

Welcome: Paula M. Poindexter, Chair, News Engagement Day Committee

Round 1: Celebrating 10 Years of News Engagement Day! Book Drawing

- *Newsroom Confidential: Lessons (and Worries) from an Ink-Stained Life* by Margaret Sullivan
- *Genius Makers: The Mavericks Who Brought AI to Google, Facebook, and the World* by Cade Metz
- *How Democracies Die* by Steven Levitsky and Daniel Ziblatt

Keynote: "Perceptions of Social Media's Effects on Democracy in the U.S. and Around the World" by Richard Wike, Director, Global Attitudes Research, Pew Research Center

Round 2: Celebrating 10 Years of News Engagement Day! Book Drawing

Presentation of 2023 News Audience Research Paper Award*

- Comparing Effects of News Subscription Motivation and News Lifestyle and Their Impact on Subscription Retention by Weiyue Chen, Butler, and Esther Thorson, Michigan State
- News for the Ages: An Examination of Trust Factors by Generational Cohort by Amy Jo Coffey and Chris DeFelice, Florida

* After receiving exceptional reviews and almost perfect scores, both research papers won the 2023 News Audience Research Paper Award. With two winning papers, the $1,000 cash prize is awarded to both papers which the authors split, and each author receives a certificate.

Round 3: Celebrating 10 Years of News Engagement Day! Book Drawing

Sharing Great Ideas to Celebrate Our 10th News Engagement Day, Tuesday, October 3, 2023

Closing Remarks: "News Engagement Day is More Important Than Ever But It's Not Enough" by Paula M. Poindexter, Chair, News Engagement Day Committee

Thank You!

Without you, we would not be celebrating 10 Years of News Engagement Day

&

10 Years of the News Audience Research Paper Award:

News Engagement Day Committee

Participants in News Engagement Day Activities, 2014–2023

News Audience Research Paper Award Recipients, 2014–2023

News Audience Research Paper Award Reviewers, 2014–2023

News Audience Research Paper Award Committee Chair:

Maxwell McCombs

AEJMC Board of Directors, 2014–2023

AEJMC Staff

Designer of News Engagement Day Logo: Amy Zerba

For News Engagement Day's History & More, please visit Newsengagementday.org

· Appendix E ·

VOTING & ENGAGING WITH NEWS ABOUT THE 2022 MIDTERM ELECTIONS

A Guide for Gen Z Voters
By Paula M. Poindexter
Used with Permission from Paula M. Poindexter

APPENDIX E

Voting & Engaging with News about the 2022 Midterm Elections: A Guide for Gen Z Voters

by
Paula M. Poindexter, Ph.D.
Past President of the Association for Education in Journalism and Mass Communication (AEJMC); Chair, AEJMC's News Engagement Day Committee

Waiting in Line to Vote, 2018 Midterm Elections (Photo Credit: Paula M. Poindexter)

Copyright © 2022 by Paula M. Poindexter

Voting & Engaging with News about the 2022 Midterm Elections: A Guide for Gen Z Voters

Contents

1. How Gen Z Can Have an Impact with Their Right to Vote

   Table 1.1: Registration and Voting in 2016 and 2020 U.S. Presidential Elections: Gen Z Citizens and All Citizens 18+

2. Verify Your Voter Registration & Know Your States' Voting Rules & Dates

   Figure 2.1: Click a Topic and Get Answers to Your Questions About Registering and Voting

3. What's on the Ballot?

   Figure 3.1: Candidates and Issues on the Ballot for the 2022 Midterms

4. Engage with Credible News *Before* You Vote

5. Vote!

6. Resources & Links

7. Special Thanks

1. How Gen Z Can Have an Impact with Their Right to Vote

In the United States, the vote of each citizen who is eligible to vote, counts as one vote. The sum of these votes determines the outcome of an election whether at the national, state or local level. It is the results of this democratic election process--casting and counting votes--that each of us can have an impact on who our elected leaders are and the laws and policies that govern our country and the state in which we live.

Through our votes, we also have the power to influence the country's direction, the treatment and safety of its citizens, the health of our democracy, and much more. But in order to exercise the power that each of us has, we must vote. But before we can vote, we must register.

Unfortunately, as Table 1.1 shows, every American citizen does not exercise the voting power they have. In 2016, only 43% of Gen Z citizens who were of voting age were registered, which means 57% were not, making them ineligible to vote. And although by 2020, 60% of Gen Z citizens who were eligible to vote, were registered, two-fifths were not, prohibiting them from voting.

Table 1.1 also underscores that registering to vote is not a guarantee a vote will be cast. In 2016, for example, 43% of Gen Z citizens were registered but only 34% voted. And in 2020, just over half of registered Gen Z voters cast a vote even though another 9% were registered.

Table A.1 Registration and Voting in 2016 and 2020 U.S. Presidential Elections: Gen Z Citizens and All Citizens 18+

	Registered in 2016	Voted in 2016	Registered in 2020	Voted in 2020
Gen Z U.S. Citizens	43%	34%	60%	51%
All U.S. Citizens, 18+	70%	61%	73%	67%

Note: Using the Pew Research Center's definition of Gen Z, the birth years of this cohort are 1997–2012. Based on these birth years, Gen Z voters would have been 18 and 19 years old in 2016 and ages 18 through 23 in 2020. These data are compiled from U.S. Census data from the 2016 presidential election and 2020 presidential election.

This failure to vote after registering is not limited to Gen Z; it's true across all registered voters 18 and older, according to Table 1.1. For the 2016 presidential election when Democratic nominee Hillary Clinton ran against Republican nominee Donald Trump, 70% of all U.S. citizens 18 years and above were registered but only 61% voted.

And in 2020 when Democratic nominee Joe Biden ran against Republican nominee Donald Trump, the incumbent president, both the percentage of registered voters and percentage of those who voted increased. Still only 67% voted despite the fact that almost three-quarters of eligible American citizens had registered to vote in the 2020 presidential election.

With registration not exceeding 73% for all U.S. citizens and 60% for Gen Z citizens during the past two presidential elections, it's not surprising that registration has been singled out as a barrier to casting a vote. But it's not the only barrier.

Other barriers that prevent young citizens from voting, according to University of Virginia professor John Holbein, include locating and traveling to polling locations, navigating long lines, and even finding time to vote. And, of course, some eligible citizens may not be interested in voting and others may not be aware of an upcoming election until it's too late to register.

But the biggest impediment to voting for some first-time voters may be as simple as not knowing what's required to vote or how, when, and where to vote. It's also the case that because some are not informed about the candidates and issues and are unsure about where to find information they can trust, they decide not to vote, even though they're registered.

Regardless of the voting barriers, they are not insurmountable, that is, if you have access to the information required to navigate the voting process. Our News Engagement Day election guide, "Voting & Engaging with News about the 2022 Midterm Elections: A Guide for Gen Z," provides that information. The guide will also help Gen Z get informed about the candidates and issues before they vote, thus making them more confident about voting as well as their ballot choices.

It's not a coincidence that this guide emphasizes the importance of being an informed voter and provides strategies to accomplish that goal. That was the plan when in the first edition of my book, *Millennials, News, and Social Media: Is News Engagement a Thing of the Past?* I proposed a day to engage with news and said it should be held the first Tuesday in October, approximately one month before Election Day, a period when citizens feel a responsibility to follow the news.

And as the 2013–2014 President of the <u>Association for Education in Journalism and Mass Communication</u> (AEJMC), the largest association of journalism and communication professors, professionals, and graduate students, I launched <u>News Engagement Day</u> which is now in its ninth year.

In 2018, 2020, and now 2022, when News Engagement Day occurred during an election year, we have produced election guides that explain how to register to vote and the voting process. But we don't stop with information about navigating the voting process.

We also emphasize the importance of getting informed *prior* to voting. And we explain how to evaluate news as well as the platforms where news can be engaged with, whether by reading, watching, listening to, posting, liking, or sharing. Additionally in our election guide, we have strategies for increasing your News IQ so that when it's time to vote, whether on Election Day, during early voting or through the mail, Gen Z can cast an *informed* vote that has the potential to have the impact they're voting for.

2. Verify Your Voter Registration & Know Your States' Voting Rules & Dates

If you're *eligible* to vote but are *not* registered, you cannot vote! So to avoid missing out on voting in the 2022 Midterm Elections, use Vote.gov, the U.S. government's official election website, to check your voter registration status.

By clicking your state (or territory or the District of Columbia), Vote.gov will take you to your state's election site where you can enter your name, county, date of birth, and zip code to learn the status of your voter registration. If you're not registered, the site will provide the information you need to register and the deadline for doing so.

Once you've taken care of your registration, you can make your voting plans, including when and how you'll vote. As you're making these plans, keep in mind that voting in the United States is handled by individual states—not the federal government.

Individual state legislatures pass election laws, governors sign election laws, and the state's top election official, usually called secretary of state, oversees the election but elections are conducted at the county level under the leadership of the county clerk. The county that you live in, is where you will register and vote.

In some states, election laws make it easy to vote; in other states, since the 2020 presidential election, state legislatures have passed and governors have signed new election laws that have made it harder to vote. Some states have even made it more difficult to register.

But if you plan *early* and carefully read and follow rules for registering to vote and voting, you should be able to vote without any problem. Still, you need to be knowledgeable about the voting process so that you don't get tripped up by things you don't know and end up on the voting sideline, disappointed that you missed out on exercising your right to vote in the midterm elections of 2022.

So how do you find out what you don't know? Vote411.

Vote411, an election website sponsored by the League of Women Voters, the preeminent non-partisan voter education non-profit, has answers to questions about registering and voting that you didn't know to ask. From their First Time Voter Checklist, I have selected the topics most relevant to successful registration and voting in the upcoming election and displayed them in Figure 2.1. When you click on the topic, and enter the information requested, the site will take you to the state where you live and provide you with the information you need to vote.

Figure A.1 Click a Topic and Get Answers to Your Questions About Registering and Voting

Absentee Ballot Process
Drop Boxes
Early Voting
Election Dates
Eligibility Requirements
ID Needed for Voter Registration
ID Needed for Voting
Official Results
Overseas and Military Voters
Polling Place Hours
Polling Place Locator
Provisions for Voters with Disabilities
Registration Deadline
Time off to Vote
Verify Voter Registration

Note: Topics selected from the League of Women Voters' First Time Voter Checklist

As you click on topics in Figure 2.1, remember that each state has its own voting laws and rules and you have to know and follow your state—not a different state where a friend or family member lives. For example, Texas does not allow a student ID card to vote but Kansas does. Kansas has "no excuse" absentee voting but in Texas, to vote absentee, you have to be at least 65 or have one of five excuses such as giving birth to a baby three weeks before Election Day.

3. What's on the Ballot?

A phrase that has been heard a lot during the 2022 election season is: "____ is on the ballot." Instead of filling in the blank with a candidate, the phrase is used to call attention to issues that, although not literally written on the ballot, will be affected by which candidates win (see Figure 3.1a).

Figure A.2 Candidates and Issues on the Ballot for the 2022 Midterms

National Candidates for Congress	
Senator	Representative
State and County Candidates	
Governor	State Senators
Attorney General	State Representatives
Secretary of State	County Clerks
Issues in the News That Can Be Affected by Candidates Voted For	
Abortion Rights	Domestic Violent Extremism
Access to Affordable Healthcare	Gun Safety
Accurate Vote Counting & Certification	Hate Crimes
Affordable Prescription Drugs	Home Ownership
Assault Weapons Ban	Immigration Reform
Childcare Quality and Affordability	Income Inequality
Climate Change	Infectious Disease Threats
College Affordability	Inflation & Economy
College Student Debt Relief	K-12 Education
Crime	LGBTQ Rights
Criminal Justice Reform	Marijuana Legalization
DACA	Pre-K Universal Access
Democracy	Race & Ethnicity Issues
Disinformation Threats	Voting Rights

When voters vote during the 2022 midterms, they will, of course, determine which candidates are elected to the U.S. Congress and state legislatures. But because members of Congress and state legislators pass laws that address issues of concern to the leaders and members of their political party, make no mistake: Issues are always on the ballot.

That's why it's essential that before voting, you inform yourself about these issues and where candidates for Congress, governor, attorney general, secretary of state, the state legislature, and county clerks who conduct elections across the state, stand on these issues. Only by informing yourself from credible sources will you know whether the candidates you're considering voting for are aligned with you on the issues that matter to you.

So as you prepare to vote in the 2022 Midterm Elections, remember that candidates as well as issues are on the ballot and both deserve your attention.

4. Engage with Credible News *Before* You Vote

When in 2020, a Pew Research Center survey asked how important <u>following news</u> was to being a "good citizen," 86% said it was very or somewhat important. Following news reported by independent, trustworthy news outlets is not just important to being a good citizen, it's essential in a democracy. When informed citizens vote, it strengthens our democracy and safeguards it against threats, a concern that has become one of the "most important" issues facing the country, according to an <u>NBC News poll</u>.

Although in the United States, it's never been easier to get news, the reality is that easy access to news, especially from social media, is not a guarantee that one will be fully informed. In fact, a <u>Pew study about getting news on social media</u> found that "Americans who primarily turn to social media for political news are less aware and knowledgeable about a wide range of events and issues in the news."

Plus, according to that study, relying on social media platforms for news increases the likelihood of "being exposed to false or unproven claims." And because young adults are more likely to get news from social media, the chances increase that they're less aware and less knowledgeable about election issues.

The good news is this news knowledge deficit can be reversed. By adopting the following news literacy tips, you can raise your News IQ, that is, your knowledge about news and how it's produced. Additionally, you can sharpen your critical thinking skills and be better able to evaluate news and distinguish it from non-news content, especially disinformation.

News Literacy Tips That Can Raise Your News IQ

1. **Be skeptical.** Unless the platform you're engaging with has a reputation for and a commitment to distributing credible news reported by experienced journalists, be skeptical and independently vet the journalism credentials of the individual who shared the story.
2. **It's not about the packaging.** It doesn't matter whether the information is packaged as an article, a video, a podcast, a photo essay, a poll, an infographic, a tweet or is distributed via app, website, text, radio, newsletter, smartspeaker, notification, YouTube or as a local, network or cable program. What matters is that if the content is represented as news, there should be evidence that it was produced by journalists.
3. **The first step in having confidence in the news you're engaging with is knowing what news is and isn't.** News is the outcome of the

information and images that journalism professionals gather, verify, edit, and report in accordance with journalism principles and a journalistic code of ethics.

4. **Opinion and advertising are *not* news.** Editorials, op-ed columns, cable news, radio, and podcast host opinions, experts' perspectives, pundit commentary, and advertising should be labeled as the non-news content they are. Additionally, this persuasive communication should be approached with skepticism because some will try to fool you into thinking they are news when they are not.

5. **Keep your disinformation antennae up!** The more informed you are from credible news outlets, the easier it is to detect disinformation which has increasingly polluted the news media landscape. Merriam-Webster defines disinformation, which some media outlets call misinformation, as "false information deliberately and often covertly spread (as by the planting of rumors) in order to influence public opinion or obscure the truth." The false information can be deceptive assertions, conspiracy theories, and outright lies.

    Disinformation can be distributed in any form, at any time, and by anyone, including individuals, organizations, political groups, elected officials, and countries. Even family and friends can share disinformation. When disinformation is encountered, and it will be, because it's everywhere, it should be ignored, deleted, or reported but definitely not shared.

6. **Don't wait for news to find you.** Be proactive. Take charge of your news diet and news engagement plan. Commit to engaging with news several times a day between now and Election Day. It's important to follow top news stories as well as news about candidates running for office from your state. Plus, make sure to keep up with the latest news about the issues that matter to you and where candidates stand on them.

7. **If you primarily rely on social media for news, balance your news diet with non-social media news platforms.** Download at least two free news apps such as NPR, NBC, or AP and turn on the notifications. You can also subscribe to their newsletters and listen to their podcasts. Additionally, every week, plan to watch at least one public affairs programs such as NBC's "Meet the Press," PBS' "Washington Week," or CNN's "Inside Politics." Because these public affairs programs feature roundtable discussions with the reporters who actually

cover the news, they are very insightful about today's pressing issues and they can significantly elevate your News IQ.

8. **Add TikTok to the list of social media platforms infected by disinformation.** TikTok's popularity does not mean it should automatically be trusted as a platform for news. TikTok should earn your trust as a place to go for news. According to the *New York Times*, "ahead of the midterm elections this fall, TikTok is shaping up to be a primary incubator of baseless and misleading information, in many ways as problematic as Facebook and Twitter."

9. **Don't just read, watch, or listen to one news outlet's report on a major story.** Regularly read and compare reports from at least three different news outlets to better inform yourself and improve your skills in critically evaluating news and the outlets that report the news.

5. Vote!

Voting in the 2020 Presidential Election during a Pandemic (Photo Credit: Paula M. Poindexter)

In a *New York Times* op-ed column published after his death on July 17, 2020, civil rights icon Congressman John Lewis wrote:

> The vote is the most powerful nonviolent change agent you have in a democratic society. You must use it because it is not guaranteed. You can lose it.

Unfortunately, according to "The 'Cost' of Voting in America: A Look at Where It's Easiest and Hardest," all states do not make it easy for citizens who are eligible to vote to use the "most powerful nonviolent change agent" in our democracy.

In fact, Texas, Wisconsin, Arkansas, Mississippi, and New Hampshire make it hardest to vote, according to the article.

Whether your state is among the hardest or easiest to vote in, do not delay in making plans to vote in the 2022 midterms. If you haven't already registered, check today about getting registered before the deadline. Remember if you're not registered, you cannot vote.

There are other things you need to know about voting in the election and the Vote411 election site sponsored by the League of Women Voters, can provide the information you need to plan your vote. Through Vote411, you can learn the voting methods available in your state—mail/absentee, early voting, Election Day—and plan how and when you will vote as well as the information or materials you need to exercise your right to vote.

For example, if mail voting is allowed in your state, what do you need to vote by mail? What excuses, if any, are required for absentee voting? How do you return a mail ballot? Is there a drop-off box near where you live or do you have to mail your ballot at the post office?

What if you want to vote early? Does your state have early voting? If so, what are the hours and where is the polling place? Is early voting available on the weekend and what ID do you need?

Voting the First Time Can Be Overwhelming But You're Ready
The last day you can vote in this year's midterms is Election Day, Tues., November 8, 2022. If you're planning to vote on Election Day, you need to know the street address of your assigned polling place as well as the voting hours and required ID.

For Gen Z citizens who are planning to vote for the first time, the election guide we have published as part of activities for News Engagement Day 2022 provides the information you need to vote.

Because we believe it is important to inform yourself prior to voting, this guide has also provided tips that will make you more knowledgeable about journalism, news, and the platforms that make news available. This knowledge plus the recommended balanced news diet will benefit the voting decisions you make during this election season.

If it wasn't clear before reading our election guide, it should be clear now that in order to exercise your right to vote, you have to know the voting requirements, navigate the voting process that may have bumps along the way, and you have to meet strict deadlines for registering and voting.

The truth is voting for the first time can be overwhelming. But we hope any feeling of being overwhelmed will be temporary and will be replaced with feelings of empowerment and pride, knowing that with your vote, will become the "non-violent change-agent" that Congressman John Lewis described in his final op-ed column.

By voting you will help influence the direction of our country. With your vote, you will help have an impact on the treatment and safety of all citizens and future citizens. With your vote, you will make our democracy stronger and work better for everyone today and in the future.

Please share our Gen Z "Voting & Engaging with News" guide with others so they too will have the information they need to vote and become non-violent change agents.

APPENDIX E

6. Resources & Links

AEJMC. https://www.aejmc.org/

Corasaniti, N., & McCann, A. (n.d.). *The "cost" of voting in America: A look at where it's easiest and hardest.* https://www.nytimes.com/interactive/2022/09/20/us/politics/cost-of-voting.html?smid=nytcore-ios-share&referringSource=articleShare

Defining generations: Where Millennials end and Generation Z begins. https://www.pewresearch.org/fact-tank/2019/01/17/where-millennials-end-and-generation-z-begins/

Forman-Katz, N., & Matsa, K. E. (n.d.). *News Platform Fact Sheet.* https://www.pewresearch.org/journalism/fact-sheet/news-platform-fact-sheet/

Holbein, J. (2020, March 11). *Why so few young Americans vote.* https://theconversation.com/amp/why-so-few-young-americans-vote-132649

Hsu, T. (n.d.). On "TikTok, election misinformation thrives ahead of midterms." https://www.nytimes.com/2022/08/14/business/media/on-tiktok-election-misinformation.html?referringSource=articleShare

League of Women Voters. https://www.lwv.org/

Lewis, J. (n.d.). Together, you can redeem the soul of our nation. https://www.nytimes.com/2020/07/30/opinion/john-lewis-civil-rights-america.html

Merriam-Webster. https://www.merriam-webster.com/dictionary/disinformation

Mitchell, A., Jurkowitz, M., Oliphant, J. B., & Shearer, E. (n.d.). *Americans who mainly get their news on social media are less engaged, less knowledgeable.* https://www.pewresearch.org/journalism/2020/07/30/americans-who-mainly-get-their-news-on-social-media-are-less-engaged-less-knowledgeable/

Montanaro, D. (n.d.). *Poll: Abortion and inflation collide as top issues in midterm elections.* https://www.npr.org/2022/09/08/1121535686/poll-abortion-inflation-midterm-elections

Murray, M. (n.d.). *NBC News poll: 57% of voters say investigations into Trump should continue.* https://www.nbcnews.com/meet-the-press/first-read/nbc-news-poll-57-voters-say-investigations-trump-continue-rcna43989

News Engagement Day. http://www.newsengagement.org/[1]

Pew Research Center. (2020). *News Consumption Survey topline.* https://www.journalism.org/wp-content/uploads/sites/8/2020/12/PJ_2020.12.08_News-Consumption_Survey-Toplines.pdf (Metered, p. 38)

Poindexter, P. M. (n.d.). *Millennials, news, and social media: Is news engagement a thing of the past?* https://www.amazon.com/Millennials-News-Social-Media-Engagement-dp-1433150034/dp/1433150034/ref=dp_ob_image_bk

Poll: Abortion and inflation collide as top issues in midterm elections. https://www.npr.org/2022/09/08/1121535686/poll-abortion-inflation-midterm-elections

---

1 Effective News Engagement Day 2023, News Engagement Day activities moved to https://www.aejmc.com/home/events/newsengagementday/

Social media and news fact sheet. https://www.pewresearch.org/journalism/fact-sheet/social-media-and-news-fact-sheet/?utm_source=Pew+Research+Center&utm_campaign=15de90170c-Weekly_2022_09_24&utm_medium=email&utm_term=0_3e953b9b70-15de90170c-399708021

Society of Professional Journalists (SPJ) *Code of Ethics.* https://www.spj.org/pdf/spj-code-of-ethics.pdf

Vote411. https://www.vote411.org/

Voting and registration in the Election of November 2016. https://www.census.gov/data/tables/time-series/demo/voting-and-registration/p20-580.html

Voting and registration in the Election of November 2020. https://www.census.gov/data/tables/time-series/demo/voting-and-registration/p20-585.html

7. Special Thanks

Thank you to the News Engagement Day Committee and all AEJMC members who support News Engagement Day every first Tuesday in October and make it come alive!

And a very special thank you is sent to Samantha Higgins and Kyshia Brown! Samantha is AEJMC's Communications Director who manages NED's promotion, social media, and TikTok Competition. And Kyshia is AEJMC's Website Content/Graphic Designer who designed our beautiful website and keeps it updated and engaging. Samantha and Kyshia, you're creative, supportive, enthusiastic, and patient. You're the best!

INDEX

A

Adoption of Social Media, 128
   Relative advantage of social media as source of news, 128
   Attributes that influence adoption rate of an innovation, 128
AEJMC. *See* Association for Education in Journalism and Mass Communication
AI (Artificial Intelligence), 15, 16, 24–25, 111, 115–117
   ChatGPT, 25
   Dr. Geoffrey Hinton, AI pioneer, 117
   Texas A&M- Commerce professor accuses class of using ChatGPT to write paper, 25
   University of Texas at Austin professor advocates for using AI in teaching, 25
Amendments to the U.S. Constitution
   First Amendment, 109
   Fifteenth Amendment, 98
   Nineteenth Amendment, 98
   Twenty-Fourth Amendment, 98
   Twenty-Sixth Amendment, 98
Artificial Intelligence. *See* AI
Association for Education in Journalism and Mass Communication (AEJMC), xiii, xix, 110, 129, 141

B

Bandura, Albert, 64
"Barbie," 25–26
Barriers to Becoming Informed, 110
   Disinterest in paying for news, 110
   Excessive time spent on social media, 110, 112–113
   Inability to distinguish credible news from disinformation, 110, 115

Lack of news engagement routine, 110, 114–115
Limited supplemental news engagement benefits, 110, 111–112
Marginal news app use, 110, 113–114
Minimal attention paid to news about government, elections, the Supreme Court, court cases, 110
Weak civic duty to keep informed, 110, 111
Weakening news engagement socialization, 110–111
Beyoncé, 25–26
Biden, Joe, 46th President
   2020 Presidential Election
      Defeats 45th President Donald Trump, winning both the popular vote and Electoral College vote, 92
      After President Trump's supporters violently attacked the U.S. Capitol, January 6, President-Elect Biden addressed the nation and called on President Trump to fulfill his oath, defend the Constitution, and demand an end to the insurrection by his supporters, 19
   2024 Presidential Election
      After a poor debate performance, President Biden dropped out of the 2024 Presidential Election race and endorsed Vice President Kamala Harris to be the Democratic Party's 2024 nominee for president, 29
   Historic Biden Administration Diversity, 10–12
      Assistant Secretary of Health Rachel Levine, 11
      Secretary of Defense Lloyd Austin, 11
      Secretary of Transportation Pete Buttigieg, 11
      Secretary of Treasury Janet Yellen, 10
      Secretary of the U.S. Department of Interior Deb Haaland, 10
      Supreme Court Nomination Ketanji Brown Jackson, 11, 12
      Treasurer of the United States Marilynn Malerba, 10
      Vice President Kamala Harris. *See also* 2024 Presidential Election
      White House Press Secretary Karine Jean-Pierre, 11
Bill of Rights, 53
Black Lives Matter, 4, 7–8, 12–14
Brown, Kyshia, xix

C

CDC Director Declares Racism "Serious Public Health Threat," 8
Celebrating 10 Years of News Engagement Day! Souvenir Program, 178–182
Center for News Literacy, Stony Brook, NY, 141
   Howard Schneider, Founder, 141
ChatGPT. *See* AI
CIRCLE (Center for Information & Research on Civic Learning) at Tufts University), 111
Clarin, John Ray, xviii
Clinton, Hillary
   Made history as the Democratic Party nominee in the 2016 presidential election; won popular vote but lost Electoral College vote to Republican Party nominee Donald Trump, 91
College Board's First AP Course for African American Studies, 15
Content Creators, *See* Influencers
Critical Race Theory, 14
   Definition, 14
   Legal theory, 14
   Fox News talking point, 14

D

Deepfakes. *See* Disinformation
Democracy, 18, 20, 121, 127, 128, 131, 134, 138, 140, 141, 143, 144, 145, 147
    Democracy Participants, 134
Demographics of Gen Z
    Gender, 45
    Race/Ethnicity, 44–45
    Education, 44–45
    Income, 46
Disinformation, 15–18, 110, 115, 129, 134, 135, 141. *See* also Barriers to Being Informed
    Deepfakes, 15–16, 115
    Familiarity with, 118
    The Big Lie, 17
Dynata, xviii

E

Electoral College Vote 91–92
    Article II, Section 1, U.S. Constitution, 91

F

Facebook, 5–6, 128. *See also* social media mental health effects
    Founding and growth, 5
    Mental health effects, 6
First Amendment, 109, 134. *See also* Amendments
Floyd, George, 4, 7–8, 13–14

G

Garrick, Alexandra Elizabeth, xvii
Gen Z
    Contributing events and issues in defining Gen Z

    Active shooter drills, 3–4
    AI (Artificial Intelligence), 24–25
    Attack on U.S. Democracy, 18–20
    Barbie, Greta, Beyoncé, and Taylor, 25–26
    Censorship laws and bans, 12–15
    Climate change, 21–22
    DEI (Diversity, Equity, and Inclusion) death, 22–23
    Disinformation, 15–18
    Global pandemic, 5–8
    Hamas' attack on Israel and Israel's war on Hamas, 27–28
    Historic Diversity at Highest Level of Government, 10
    LGBTQ+ State of emergency, 23
    Pandemic Reading and Math Loss, 4
    Roe v. Wade Overturned, 12
    Reset of 2024 President Election, *See* ____
    Social Media and Mental Health Harm, 5–6
    TikTok Ban, 20–21
    Vaping Epidemic, 24
    Video Murder of George Floyd, 4
    Women Still Earn Less than Men 26–27
    Young Voter Political Power, 9
Generations
    Categories
        Born since 1901, 30
        Defined by Years Born, 46
        Generation Names Lack Scientific Rigor, 31
        Not scientifically defined, 30–31
        Surveyed for The National Gen Z, Social Media & News Engagement Survey, 46
Grading General News Coverage, 80
    Gen Z Grades, 80
    Gen Z Reasons for High Grades, 81
    Gen Z Reasons for Low Grades, 81
Grading News Coverage of Their Generation, 82

Gen Z Reasons for Grades, 83–84
Perceptions and Expectations of News and News Media, 84–87
   Important for News Media to be Watchdog, 87
   Independent Press is Good for Democracy, 87
   News Media Accurately Represent Groups in U.S., 87
   News Media Accurately Represent your Generation, 87
   News Media Care Little About People Like You, 87
   News Media Protect Democracy, 87
   News Media Should be like a Good Neighbor, 87
   News Organizations More Concerned about Being First, 87
   News Organizations Willingness to Admit Mistakes, 87
   News on the Internet Should be Free, 87, 120
   Paying for News Supports Independent Press, 87, 120
Voter Political Profile, 97–102
   Ideology, 97
   Importance of Voting Belief, 98
   Most Important Issue Facing Generation, 101–102
   Political Party, 97
   Presidential Election News Engagement, 104
   Voter Registration, 99
   Reasons for not Registering to Vote, 100–101
   Voted in 2020 Presidential Election, 99
   Voting Intentions in 2024 Presidential Election, 99–100
   Impediments to Voting Intentions, 102
   Reasons for Voting Intentions, 103
Gerwig, Greta, 25–26
Groups Responsible for Future Informed Generations, 131
   Elementary-through-College Educators and Librarians, 131, 133
   News Outlets, Associations, and Journalists, including Student Journalists, 131
   News Literacy, Civic Education, Journalism Groups, Non-Profits, Foundations, and Centers, 131
   Parents, 131–133
      Importance of Explaining Engaging with News on Smartphone, 132
      Introduce Kid-Friendly News, 132–133
      Social Learning Theory Explained and Applied in Smartphone World, 131–132
Growing Up with News, 66
   Advised Important to be Informed, 67
   Discussions about News at Home, 66
   Newspapers at Home, 66
   Raised to Believe It's Important to be Informed, 66
   TV News at Home, 66
   News Included in Classroom, 67
   High School Civics Education

H

Harris, Kamala, 96
   Events Upending 2024 Presidential Election, 93–96
   First Woman of Color to be Nominee of Major Political Party, 96
   Vice President Kamala Harris vs. Former President Donald Trump, 29–30
   Loses 2024 Presidential Election, 97
Harvard Institute of Politics Youth Poll, 9, 111, 121, 134, 135
Higgins, Samantha, xix
High School Civics Education, 134
Hinton, Geoffrey. See AI
How Democracies Die, 20
Howard, Elizabeth (Lizzie), xviii, xix
Hutchins Commission (Commission on Freedom of the Press), 109–110
   Responsibilities of journalism process to gain public trust, 110

Reporter responsibilities, 110
Keep fact and opinion separate, 110

I

Influencers, 8, 15, 136
iPhone, 46–47

J

Jan. 6 attack on U.S. Capitol, 18–20
Journalism and Mass Communication Quarterly, 129
Jobs, Steve 46

K

Kid-Friendly News, 132–133
   NBC Nightly News: Kids Edition, 132
   Time for Kids, 133
Kovach, Bill. See *The Elements of Journalism*

L

Legacy Media explained, 51–53
LGBTQ+, 13
Luce, Henry, 110

M

Markowitz, Frank, xviii
McCombs, Maxwell, xix, xx
Media Literacy Now, 135
Millennials, News, and Social Media: Is News Engagement a Thing of the Past?, xiii, xiv, xix, 130, 136
Millennial News Coverage Grades in 2012 Compared with Gen Z News Coverage Grades in 2023, 137

"Millennials and news: What kids say about the news" Vimeo. See mynews@school
Misinformation. See Disinformation
Modeling Theory, 64
mynews@school, 134
   News-in-the-classroom program developed with the Austin *American-Statesman*, 134
   "Millennials and news: What kids say about the news" Vimeo on mynews@school, 134.

N

National News Literacy Week, 141
National Gen Z, Social Media & News Engagement Survey Method, 157–160
National Gen Z, Social Media & News Engagement Survey Questionnaire, 161–176
News Avoidances, 63, 70
News Categories Paid Attention to Often, 56
News Credibility Quick Check, 136
News Deserts, 140
News Engagement
   Digital Platforms
      Social Media, 49
      YouTube, 50
      Google, 50
      Notifications, 50
      News Apps, 50
      Podcasts, 50
      Newsletters, 50
      Smart Speaker, 50
   Interpersonal Platforms
      Family, 49
      Friends, 49
   Legacy Media
      Explained, 51–52
      Cable, 50
      Local TV, 50, 129
      Magazines (Print), 50
      Network TV, 50, 129
      Newspapers (Print), 50, 129

News Engagement Day (NED), xix, 130, 133, 141
   History, 130
News Engagement Routine
   Defined, 71, 135
   Increased News Engagement Frequency, 71–72
   Descriptions, 73
News Engagement Socialization Defined, 64
   Disruption of news engagement socialization, 69
   Smartphone disruption of news engagement socialization, 69
News Literacy
   Defined, 133, 134
News Literacy Education, 134
News Literacy Project, 141
   Alan C. Miller, Founder, 141
News Literate Person
   Defined, 134
News Media Action Plan for Covering and Engaging Gen Z, 138–140
   Consult Style Guides Produced by Journalism Associations of Color, 139
   Include LGBTQ+ Voices in News Stories
   Discount Digital News Subscriptions, 138
   Produce and Distribute Election Guides during Election Seasons, 138
   Re-think and Re-brand NIE for the Digital Age, 140
   Know Stereotypes and Avoid Them, 139
   Include Gen Z Sources in News Stories, 139
News Topics Often Paid Attention To, 57
News Topics Paid Attention to by Gender, 58–59
Newspaper Reading. *See also* Legacy Media.
   Daily Newspaper Non-Reader, 129
      "A Profile of the Daily Newspaper Non-Reader, 129
         Newspaper Reading Compared with Network, Local TV News Viewing, Online News, 1990s-Early 21st Century, 129–130
   Newspaper Reading Decline, 129–130

Institutionalized Behavior of Americans, 129
News for a Mobile-First Consumer, xiii, xiv

O

Overview of *Gen Z, Social Media, and News: Implications for the Future of News Engagement, Journalism, the U.S., and Democracy*, 30–33

P

Pandemic, 7. *See also* WHO declares Global COVID-19 Pandemic
Pen America, 13–14
Pew Research Center, 20–21, 30, 48, 68–70, 98, 111–112, 117, 127, 129–131, 139, 144–145, 157, 186, 193
Poindexter, Alfred and Rachael, xix

Q

Questionnaire. *See* National Gen Z, Social Media & News Engagement Survey Questionnaire
Questions and Reflections
   Chapter 1, 33
   Chapter 2, 60
   Chapter 3, 75
   Chapter 4, 88
   Chapter 5, 104–105
   Chapter 6, 122
   Chapter 7, 148
   List of Questions and Reflections, 153–155

R

Racial disparities, 8

Racial reckoning, 8
  Backlash, 8
Reporters Without Borders, 142
  Press Freedom Index, 142
    China Press Freedom Rank, 142
    France Press Freedom Rank, 142
    Norway Press Freedom Rank, 142
    Russia Press Freedom Rank, 142
    Ukraine Press Freedom Rank, 142
    United States Press Freedom Rank, 142
Rosenstiel, Tom. See *The Elements of Journalism*

S

Shaw, Donald, xx
Social Media
  Use, 47–48, 51
  Mental health effects, 5–6 See also Surgeon General
  What users like about news on social media, 128
  What users dislike about news on social media, 129
  Relative advantage of social media for news. See adoption of innovations
Society of Professional Journalists ethics code, 138
"Stop the Steal" Rally, 18 See also Donald Trump
Subscriptions, Digital, 120
  Movie/TV, 120
  Music, 120
  Sports, 120
  News, 120
Supreme Court
  1954 Brown v. Board of Education Landmark Supreme Court Ruling, SLandmark Ruling, Brown v. Board of Education,
  1973 Landmark Roe v. Wade Supreme Court Ruling Overturned, 12
  Historic Nominations

Thurgood Marshall, First Black Person to Serve on Supreme Court, 11
Sandra Day O'Connor, First Woman to Serve on Supreme Court, 11
Sonia Sotomayor, First Hispanic Woman to Serve on Supreme Court, 12
Ketanji Brown Jackson, First Black Woman to Serve on Supreme Court, 12
Overturning Roe v. Wade
Surgeon General
  Social Media and Youth Mental Health Advisory, 6
Special Counsel Jack Smith, 92
Stylebooks produced to improve reporting about people of color, LGBTQ+ communities and American Muslims
  National Association of Black Journalists (NABJ), 139
  National Association of Hispanic Journalists (NAHJ), 139
  Asian American Journalists Association (AAJA), 139
  Indigenous Journalists Association (IJA), 139
  The Association of LGBTQ+ Journalists (NLGJA), 139
  Trans Journalists Association (TJA), 139
  Covering American Muslims, 139
Swift, Taylor, 25–26

T

"The 1619 Project," 15
  Nikole Hannah-Jones, 15
The American Journalist Survey, 138
The Big Lie, 15, 17. See also Disinformation
The Elements of Journalism by Bill Kovach and Tom Rosenstiel, 109, 143
The Learning Network (*New York Times*), 140
The Trust Project, 138
TikTok

Popular among teens, 20
Banned by countries, state governments, and universities, 21
Time Magazine, 109
   Taylor Swift *Time* Magazine Person of the Year, 26
Trump, Donald, 19–20
   45th and 47th President, 97
   Assassination Attempt, 94–95
   Four Indictments; One Conviction, 92–93
   January 6 Insurrection, 19–20, 92–93
   "Stop the Steal" Rally, 18–19
   The Big Lie, 15, 17
Trustworthiness of News Story, 117–118
Twitter
   Founding, 128
   Adopted by Millennials as go-to news source, 128
   Distributor of news reported by journalists, 128
   Purchased by Elon Musk who changed name to X, 128

U

U.S. Media Literacy: A State-by-State Status of Media Literacy Education Laws for K-12 Schools, 135

U.S. Presidential Election. *See* Presidential Elections
Uses and gratifications, 112

V

Voting Guides, 135
Voting & Engaging with News about the 2022 Midterm Elections: A Guide for Gen Z Voters by Paula M. Poindexter, 184–200

W

WHO declares Global COVID-19 Pandemic, 7
Winters, Colton xviii
Wired magazine, 47

X

X, the social media platform. *See* Twitter

Made in the USA
Monee, IL
03 May 2026

49437775R00127